LINE UPON LINE

LINE UPON LINE

BY
TOMMY ROBBINS
(1948-2011).

FOR PRECEPT *MUST BE* UPON PRECEPT, PRECEPT UPON PRECEPT; LINE UPON LINE, LINE UPON LINE; HERE A LITTLE, *AND* THERE A LITTLE: (ISAIAH 28:10).

Produced and published by
GRACE-EBOOKS.COM
Contact: GraceEbooks@gmail.com

Cover photo and design by Caroline Rutland

ISBN 978-1-936990-00-9

CONTENTS

FOREWORD

Tommy Robbins was Pastor of Fairmont Grace Church in Sylacauga, Alabama. He faithfully preached the Gospel of God's free grace in Christ Jesus to the people of God there for seventeen years. Each week he wrote an article for the church bulletin and each week those who knew about them waited to read them, knowing a blessing was to be had. This book contains those Christ honoring articles in the same rich, Gospel language with which the Lord blessed him when he preached.

I came to know Tommy at a New Caney, TX Bible Conference at which he and I preached together. I had known of him before and perhaps briefly met him at other such conferences, but then I was blessed of the Lord to have the luxury of leisurely sitting with him on the porch of the parsonage and talking for hours. It didn't take long for me to realize that I had just received that which is among the most precious of God's gifts in this world, a true friend. A friend, not just in the typical sense of having some things in common and being able to "get along good," but a real friend to my soul. In the following years, we fished together, ate together, did quite a bit more porch sitting at his house or mine, cried and laughed together, and stood in one another's pulpits now and then. He ministered to me in his preaching, his writing, and in conversation.

Not long before he died, someone wrote to me that another Pastor friend was going to visit Tommy, and expressed the prayer that the Lord would give that Pastor something to say that would be a blessing to Tommy. My reply was that would be good, but that I expected perhaps the Lord would give Tommy something to say that would be a blessing to the visitor. That was always the way it was when I visited him. That was Tommy's gift. He was a blessing to all who knew him, and you will see it in the words of this book.

Pastor Chris Cunningham
College Grove Grace Church, College Grove TN

FOUR QUESTIONS

There are four vital questions set forth in the Gospel of our Lord Jesus Christ that we all will have to deal with and answer, both now and when we are brought before the bar of truth, when this life is over. Universally, mankind refuses to recognize and deal with these humbling truths because the answers are not that which is agreeable to the flesh. Man deals with these issues now by ignoring them and stopping their eyes and ears to the eternal truth of Scripture. This is the same response that man had toward our Lord when he was on the earth. Need we suppose it would be different now? Man's hatred for God and truth has never changed, and never will, until and unless, God in sovereign mercy and grace gives them a new heart.

    1. IS GOD REALLY GOD? What does this question imply? If God is God, then he is exactly as the Bible declares him to be! God is HOLY, JUST, INFINITE, MAJESTIC, GLORIOUS AND SOVEREIGN. He does as he pleases, when he pleases, with whom he pleases and none can give him counsel, nor question what he does. God is God, or he is no God at all. Is your God the God of the Bible or another?

    2. WHO IS THE LORD JESUS CHRIST? If Jesus Christ is Lord, then he is exactly that! He is LORD! He is God incarnate. The Word made FLESH. He is the divine and perfect MAN in one body. The Lord Jesus Christ is one. In him dwells all the fullness of the Godhead bodily. He is God's Son—God's Lamb; God's image of himself. He is the visible image of the invisible God. The Lord Jesus Christ, as a man, is exalted at God's right hand

having all power in heaven and earth. Is this the Jesus you love and bow to? If he is not, then you do not know the ONE LORD JESUS CHRIST!

3. HOW DOES GOD, WHO IS HOLY, JUST AND RIGHTEOUS SAVE SINNERS, AND YET REMAIN AS HE IS? God saves sinful men by substitution. God saves sinners in the Lord Jesus Christ. God made him to be sin, that he might make sinners righteous. The final judgment and punishment for sin is eternal death. The Lord Jesus Christ, in his suffering and death underwent the equivalent of the sinner's eternal punishment to the satisfaction of the just and holy God. The blood and righteousness of the Lord Jesus Christ guarantees the eternal salvation of all those for whom God intended it.

4. ARE YOU A SINNER? Men make a joke of sin and being a sinner. David's thoughts about himself were scriptural. He said, *against thee, and thee only have I sinned and done this evil in thy sight.* Paul wrote, *all have sinned and come short of the glory of God.* The question is NOT, "Have I made some mistakes?" or, "Am I imperfect?" The question IS "Am I a SINNER before God?"

Scripture references: Is 40 & 43; Jn 1; Acts 4; Rom 3.

GOOD NEWS!

Everyone likes to receive glad tidings. But not every thing that is proclaimed to be good news is so great. Sometimes what seems to be good news is not so good when the results are in. This is especially true in religion. False religion has an incredible ability to present a damnable lie (salvation by works) in the guise of truth and the multitudes gladly receive it. The fact is that there is no good news for sinful man apart from JESUS CHRIST and him crucified (1 Cor 2:2). Chosen by God in CHRIST

(Eph 1:4); redeemed by the blood of CHRIST (1 Pt 1:18-19); clothed with the imputed righteousness of CHRIST (Rom 4:24); CHRIST revealed by his Spirit (1 Cor 2:1-10) and given faith in Christ in regeneration by the preaching of CHRIST, *kept by the power of God through faith in CHRIST* (Eph 2:1-10)—This is GOOD NEWS! If one could but read and believe Ephesians chapter one, (as well as all other Scriptures), they could not deny that the good news is CHRIST! On the other hand anything that originates in man is bad news. Anything that man finishes is bad news. And everything in-between is the same. *Behold, thou hast made my days as an handbreadth; and mine age is as nothing before thee: verily every man at his best state is altogether vanity* (Ps 39:5).

"On Christ the solid rock I stand,
All other ground is sinking sand!"

ASSURANCE

The child of God (the true child of God), like every professor of Christianity, is continually looking for assurance. The mere professor of Christ who is not a possession of Christ, looks for assurance in all the wrong places. He looks to the flesh. He looks to his experiences, his feelings, his faithfulness, his longevity in religion, his knowledge of the Bible, his knowledge of doctrine, and at every thing and in every place and person, except in the one who is the believer's assurance—THE LORD JESUS CHRIST!

The child of God may from time to time be distracted from Christ, but not for very long. Every believer has GOD GIVEN FAITH, and the OBJECT of *the faith of God's elect* is the LORD JESUS CHRIST! Without faith there is no assurance, and without assurance there is no view of Christ, and without a view of Christ by faith there is no spiritual life. The child of God continually looks to Christ, while the unbeliever (though religious) looks to himself. We see our Lord in his Word (the Bible); we see him in the Gospel (the ministry of the Word); and we see him in everything that transpires in our life. The believer's assurance is in our OMNISCIENT, OMNIPOTENT, OMNIPRESENT REDEEMER!!

REJOICE ALWAYS

There is every reason for the child of God to rejoice. We live in a world and a body that daily reaps the result of the ravages of sin, but not to despair. Are you sick in body?—Then rejoice in the Lord! Is there trouble in the family?—Then rejoice in the Lord! Are you tired, weary, weak, heavy-laden with life itself—then rejoice in the Lord! Our blessed Redeemer underwent every trial and temptation that will accost the believer. This he did so that he might be touched with the feeling of our infirmities. As he was tried, tested, and tempted, he looked to the love, wisdom, and will of his Father and rejoiced and rested in his goodness. Although we all know and can quote Rom 8:28, sometimes we forget and find it hard to believe this great promise to us—*For we know that all things work together for good to them that love God; to them who are the called according to his purpose.* In John 14, Christ told his disciples not to let their souls be troubled, to believe in Him. There CAN be rejoicing in the Holy Ghost when we are *looking to Jesus, the author and finisher of our faith.* Being occupied with temporal things will not bring the saint any happiness and pleasure, only the conscious presence of the Lord Jesus Christ makes everything ALL RIGHT. We rejoice in his strength when we are weak. We rejoice in his power when we are low. Only the true child of God understands the workings of grace in the heart.

ENCOURAGEMENT

I have found that even the saints are prone to dwell too much upon things that discourage. At least this is my experience. It is good to be able to confide in one another and talk about the things that trouble us. But it is not good to let our burdens and difficulties become a load that we always carry and a burden that we always place upon the brethren. If we would stop and consider, for every burden that the child of God has, there are ten thousand blessings! And all these blessings are in Christ! If we have burdens and trials (and every child of God does), in the long run they will prove to have been a blessing from God. Never make light of a brother's complaints nor brush them off and ignore him, but try to encourage him by speaking of the good things, the things that we have in Christ, such as life, peace, righteousness, and redemption. We must continually remind ourselves and others, that *all things work together for good to them that love God, to them who are the called according to his purpose* (Rom 8:28).

PARTICULAR REDEMPTION

This term "particular redemption" is familiar to most, if not all of us. It simply means that the Lord Jesus Christ redeemed a certain number of individuals whom his Father gave him in the eternal covenant of grace before the world was. He redeemed them by his precious blood. The doctrine of particular redemption is taught throughout the Bible. To deny that it is taught in the Bible would be to deny virtually the whole sacred writ. Those who refute this blessed truth are not Christians and are not Gospel preachers. They are enemies of God and his Christ. Those whom Christ has redeemed with his sacrificial blood and called by his sovereign grace through the preaching of his Gospel do not and will not compromise the glory of God, nor the honor and integrity of the holy person and the perfect, effectual and complete work of their Redeemer.

If this blessed doctrine be not so, then the attributes of God mean absolutely nothing, and the living and dying of the Lord of glory was a misnomer. On the contrary, the doctrine of particular redemption establishes and magnifies all the attributes of God, and glorifies and honors the Lord Jesus Christ and his work of redemption. The particular redemption of the Lord Jesus Christ is the heart of the true Gospel of God. It is the child of God's only hope. What hope have we if Christ died universally for everyone, and some for whom he died will be cast into the Lake of Fire to be punished forever for their sins?

Someone may ask the question, "Does one have to believe in particular redemption to be saved?" My answer would be this, "It is only those that believe on the Lord Jesus Christ that are saved. And to not believe in the effectual redemption of Christ can only be true of an unbeliever." I would not be so foolish as some, to insinuate that one must meet a long list of criteria before God will save them. It is simple heart faith, which God gives, that joins the sinner to Christ. But this I will boldly, without apology, declare—We must believe on the Christ of the Bible—that ONE who *obtained eternal redemption for us!*

LET THERE BE LIGHT

God Said, Let There Be Light, And There Was Light.
Genesis 1:3

We cannot help but bow in wonder and amazement as we behold the sovereign power and the intrinsic glory in the majestic display of the incomprehensible being of the triune God. Our feeble minds can grasp but little (even with the assistance of his blessed Spirit) of the infinite and glorious works of the Almighty. In Psalm 33:6 it is written, *By the word of the LORD were the heavens made; and all the host of them by the breath of his mouth.*

As we see our Lord's sovereign power and unalterable purpose unfold in the creation of all things, in this passage *(God said, Let there be Light, and there was Light.)*, we see a beautiful picture of the impartation of his divine nature to chosen dead sinners in regeneration. Before we knew Christ we were like the earth before God said, *Let there be Light.* We were without the image of Christ within and without. We were void of the life of Christ. We were in spiritual darkness and death. There was no hope that we would be otherwise had not God said, *Let there be Light.* The raising of a dead, helpless, hopeless wretch from the depths of wreck and ruin is the sovereign work of almighty grace in Christ our Redeemer. Let it be understood that this preacher not only believes the Biblical account of CREATION, I believe the Biblical account of SALVATION. May we shout with brother Jonah, *Salvation is of the Lord!* May we sing with Newton,

> Amazing grace, how sweet the sound,
> That saved a wretch like me!

The *Light* that God hath shinned in our hearts is none other than the Lamb who is the light, and he who dwells in the midst of the throne of God. The Lord Jesus Christ is the Light and life of every believer. *For God, who commanded the Light to shine out of darkness, hath shined in our hearts, to give the light of the knowledge of the glory of God in the face of Jesus Christ* (2 Cor 4:6).

Unless and until God, in efficacious grace and mercy, raises spiritually dead sinners and imparts to them spiritual life, they will remain dead. This nonsense of LET GOD SAVE YOU that is being preached and promoted by the so-called evangelicals of our day, is nothing more than a herald from hell.

Thank God he said, *Let there be Light, and there was Light!*

BEHOLD, IT WAS VERY GOOD

And God saw every thing that he had made, and, behold, it was very good. And the evening and the morning were the sixth day.
Genesis 1:31

God does everything, and EVERYTHING that he does is GOOD. I make no claim to understand all that is implied in the Bible or in the statement that I just made concerning this truth, but I know it is so because the Scriptures declare it to be so. He is the first cause of all things. He can do no less than good because he is good. *For THE LORD IS GOOD; his mercy is everlasting; and his truth endureth to all generations* (Ps 100:5). The great work of redemption, from election to glorification, is the work of God alone. Therefore the work of regeneration and the preservation of the saints in Christ is his work and is GOOD. *Being confident of this very thing, that he which hath begun a good work in you will perform it until the day of Jesus Christ* (Phil 1:6). Why should we emphasize this? Because, it is the truth and it glorifies the Father, the Son, and the Spirit, and is the foundation of the hope of every believer, and because the vast majority of preachers and professors of Christianity deny this truth. God is good had he not chosen to save anyone. But he did, and the revelation of his goodness is most wondrously seen in the context hereof spoken—*But after that the kindness and love of God our Saviour toward man appeared, Not by works of righteousness which we have done, but according to his mercy he saved us, by the washing of regeneration, and renewing of the Holy Ghost; Which he shed on us abundantly through Jesus Christ our Saviour* (Ti

3:4-6). As God looked upon his handiwork in Genesis chapter one and saw that it was very good, so he looks upon his new creation in Christ and sees that it is very good. This is how God sees it— GOOD! For *we are his workmanship, created in Christ Jesus* (Eph 2:10). It is good because of the ONE who did it and he is good— *there is none good but one, that is, God* (Mk 10:18). If we had anything to do with it, it would not be good. *They are all gone out of the way, they are together become unprofitable; there is NONE THAT DOETH GOOD, no, not one* (Rom 3:12). The heart and soul of free will doctrine is NO GOOD because it emphasizes the imaginary, God-dishonoring, goodness, works, and supposed ability of man in the execution of, and in the performance of salvation. The Bible plainly declares that; *it is not of him that willeth, nor of him that runneth, but of God that sheweth mercy* (Rom 9:16). The God of purpose and the purpose of God is good; Christ and his redemptive work is good; the great work of his Spirit in regeneration is good; and all those whom God views in Christ are good, simply and singularly because God is good.

SATAN'S GRIEF; THE CHILDREN OF GOD

The more they afflicted them, the more they multiplied and grew. And they were grieved because of the children of Israel.
Exodus 1:12

As Satan and the world is no match for God, neither is sin and Satan a victor over the children of God. *Nay, in all these things we are more than conquerors through him that loved us* (Rom 8:37). The more the child of God is afflicted, the more

24

we grow in grace and knowledge of Him. This is because of Christ, not ourselves. *Ye are of God, little children, and have overcome them: because greater is he that is in you, than he that is in the world* (1 Jn 4:4). Our Lord knows nothing of defeat. He has won every battle and defeated every enemy that comes against us. *What shall we then say to these things? If God be for us, who can be against us?* (Rom 8:31). We but need to stand on the bank of the river and watch the final destruction of Pharaoh and his army to calm our fears. The deliverance of the children of Israel is but a picture of a greater deliverance. It was by the affliction of our Lord Jesus Christ that grace was multiplied for his sheep.

The grief of Satan is the growth of God's kingdom through Christ's suffering and death. Shall those whom Christ purchased with his own blood suffer loss? Emphatically, NO! *This is the Father's will which hath sent me, that of all which he hath given me I should lose nothing, but should raise it up again at the last day* (Jn 6:39). As the children of Israel were an uncontrollable burden and grief to the Egyptians, so is Christ and his church to the world.

Adversity is sent from the loving hand of God to graciously force us to himself. *These things I have spoken unto you, that in me ye might have peace. In the world ye shall have tribulation: but be of good cheer; I have overcome the world* (Jn 16:33). What Satan means for evil, God uses for his people's good. *We know that all things work together for good to them that love God, to them who are the called according to his purpose* (Rom 8:28).

IDOLATRY: MOSES' ANGER

He saw the calf, and the dancing: and Moses' anger waxed hot.
Exodus 32:19

M oses' anger raging hot against the Israelites, as they worshiped the golden calf, represents the law of God condemning all idolaters. God Almighty has zero tolerance for idolatry no matter in what shape, form or fashion it manifests itself. Ignorance and spiritual darkness is no excuse. We are natural born worshippers of false gods. The SELF-GOD of freewillism is the personification of all idolatry. The Scriptures plainly tell us there is but one God and he alone is to be worshipped. *There shall no strange god be in thee; neither shalt thou worship any strange god* (Ps 81:9); *Then saith Jesus unto him, Get thee hence, Satan: for it is written, thou shalt worship the Lord thy God, and him only shalt thou serve* (Mt 4:10). If we will be spared from God's wrath and indignation it is of the Lord's doing. There is no loophole in God's unalterable, inflexible justice. We must be given a new nature appropriated by the person and work of our Redeemer and imparted by the omnipotent work of the Spirit of the living God. This divine nature institutes and perseveres in *new heart* worship (covenant worship) of the true and living God—*And I will give them an heart to know me, that I am the* LORD: *and they shall be my people, and I will be their God: for they shall return unto me with their whole heart* (Jer 24:7).

Old Israel was known for their rebellion, stiff necks, hard hearts, and idolatry. Spiritual Israel is known by their worship of the true and living God. *For they themselves shew of us what manner of entering in we had unto you, and how ye turned to God from idols to serve the living and true God* (1 Thes 1:9). Our precious Lord drank the dregs of the golden calf and fell under the wrath of divine justice by the demands of the thrice-holy God for his loved ones to purchase us the privilege of divine worship. Those who habitually forsake the worship of God habitually worship a false god.

A STRANGE MESSAGE

And he said, I will make all my goodness pass before thee, and I will proclaim the name of the LORD before thee; and will be gracious to whom I will be gracious, and will shew mercy on whom I will shew mercy.
Exodus 33:19

The message of the Bible (Christ and him crucified) may be unfamiliar to the ears of those who do not hear Christ preached consistently, and do not study for themselves, and take someone's word for the truth. The religion of multitudes is superficial, to say the least. When most people hear the true message of the Gospel their response is, "What in the world is he saying, I have never heard anything like that!" Without taking the time to inquire and study and seek God to see if these things be true, they usually become angry and offended and judge it not to be so. I feel that I can speak freely concerning this because I was once there myself.

The heart of false religion is focused upon SELF. The theme of a false Gospel is GOD LOVES EVERYONE; CHRIST DIED FOR EVERYONE; SALVATION IS UP TO ME; I AM A GOOD PERSON;

AND I KNOW I AM GOING TO HEAVEN BECAUSE I AM DOING GOOD THINGS. The glory of God, the effectual work of Christ, the depravity of the human heart, and the sovereign grace of God is a strange message to those that are strangers to the truth. The great concern of the flesh is health and prosperity here, and heaven and hell hereafter. The great concern of the Christian message is the glory of God, here and hereafter.

If it were not for the programs, recognitions, theatrics, entertainment, pastors telling stories and dealing with moral issues, and telling people how good they are and begging for money, most church services could be cancelled. Contemporary religion's purpose is to make their message and methods palatable to fallen creatures at the expense of the glory of God and truth. The message of the Gospel is as old as God himself and has never changed and never will. May God in grace and mercy reveal to this generation his sovereign glory in Jesus Christ our Lord.

I will make all my goodness pass before thee, and I will proclaim the name of the LORD before thee; and will be gracious to whom I will be gracious, and will show mercy on whom I will show mercy (Ex 33:19).

THE SALT ROOM

Every oblation of thy meat offering shalt thou season with salt; neither shalt thou suffer the salt of the covenant of thy God to be lacking from thy meat offering: with all thine offerings thou shalt offer salt.

Leviticus 2:13

Every minute detail, both in substance and service in the ceremonial law ordained by God for the nation of Israel in the Old Testament, points to and is a picture of our blessed Redeemer. The significance of salt is obvious in this verse and is no less than required hereafter with every meat sacrifice offered.

Salt has at least two outstanding and beneficial uses. One is to give desirable and satisfying flavor to food. Another is to preserve food from perishing. Not only is the meat offered a type of our substitute, the salt is as well. He is the Salt of the everlasting covenant of grace. Without him there would only be a covenant of works and it would be tasteless and even less satisfying and consequently a ministration of death.

As we eat of Him, he is that meat which is salted with all of his graces in his accomplished work, as he is our Redeemer and satisfies his Father and the taste of the inward man. *Can that which is unsavoury be eaten without salt? or is there any taste in the white of an egg?* (Jb 6:6). It is *Christ in you* that makes his people the salt of the earth. *Ye are the salt of the earth* (Mt 5:13).

The Lord Jesus Christ is our preservation as well. The covenant of grace is an everlasting covenant because Christ is the salt, or surety of that covenant. As long as he endures we will endure. *Labour not for the meat which perisheth, but for that meat which endureth unto everlasting life, which the Son of man shall give unto you: for him hath God the Father sealed* (Jn 6:27). A message without Christ is a message without salt. It has no desirable taste and absolutely no enduring benefits.

In the *Salt Room* there was an abundance of salt to saturate the sacrifice. In the Gospel there is an abundance of Christ. By God's grace may we labor for that Meat which satisfies the soul and endureth unto everlasting life.

THE POWER OF THE BLOOD

And he brought the bullock for the sin offering: and Aaron and his sons laid their hands upon the head of the bullock for the sin offering. And he slew it; and Moses took the blood, and put it upon the horns of the altar round about with his finger, and purified the altar

Leviticus 8:14-15

It is the blood of Jesus Christ that appropriates justification for the chosen guilty sinner before the holy God. The law of God must say either "guilty" or "not guilty." Without the blood all the law can do is condemn. The horns of the altar typifies power— that is power to execute condemnation to eternal death for sin— that is until Moses dipped his finger in the blood and smeared it upon the horns of the altar. The finger of God's wrath penetrated the sinless sacrifice, opening a fountain of blood, which spewed forth and saturated the law of God to the extent that all the law can say concerning those for whom it was shed is, NOT GUILTY! With the blood applied, all the law can do is justify. Without the blood the altar meant death, someone MUST die. With the blood, the altar meant life. Someone MUST live.

God's altar is purified by the blood of Jesus Christ. It is forever no more death for the elect of God because, *this man, after he had offered one sacrifice for sins for ever, sat down on the right hand of God* (Heb 10:12). This is where, and in whom, *mercy and truth are met together; righteousness and peace have kissed [each other]* (Ps 85:10). The blood of Jesus Christ our Lord is not TYPICAL blood. Neither is his blood worthless in substance (as some would propagate). Neither is his blood in the hands of man to appropriate to themselves or to others. The blood of THE LAMB OF GOD is God's offering to himself, powerful to make satisfaction for the sins of those for whom it was shed. The application of his blood is in the hands of sovereign mercy and grace, which was promised and given to his elect in covenant before the world began. His blood is the blood of the everlasting covenant.

PERFECT SINFULNESS

Then the priest shall consider: and, behold, if the leprosy have covered all his flesh, he shall pronounce him clean that hath the plague: it is all turned white: he is clean.
Leviticus 13:13

O ur Lord saves only complete sinners. No one can come to Christ with one little bit of his own supposed righteousness to claim. The plague of leprosy is a picture of the plague of sin, which infests every fiber of fallen man both inwardly and outwardly. *From the sole of the foot even unto the head there is no soundness in it; but wounds, and bruises, and putrifying sores:*

they have not been closed, neither bound up, neither mollified with ointment (Is 1:6). This truth God our Saviour reveals to all his chosen in his call in electing grace. When he reveals Christ in his perfection in sovereign regeneration God the Spirit reveals our complete sinfulness.

We cry unto him as the leper of old "unclean, unclean!" By virtue of our sinful nativity we are permeated with the plague of which we cannot rid ourselves. We are perfect (complete) sinners. By virtue of Christ and his perfect (complete) sacrifice we are made perfectly righteous. A perfect salvation for perfect sinners! If our Priest pronounces us clean, we are completely free of sin before God—*but now once in the end of the world hath he appeared to put away sin by the sacrifice of himself* (Heb 9:26), *And you, being dead in your sins and the uncircumcision of your flesh, hath he quickened together with Him, having forgiven you all trespasses* (Col 2:13).

We may not be able to rest in the living experience of this wonderful and miraculous work of grace every moment of every day, however this is the way God sees it and this is how it really is! Those whom he has cleansed and revealed it to, believe it! There are two things, which every child of God will absolutely know.

1. His own complete sinfulness and unworthiness, and
2. Christ our Lord and his complete salvation.

I AM NOT AMONG YOU

And the LORD said unto me, Say unto them, Go not up, neither fight; for I am not among you; lest ye be smitten before your enemies.

Deuteronomy 1:42

A lthough God, by the mouth of Moses, forbade (religious, earthly) Israel to go up against, or engage in battle with the Amorites, they *went presumptuously up into the hill* anyway and were destroyed *in Seir even unto Hormah*. Those that were not immediately destroyed *returned and wept before the LORD, but the LORD would not hearken to their voice, nor give ear unto them.*

The reason for their severe judgment and defeat was threefold; they disobeyed God in unbelief; they trusted in themselves; and this was a work ordained for Joshua in a time appointed by God. *Joshua the son of Nun, which standeth before thee, he shall go in thither. He shall cause Israel* (spiritual Israel) *to inherit it.* God had clearly told them *I am not among you* to do this.

There is a vital Gospel lesson to be learned here. It is our Joshua (Jesus Christ) that has and will successfully conquer every enemy, and bring those chosen ones who have no sin (because of his redemptive work) to their promised abode in that day—*They shall go in thither, and unto them will I give it, and they shall possess it.* In all the Bible, God's command to his people is to *stand still and see the salvation of the Lord.* The Lord God is not with those who go presumptuously up into the hill.

God's judgment is always the same for those who presume that salvation is in some way according to their own will and efforts. *Many will say to me in that day, Lord, Lord, have we not prophesied in thy name? and in thy name have cast out devils? and in thy name done many wonderful works? And then will I profess unto them, I never knew you: depart from me, ye that work iniquity* (Mt 7:22).

God will never be savingly found among the Armenian, free will, works religionist, or the legalistic, Calvinistic intellectuals. The element of prideful self-righteous supremacy over the humbling work of Christ in sovereign redemption reveals the absence of his presence and blessing. May God help us to; *Go not up, neither fight.*

CLOTHES AND SHOES FOR LIFE

I have led you forty years in the wilderness: your clothes are not waxen old upon you, and thy shoe is not waxen old upon thy foot.
Deuteronomy 29:5

This miracle wrought by God for the children of Israel as they journeyed through the wilderness represents a far greater miracle of grace.

THE FORTY YEARS in the wilderness represents the believer's life in this world.

THEIR AGELESS CLOTHES represents the righteousness of Christ, by and in which we are adorned before God as he leads us to our predestinated abode.

THE SHOES upon their feet represents his sustaining grace, as we walk by faith through this world of adversity.

Every day for forty years, as they grew and persevered, their clothes and shoes remained new and suited for them. He has lovingly clothed his children with an everlasting righteousness. Thy *righteousness is an everlasting righteousness, and thy law is the truth* (Psalm 119:142). *He* has *shod our feet with the preparation of the gospel of peace* (Ephesians 6:15), *and his mercies are new every morning. It is of the LORD's mercies that we are not consumed, because his compassions fail not. They are new every morning: great is thy faithfulness* (Lam 3:22-23).

Our Lord in love, mercy and grace has provided for his people all that we will ever need for time and eternity in his blessed Son. We are kept by the power of God through faith in Christ Jesus as we journey through this valley of the shadow of death. We are clothed with the righteousness of Christ to one day stand in his glorious presence. My friends, nothing grows old in Christ. He is the same yesterday, today and forever. That which is in Christ remains the same, yet is always new! *The thing that hath been, it is that which shall be; and that which is done is that which shall be done: and there is no new thing under the sun* (Eccl 1:9). This verse speaks specifically of Christ and his redemptive work in its infinite purpose and perfection. The salvation of the Lord is as old as God himself, yet will remain new and enjoyed by the elect for all eternity.

YE CANNOT SERVE THE LORD

And Joshua said unto the people, Ye cannot serve the LORD: for he is an holy God; he is a jealous God; he will not forgive your transgressions nor your sins.

Joshua 24:19

God the Spirit here reveals the impossibility of any one, by the mere changing of the mind and determination of the natural will, forsaking their false god and serving the true and living God, or of God forgiving our sin while worshipping a false God. In verse 15 Joshua told the nation of Israel to choose them a god. It made no difference, either the false gods of their fathers before the flood or the false god of the Amorites.

It makes no difference whether we worship Gautama or John Calvin, Buddhism or Calvinism; we worship a false god and remain in our sin. *No man can serve two masters: for either he will hate the one, and love the other; or else he will hold to the one, and despise the other* (Mt 6:24). We cannot worship the Lord God of glory and embrace the false god of freewillism and legalism. We cannot bow to Dagon and receive the blessing of the atonement of God's blessed sacrifice, the Lord Jesus Christ. God, by his spokesman Joshua, is telling us here that salvation is by the purpose and power of God alone, and in Christ alone. Apart from God-given faith in Christ it makes little or no difference what we profess to believe or who we profess to worship. *I said therefore unto you, that ye shall die in your sins: for if ye believe not that I am He, ye shall die in your sins* (Jn 8:24). *I am He*—that is, God incarnate—God's only Propitiation for sin. He is all of God's salvation—None other. *Neither is there salvation in any other: for there is none other name under heaven given among men, whereby we must be saved* (Acts 4:12). There is no serving God or assurance of forgiveness of sin apart from spiritual union with Christ in regeneration. Do not expect God to forgive you of your sin while bowing in your self-righteousness to an impotent false Christ. May God cause us to die that we may live!

THE GOSPEL; A PRECIOUS GIFT

The word of the LORD was precious in those days
1 Samuel 3:1

O ur Heavenly Father has bestowed upon his children the precious gift of eternal life in his blessed Son. The gift of Christ to us is owing completely to his sovereign love, grace and mercy. It is he alone that merits worship, praise and thanksgiving for his unspeakable Gift. *God so loved that he sent*—tells it all! It is evident that those to and for whom he has revealed his great love, esteem him and his Gospel most precious.

Those who ONLY PROFESS to know him and love him are consumed with themselves, the cares of this life, and the pleasures of this world. To the child of God, even the most dear things to the flesh is but a trial of faith and a hindrance that sorrowfully dims our view of his precious face.

The Word of the Lord, the Gospel, is precious to those that love Him—To ALL those that love Him, without exception. What an honor! What a privilege! What a blessing, that our Lord would take us by the heart and set us at his table and feed our souls with heavenly portions! Why would we want to be anywhere else? No wonder Job said, *neither have I gone back from the commandment of his lips; I have esteemed the words of his mouth more than my necessary food* (Job 23:12). The means whereby God has graciously ordained to feed and care for those whom he loves, with an everlasting love, is not taken lightly or passed over by them. If God permits them to deny him for a brief moment, they like Peter, will repent with bitter tears. They will not have a hard, cold heart and the attitude that No matter what God or the preacher says, I WILL DO AS I PLEASE.

The prayer of the one to whom Christ and his Gospel is precious is, "Lord, take not thy Spirit from me. Teach me thy way. Help me to commit myself to you and your Word." When the Lord said to Peter, *If you love me, feed my sheep,* by the same token he says to the sheep, "If you love me, come and dine." Whether Christ is precious to us or not is a matter of the heart. May God in mercy and grace empty us of ourselves and fill us with Christ our Redeemer, love for Him, and commitment to Him.

OUR BEST IS WORTHY OF DEATH

And Saul said, . . . the people spared the best of the sheep and of the oxen, to sacrifice unto the LORD thy God; and the rest we have utterly destroyed. (33) And Samuel hewed Agag in pieces before the LORD in Gilgal.
1 Samuel 15:15

The only sacrifice that the Lord God will accept is that which he provides. The best that sinful man can offer in any shape, form or fashion is detestable in God's sight and will not be accepted by Him. Sinful man can only offer that which he IS; sinful and unworthy of the infinite and holy God. Saul in brazen disobedience attempted to offer to God that which God had refused and condemned to death. The inevitable consequence of his irreverent and blasphemous act was death.

The best of our storehouse of offerings acquired by our own doings is rotten and vile. *We are all as an unclean thing, and all our righteousnesses are as filthy rags; and we all do fade as a leaf; and our iniquities, like the wind, have taken us away* (Is 64:6). Our best compared to Christ our Lord and his sacrifice is repugnant and a stench in the nostrils of God. However, the sacrifice of Christ is a sweet smelling savor unto God, *as Christ also hath loved us, and hath given himself for us an offering and a sacrifice to God for a sweetsmelling savour* (Eph 5:2). Those that offer the works of their own hands unto God for acceptance will be hewn to pieces by God Almighty in his anger and wrath and suffer eternal damnation for their effort.

Those who come to God by his efficacious grace pleading the blood and righteousness of Christ alone for acceptance will eternally live in his presence enjoying the Light of his love and countenance, being fully and completely accepted before God in Him. Remember, the best Abraham had to offer was Isaac his only son. This was not good enough. *Abraham said, my son, God will provide himself a Lamb* (Gn 22:8). This he said before they ever arrived at the appointed place of sacrifice. The object of Abraham's God given faith was THE LAMB OF GOD'S PROMISE, not his own offering!

GLORIFIED DOGS

He bowed himself (Mephibosheth), and said, What is thy servant,
that thou (David) shouldest look upon such a dead dog as I am?
2 Samuel 9:8

A s Mephibosheth compared himself to a worthless dead dog
in the presence of King David for the great kindness shown
to him, so is the consideration of every child of sovereign grace.
As we sit at the King's table day after day reflecting upon and
delighting in the bounty of God's perpetual blessings in Christ we
can only bow and worship.

Though but dogs by nature, as Mephibosheth's feet were
under the table, our despicable shame and inabilities are under
the table, out of sight, out of God's sight by his tender mercies.
He *has raised us up in Christ and sat us together with Christ in
heavenly places.* Though we often see ourselves, and feel our
infirmities, in our native condition, God never does. He always
smiles upon his own as we feast with Him.

What a position for a dog! Accepted! Glorified! *Moreover
whom he did predestinate, them he also called: and whom he
called, them he also justified: and whom he justified, them he
also glorified* (Rom 8:30). As David's thoughts of love fell upon
Jonathan, and consequently upon Mephibosheth, he manifested
that love according to the desire of his heart. So it is with God's
love for Christ and his sheep. *In this was manifested the love of
God toward us, because that God sent his only begotten Son into
the world, that we might live through him* (1 Jn 4:9).

The love of God is the heart and soul of the sinner's salvation, from election to glorification. There is nothing mechanical or systematic involved in God's salvation. May God save us from legalizing and systemizing the glories of God's amazing, wondrous, love-saturated grace!

"Oh, love of God, how rich and pure!
How measureless and strong!
It shall forevermore endure
The saints' and angels' song."

INFINITE MERCY

O give thanks unto the LORD; for he is good; for his mercy endureth for ever.
1 Chronicles 16:34

It is only the believing sinner that has an interest in sovereign mercy. Those who imagine themselves to be righteous within themselves find the infinite mercy of our sovereign God to be quite offensive. But the child of God has been made to know by the grace of God that he is in desperate need of the mercy of God all the time. We understand that if God, for one split second, ceased to be merciful, we would perish without his Son and without recovery. *I will be merciful* is the ETERNAL WORD OF GOD! This declaration is more than prophetic.

God is declaring that he will be FOREVER MERCIFUL! God must be merciful, because mercy is his very nature—He has declared it. God has chosen, by necessity of his character, to manifest his mercy for sinful man in the Lord Jesus Christ. It is in the eternal Son of God, who was manifest as the eternal Son of

Man, that we poor sinners are objects of infinite mercy. *I will be merciful* was not God's declaration made first in time, but in eternity. This is his oath made to his Son in the eternal covenant of grace before the world was and repeated unto Moses for the assurance and comfort of all the elect of God. There is no mercy for fallen creatures apart from the person and work of God's appointed substitute, the Lord Jesus Christ. He is our MERCY SEAT!

"I SHALL SEE GOD"

And though after my skin worms destroy this body, yet in my flesh shall I see God.

Job 19:26

God's children DO see him and WILL see Him. He whom we see is none other than the Lord Jesus Christ. He *that hath seen me hath seen the Father* (Jn 14:9). When our Lord appeared unto Thomas after his resurrection, Thomas said, my *Lord and my God.* BY FAITH we see him now as he reveals himself to us by his Spirit through the preaching of the Gospel. The glorious Father is revealed in the glorious Son. *In him dwelleth ALL the fulness of the Godhead bodily* (Col 2:9). *For God, who commanded the light to shine out of darkness, hath shined in our hearts, to give the light of the knowledge of the glory of God in the face of Jesus Christ* (2 Cor 4:6).

Job was speaking of Christ, whom he knew by faith as his substitute. *For I know that my REDEEMER liveth, and that he shall stand at the latter day upon the earth* (Jb 19:25). It is by faith in Christ that God gives, whereby we see God in all his perfections—not only as our God, as our Saviour as well. The believer sees and knows him in love, mercy and grace, as well as in holiness, righteousness and justice. All the attributes of God are manifested in the person and redemptive work of the Lord Jesus Christ. This is where and how we see Him, as Job did.

Not only do we see him now, by faith. WE WILL SEE HIM presently face to face. This was Job's anticipation—*though AFTER my skin worms destroy this body, yet in my flesh SHALL I SEE GOD.* He looked by faith to the time when in his resurrection body he would see his Redeemer, who ever lives to make intercession for him. We too shall see him for our self. *Beloved, now are we the sons of God, and it doth not yet appear what we shall be: but we know that, when he shall appear, we shall be like Him; for WE SHALL SEE HIM AS HE IS* (1 Jn 3:2).

Therefore, not many days hence we will arrive to our place appointed by God. *For we know that if our earthly house of this tabernacle were dissolved, we have a building of God, an house not made with hands, eternal in the heavens* (2 Cor 5:1). Until then we say with Job, *If a man die, shall he live again?* (YES!) *all the days of my appointed time will I wait, till my change come* (Jb 14:14).

REPENTANCE

I have heard of thee by the hearing of the ear: but now mine eye seeth thee. Wherefore I abhor myself, and repent in dust and ashes.

Job 42:5-6

Repentance is a work of God's grace in the heart of every believer. Apart from the grace of God no man will repent. Repentance toward God is an evidence of spiritual life. One great example of what repentance is, is found in 1 Thessalonians 1:9; *For they themselves shew of us what manner of entering in we had unto you, and how* YE TURNED TO GOD FROM IDOLS TO SERVE THE LIVING AND TRUE GOD. Hearing with the physical ear and giving mental accent to the truth does not bring about true repentance.

This can only change man's ways for a while and to some degree, which only tends to self-righteousness. Only when Christ is revealed in the heart by God's efficacious Spirit in the preaching of the Gospel, will a sinful man, who is an idolater by nature, repent toward and believe on Christ. Faith in Christ alone—*now mine eye seeth thee*—which is a gift of God (Eph. 2:8-9), will cause a sinner to hate himself and love God. Repentance is a heart work perpetually carried on by the indwelling Spirit and grace of God. True repentance changes a person from the inside out.

Repentance and faith are twins. They always come together. The object of both is the same—CHRIST. The cause is the same—CHRIST. Repentance is not a work of the flesh that we do which God will accept. It is produced and directed by the faith that he gives.

Being confident of this very thing, that he which hath begun a good work in you will perform it until the day of Jesus Christ (Phil 1:6).

THE BRIDE OF CHRIST

Yet have I set my king upon my holy hill of Zion.
Psalm 2:6

Though the true church of the living God is but little esteemed in the religious world, the bride of Christ is most glorious in the eyes of God. It is the object of his love and affections. It is the place of his abode here on this earth, and it is through and in his church that he saves, comforts and assures the hearts of his people. The church is not an organization, it is a living spiritual body of which Christ is the Head and very life. Its members are those whom God has chosen, Christ has redeemed, called and glorified in himself.

The Lord Jesus Christ, having pleased the Father and being exalted in glory, exalts his church with him and in Him. In Christ, the church is holy and without spot of sin. The Lord Jesus Christ is head over all things to the church. There is no more noble, honorable, exalted position than being an inhabitant of Zion because that is where Christ dwells. The God given knowledge of this wondrous truth causes the Spirit to soar to heavenly heights and at the same time humbles the heart to grateful submission before the King in the midst of Zion.

COMING INTO THE HOUSE

But as for me, I will come into thy house in the multitude of thy mercy: and in thy fear will I worship toward thy holy temple.
Psalm 5:7

WHAT A GREAT HONOR AND PRIVILEGE God has bestowed upon his church to come together at the appointed time to worship Him, as Christ our Lord is revealed to us through the preaching of the Gospel! There is no generation gap when it comes to public worship. It is believing parents' responsibility to teach their children of Christ at home and to make sure that they are in the presence of the preaching of the Gospel as well. The preaching of the Gospel is the means that God has ordained to save his people. Teaching and rearing our children in the things of God is needful and very important, but making sure they are under the ministry of the Gospel is vital for them as well as ourselves.

THE CHURCH COMING TOGETHER TO WORSHIP CHRIST IS A JOY TO THE SAINTS. *I was glad when they said unto me, Let us go into the house of the LORD* (Ps 122:1). The church rejoices in Christ and the truth. *We will rejoice in thy salvation, and in the name of our God we will set up our banners: the LORD fulfill all thy petitions* (Ps 20:5). To hear of his love, mercy and grace is the desire of our hearts.

THE ASSEMBLING OF OURSELVES TOGETHER IN HIS NAME IS ALSO A SOLEMN THING. HE is the Lord God of glory—we are his people. He is revered among his church. His Word is truth, light and life. The worship of Christ is not a frivolous and trivial thing.

46

The position of the believing sinner is one of humbleness of mind and heart before him who is glorious in holiness. *Who is like unto thee, O LORD, among the gods? who is like thee, glorious in holiness, fearful in praises, doing wonders?* (Ex 15:11).

Not only is public worship a privilege, joy and a solemn thing, WE ARE GRACIOUSLY INSTRUCTED TO MEET IN HIS NAME. *Not forsaking the assembling of ourselves together, as the manner of some is; but exhorting one another: and so much the more, as ye see the day approaching* (Heb 10:24-25). When the church meets to worship Christ in the preaching and hearing of the Gospel it is a special time. *For where two or three are gathered together in my name, THERE AM I IN THE MIDST OF THEM* (Mt 18:20).

THE LANGUAGE OF A FOOL

The fool hath said in his heart, There is no God. They are corrupt, they have done abominable works, there is none that doeth good.
Psalm 14:1; Psalm 53:1

It would be unbecoming of me to judge another to be a fool. However he who knows the hearts of all individuals makes this judgment according to the virtue of his infinite wisdom and knowledge. According to the verse above, this issue is a matter of the heart, the inward man. The Bible also declares that which is in the heart will eventually be manifested outwardly. *Of the abundance of the heart his mouth speaketh* (Lk 6:45); *Those things which proceed out of the mouth come forth from the heart; and they defile the man* (Mt 15:18). Not only what comes out of the mouth reveals the heart, but our actions reveal the heart as

47

well. *Talk no more so exceeding proudly; let not arrogancy come out of your mouth: for the LORD is a God of knowledge, and BY HIM ACTIONS ARE WEIGHED* (1 Sm 2:3).

The true and living God has been pleased to reveal himself in the Scriptures, and in the person of the Lord Jesus Christ, exactly as he is in character and virtue. To think of Him, or speak of Him, or to live before Him, in any other way than in reverence and submission is foolish. Those who do so are saying in their heart, "There is no God." There are those who profess to be Christians who speak of him irreverently and deny his claims as he declares himself to be. This is foolish as well. There are those who give accent to his claims, yet live as if he did not exist. This too is foolish and a contradiction. In professing Christianity today, for the most part, it seems that the names "God" and "Jesus Christ" are nothing more than a by-word. To profess to be a Christian and ignore his Word, his Gospel, his church and live to one's self is nothing short of blasphemy, and in essence is to say "There is no God."

The focus of contemporary religion is numbers, money, programs, entertainment, physical healing—anything to please the people and keep them coming and giving. Most could go on doing what they are doing and never know that there is a God, and would not miss him if there was no God.

My friend, don't live the life of a fool trusting in an empty profession made while going through some ritual or ceremony, or because of the persuasions of some preacher or SOUL-WINNER. *Seek ye the LORD while he may be found, call ye upon him while he is near* (Is 55:6).

THE BEAUTY OF THE LORD

One thing have I desired of the LORD, that will I seek after; that I may dwell in the house of the LORD all the days of my life, to behold the beauty of the LORD, and to enquire in his temple.

Psalm 27:4

The psalmist has here revealed his singular—*one*—desire as a worshipper of the true and living God. Yet, his desire is THREEFOLD and incorporates the whole of a believer's life. The desire of David is the desire of every child of God. Anything short of this is coming short of the glory of God. The glory and beauty of God revealed in the Lord Jesus Christ captivates the hearts of those that have been blessed to see Him. His glorious person and wondrous work consumes and enthralls the sinner whose acceptance by him has been made plain.

The desire of the believer is to be in his presence here on this earth. To be in the presence of his Gospel, his people, and never be separated from Him, is what we seek after. The earthly pleasures of this life that the Lord has given us to enjoy are trivial compared to the spiritual blessings that we have in knowing him and living in his house.

In his house we behold his glorious attributes in the beauty of holiness. To know him and be found in Him, not having our own righteousness, but His, is a wonder that we ponder with joy unspeakable. As we behold his sovereign love, mercy, and grace we are drawn to him as a moth to a flame. Gazing upon his sacrifice, we see our sin put away forever, and cannot help but bow in thanksgiving and gratitude. As we live in him we see his great hand of providence working all things to our good and his glory. His work in his people's lives is a thing of beauty and wisdom that comforts and assures those that dwell in his presence.

The desire of the believer is to know more, see more, and understand more of Him. As we grow in grace and knowledge of him we desire him and the things of God more. The child of God loves his Gospel and listens with inquiring ears to hear a word from their Master. For the people of God to meet together and worship him in the Gospel is not optional or a thing of convenience, it is a burning desire given to them by God himself.

His mouth is most sweet: yea, he is altogether lovely. This is my Beloved, and this is my Friend, O daughters of Jerusalem (Sg 5:16).

THE BELIEVER'S DESIRE

One thing have I desired of the LORD, that will I seek after; that I may dwell in the house of the LORD all the days of my life, to behold the beauty of the LORD, and to enquire in his temple.
Psalm 27:4

The child of God's desire here on earth is to know Christ, to behold Him, and to learn more of Him. He is the fairest of ten thousand to the heart and soul of all who are blessed to see him by faith. He is the singular object of their faith and worship. All else vanishes like the light of a candle in the presence of the noonday sun.

Like David, you will find those who are captivated with the beauty of the holiness which saturates and permeates his infinite being as God, and his sinless virtues as the God-man. All the days of their life are spent desiring, seeking, beholding and inquiring of Him. To those who truly know him and see him by faith, he is their life—*When Christ, WHO IS OUR LIFE, shall appear, then shall ye also appear with him in glory* (Col 3:4). When Christ is the ONE THING we desire, all else will be consumed by his perfections. The alluring glitter of this world, as well as the cares and troubles of this earthly pilgrimage, are only a bump in the road and a hindrance ordained by God to cause us to look to him the more.

By God's grace, the comforts and pleasures of this world, though real and compelling to the flesh, are cast aside by those who really desire Him; that they may enquire of him in the Gospel, and worship him as his glorious person and work is proclaimed—*I was glad when they said unto me, Let us go into the house of the LORD* (Ps 122:1). The believer's desire is evident by his gladness of heart and faithfulness to attend the things of Christ. The believer will find reason and excuse to enquire in his temple. The unbelieving professor will give reason and excuse to himself why he cannot be faithful.

Those who love and desire the pleasures of this world more than Christ are offended by this truth, while those who love and desire Christ are humbled by it. To believe the doctrines of grace as fact is one thing, and a good thing, but to know and love Christ, and those doctrines revealed in Him, is salvation and the desire of every child of God. Therefore, those who know Christ can say with David, *One thing have I desired of the LORD, that will I seek after; that I may dwell in the house of the LORD all the days of my life, to behold the beauty of the LORD, and to enquire in his temple.*

I WILL GIVE THANKS FOR EVER

To the end that my glory may sing praise to thee, and not be silent. O LORD my God, I will give thanks unto thee for ever.
Psalm 30:12

The giving of thanks is much more than words. Thanksgiving to our blessed God involves the heart and soul—all our being. *Bless the LORD, O my soul: and all that is within me, bless his holy name* (Ps 103:1). This is what is meant in our text by *TO THE END THAT MY GLORY MAY SING PRAISE TO THEE*—My HEART shall sing praise to thee. The God of Israel has given his people a heart of gratitude for all things, both spiritual and providential. *In every thing give thanks: for this is the will of God in Christ Jesus concerning you* (1 Thes 5:18).

The thankful heart is A HEART OF WORSHIP. How could one not worship and adore the ONE who is altogether lovely, simply because he loves us (we who are unworthy), and has given us all things that are good, just, and right—being PLEASED to do so? He has *blessed us with all spiritual blessings in heavenly places in Christ* (Eph 1:3). He has given us all our hearts could desire for time and eternity! Therefore, *O LORD my God, I will give thanks unto thee forever.*

The thankful heart is A HEART OF SUBMISSION. Those that enjoy the blessings of Christ, willingly, and with desire, submit to his Lordship. It is his blessed, sovereign will in which a thankful heart rejoices. The substance of our prayers is *Our Father which art in heaven, Hallowed be thy name. Thy kingdom come. Thy WILL BE DONE IN EARTH, AS IT IS IN HEAVEN.* We, by his grace and mercy, cast down our arms of rebellion and lay at his blessed feet in WORSHIP and SUBMISSION. He has made it so!

The thankful heart is A HEART OF COMMITMENT. To be committed to our Lord and Saviour is the aim and goal of every child of God. To honour and glorify our Great God and Saviour is the believer's work of faith and labor of love. *Let your light so shine before men, that they may see your good works, and glorify your Father which is in heaven* (Mt 5:16). To be faithful to him who loved us and gave himself for us is the commitment of every thankful heart. To be committed to Him, his Gospel, and his church is the believer's life. The Psalmist said, *I WILL SING PRAISE TO THEE, and be not silent.*

The thankful heart EXPRESSES HIS GRATITUDE IN HOLY COMMUNION WITH THE BLESSED TRINITY. By his Spirit we offer up praise and thanksgiving in *psalms and hymns and spiritual songs, singing and making melody in your heart TO THE LORD.*

The thankful heart ENJOYS SWEET FELLOWSHIP. *Truly our fellowship is with the Father, and with his Son Jesus Christ* (1 Jn 1:3).

THE BELIEVER'S DELIGHT

I delight to do thy will, O my God: yea, thy law is within my heart.
Psalm 40:8

The Lord Jesus Christ is the one in whom all believers delight. Delight suggests love, joy, satisfaction, pleasure, etc. Delight is a passion or an emotion of the heart. The words in the verse above are the words of our Lord, making reference to all that he did in his humanity, especially his vicarious death on the cross as his people's substitute.

It was not the suffering, shame, or the ACTUALLY BEING MADE SIN that was his delight. It was the doing of his Father's will that brought him joy, satisfaction, and delight. The child of God delights in the same—In God—In Christ—In his Gospel—in his church—In the doing of his will.

It is the Father's will that we believe on his Son, rejoice in his Word, and commit ourselves to his body—His church. This is our delight while we are here on this earth. What a privilege! What an honour! What a calling! What a delight!

The delight and satisfaction found in knowing Christ, worshipping Him, and believing his Gospel, makes the sufferings and cares of the flesh seem but little, and makes them bearable in our pilgrimage through this life. Our Lord said in John 16:33, *These things I have spoken unto you, that in me ye might have peace. In the world ye shall have tribulation: but be of good cheer; I have overcome the world.* When we are cast down in spirit and begin to murmur and complain, it is ALWAYS because we are looking at SELF, rather than looking unto him in whom we delight. *Why art thou cast down, O my soul? And why art thou disquieted within me? Hope thou in God: for I shall yet praise Him, who is the health of my countenance, and my God* (Ps 42:11).

The man that delights in the Lord is a blessed and happy man, because his faith is in THE ONE who is able, and will provide for him in all things. *Blessed is the man that walketh not in the counsel of the ungodly, nor standeth in the way of sinners, nor sitteth in the seat of the scornful. But HIS DELIGHT IS IN THE LAW OF THE LORD; and in his law doth he meditate day and night. And he shall be like a tree planted by the rivers of water, that bringeth forth his fruit in his season; his leaf also shall not wither; and whatsoever he doeth shall prosper* (Ps 1:1-3).

If he is not our delight, then we have nothing substantial in which to delight. All other pleasures and joys will eventually perish, and we will be confined to our own misery forever.

HEARTLESS FAITH

I delight to do thy will, O my God: yea, thy law is within my heart.
Psalm 40:8

These are the words of our King David, the Lord Jesus Christ, in the eternal covenant of grace. Here he reveals to his people his heart's desire for their salvation and the glory of his Father. Not only did he agree with, and to do his Father's will, he delighted to do so. Yea, even, this was in his heart. This was not something that he must do only out of obligation and fulfillment of promise, he must accomplish salvation as our substitute because of love for his Father and for his people.

The great work of redemption is more than doctrine, it is more than systematic theology, it is one perfect man dying for those sinful creatures whom he everlastingly loves, in obedience to God whom he loves. This truth makes the passage in Romans 8:38-39 *(For I am persuaded, that neither death, nor life, nor angels, nor principalities, nor powers, nor things present, nor things to come, Nor height, nor depth, nor any other creature, shall be able to separate us from the love of God, which is in Christ Jesus our Lord)* more than a dogmatic doctrinal truth. It reveals the heart and soul of Christ in the Gospel.

The desire of our Lord is not unlike his children's desire. Is this not the cry in our hearts? *I delight to do thy will, O my God: yea, thy law is within my heart?* Love for Christ, which he has given us, must be the singular motive and rule of life for what we do, no matter how noble the work, or it is even as a sounding brass and a tinkling symbol, and will be burned with fire.

I have no heart for a heartless Christ preached by a heartless preacher.

BEAUTIFUL FOR SITUATION

Beautiful for situation, the joy of the whole earth, is Mount Zion, on the sides of the north, the city of The Great King.
Psalm 48:2

There are several definitions for *situation.* The Greek definition for this word, in the context of this passage of Scripture, is ELEVATED or LIFTED UP. The English definition is CURRENT CONDITIONS THAT CHARACTERIZE SOMEBODY'S LIFE OR EVENTS IN A PARTICULAR PLACE.

Zion, the church of the living God, is gloriously exalted in the perfections of the Great King, the Lord Jesus Christ. The beauty of the saints radiates his beauty as his creation and workmanship. The condition of the church is righteous, holy and just as she abides in Him. The position of the redeemed is one of infinite elevation—He *hath raised us up together, and made us sit together in heavenly places in Christ Jesus: That in the ages to come he might shew the exceeding riches of his grace in his kindness toward us through Christ Jesus* (Eph 2:6).

Zion, the city of The Great King, is the residence of The Great King as well. *And I heard a great voice out of heaven saying, Behold, the tabernacle of God is with men, and he will dwell with them, and they shall be his people, and God himself shall be with them, and be their God* (Rv 21:3). The Light of the city of The Great King is none other than the Lamb himself, for *The city had no need of the sun, neither of the moon, to shine in it: for the glory of God did lighten it, and the Lamb is the light thereof* (Rv 21:23).

Zion is so situated that everywhere you look you see the beauty of the King, the Lamb in the midst of the throne—*Thine eyes shall see the King in his beauty* (Is 33:17). The Lord himself looks upon Zion, admiring her, and *presents it to himself a glorious church, not having spot, or wrinkle, or any such thing; but that it should be holy and without blemish* (Eph 5:27).

LET GOD BE MAGNIFIED

Let all those that seek thee rejoice and be glad in thee: and let such as love thy salvation say continually, Let God be magnified.
Psalm 70:4

The heavens and earth declare the greatness and glory of the one true and living God. All things were made by him and for his pleasure (Jn 1:1-3; Rv 4:11). This is clearly seen by all, yet believed by few. It is only those to whom Christ is revealed that clearly see God's saving glory and grace, and believe. It is *such as love thy salvation* (that) *say continually, Let God be magnified.* The love, mercy, grace and all of God's attributes is magnified in Christ and his redemptive work. The purpose of God in Christ, in the salvation of his elect, is the manifestation of his glory; *Nevertheless he saved them for his name's sake, that he might make his mighty power to be known* (Eph 1:4-6; Ps 106:8).

God's people magnify him in his Word. They love, believe, and submit to the Scriptures that declare his glory. *I rejoice at thy word, as one that findeth great spoil* (Ps 119:162).

The believer magnifies God the Living Word, the Lord Jesus Christ. He is God incarnate. In him dwells all the fulness of the Godhead bodily. *And Thomas answered and said unto him, my Lord and my God* (Jn 20:28).

His people magnify him in salvation. In Christ alone is all our salvation. *The LORD liveth; and blessed be my rock; and exalted be the God of the rock of my salvation* (2 Sm 22:47).

The child of God magnifies him in all providence. He is sovereign over all things for his people's good and his glory. *And we know that all things work together for good to them that love God, to them who are the called according to his purpose* (Rom 8:28).

He is magnified in the hearts of his people and they confess to all that he is God, and beside him there is none other. *Let the words of my mouth, and the meditation of my heart, be acceptable in thy sight, O LORD, my Strength, and my Redeemer* (Ps 19:14). *I will bless the LORD at all times: his praise shall continually be in my mouth* (Ps 34:1).

To magnify the great name of our God is the joy and delight of the church. Those who glorify and magnify man do not know the true and living God. Yet some day all will be made to submit to Him. *For it is written, As I live, saith the Lord, every knee shall bow to me, and every tongue shall confess to God* (Rom 14:11).

SELF-PROMOTION

For promotion cometh neither from the east, nor from the west,
nor from the south.

Psalm 75:6

It is peculiar to mankind (especially religious mankind) to promote themselves. A little notoriety, a little recognition, a little attention, and the flesh is launched like a rocket. They love to see their name displayed with flashing lights and to be identified with those who are highly esteemed. They want all to know of their acceptance and success. They want the world to know how much they are in demand. While they put on an air of humility their heart is bursting with pride. They have learned how to position themselves in the eyes of men to receive praise.

Promotion of this sort issues not from God. In our text-verse the NORTH is conspicuously left out. In Psalm 48:2 we see why. *Beautiful for situation, the joy of the whole earth, is mount Zion, on the sides of the north, the city of the Great King.* The Holy Spirit reveals to us that promotion for God's people and God's preachers comes from God. It is few that are able to wait on the Lord and to be content with God's promotion.

Our Lord *made himself of no reputation, and took upon him the form of a servant* (Phil 2:7). The apostle Paul wrote by the inspiration of God, *I am the least of the apostles, that am not meet to be called an apostle* (1 Cor 15:9). It is heart breaking to see some, who once seemed humbled by the Gospel, sell their soul for a mess of glorified pottage. The Gospel of Christ, made effectual by God the Spirit, does not send the soul into arrogant orbit above and beyond others, he brings his captives beneath their brethren, and to union with their brethren. May God in grace and mercy teach us who we are, who he is, and thereby may we experience our insignificance in comparison to others in God's great design.

For if a man think himself to be something, when he is nothing, he deceiveth himself (Gal 6:3).

A HAPPY MAN

For thou, LORD, hast made me glad through thy work: I will triumph in the works of thy hands.
Psalm 92:4

When Paul stood before King Agrippa to defend the Gospel, the first thing he said was, *I think myself happy.* How is it that one can be happy, when in such circumstances as this man? The Lord had made him glad! God had revealed Christ and his redemptive work to him. Like David and Paul, every true child of God is glad. He rejoices in God, and in Christ, and his work of redemption—*By whom also we have access by faith into this grace wherein we stand, and rejoice in hope of the glory of God* (Rom 5:2). The believer is happy that God is God! Religious men argue and debate over how much power God has, when in truth they deny the power of God. The child of God is glad, yea happy, that God is omnipotent.

The true Christian is glad that God is sovereign in salvation. The believer is a happy man because Christ has put away his sin forever. What could make a poor sinner happier than knowing that he is no longer condemned before God; that his sin is forgiven? This good news, that no sin can be laid to our charge because God *hath made him sin for us,* makes a happy heart. The child of God is glad and rejoices in the imputed righteousness of Christ. He is our righteousness! We do not wallow in our filthy rags; we stand in his everlasting, glorious righteousness. All of these spiritual blessings and benefits of his grace makes the believing heart rejoice and joy in our God. But the greatest blessing of all, that makes the heart glad, is our knowledge of Christ in vital union with him in regeneration.

By his grace and Spirit we experience that blessed fellowship with the Father and Son in the Gospel, and the preaching of it. By faith that he gives, we see Him, we hear his voice, we follow Him, rejoicing in his Word. Though circumstances around us may be unpleasant, though the flesh may suffer, though the outward man perish, the inward man, created in Christ Jesus, is glad and rejoices in the God of his salvation. *Whom having not seen, ye love; in whom, though now ye see him not, yet believing, ye rejoice with joy unspeakable and full of glory* (1 Pt 1:8).

DIVINE HEALING

Bless the LORD, O my soul, and forget not all his benefits: who forgiveth all thine iniquities; who healeth all thy diseases.
Psalm 103:2

This would be a perfect man—one that has no sin and no disease. I can think of only one that fits this description; The Lord Jesus Christ—The Godman. The Lord Jesus Christ became so much one with his people that he was made our sin, and we are made his righteousness. We are perfect in Him! Iniquities and disease are one and the same in this context. The HEALERS of our day like to apply this to themselves and physical healing. But this is not the case. Granted, if we are healed physically it is the Lords doing. However, the healing spoken of and portrayed in the Scriptures is the redeeming work of the great physician in the putting away of our sin and the imputation of his righteousness to us. Do I believe in divine healing? Emphatically YES! I believe Christ heals his people eternally! *Speak ye comfortably to Jerusalem, and cry unto her, that her warfare is accomplished, that her iniquity is pardoned: for she hath received of the LORD'S hand double for all her sins* (Is 40:2).

FORGIVEN

Who forgiveth all thine iniquities.
Psalm 103:3

To hear and understand that WE ARE FORGIVEN OF ALL SIN BY THE ALMIGHTY, is the best news that a poor sinner could receive. We, who are nothing but sin and can do nothing but sin, having been freely, lovingly, everlastingly forgiven from the heart of God, can do nothing but by his grace worship and praise him, for his mercy and grace shown toward us in Christ Jesus our Lord. We did not merit the forgiveness that we enjoy. As he loves us freely—*I will love them freely* (Hos 14:4), he forgives us freely—*Being justified freely by his grace through the redemption that is in Christ Jesus* (Rom 3:24).

The first cause of forgiveness is love. The means whereby we are forgiven is the execution of that love, which was manifest in the person and work of Christ, our sin bearer. Forgiveness of sin is not only a judicial work; it is a heart work. We, as David, are a people after God's own heart. True, justice must be satisfied, but God's love must be fulfilled as well. Can it not be truthfully, scripturally said that God forgave me because he loved me? *Herein is love, not that we loved God, but that he loved us, and sent his Son to be the propitiation for our sins* (1 Jn 4:10).

I fear that sometimes we are so careful to be doctrinally correct (and we should be careful) that we neglect to remember that all God and his Son is to, does for and in his people, is according to his tender mercy and everlasting love. *Have mercy upon me, O God, according to thy lovingkindness: according unto the multitude of thy tender mercies blot out my transgression* (Ps 51:1). *The LORD hath appeared of old unto me, saying, Yea, I have loved thee with an everlasting love: therefore with lovingkindness have I drawn thee* (Jer 31:3).

Therefore, forgiveness of sin is an efficacious act of sovereign love toward guilty, wretched sons of Adam. The Lord Jesus Christ appeared once in the end of the world to put away our sin by the sacrifice of himself, and *Hereby perceive we the love of God, because he laid down his life for us* (1 Jn 3:16); he put away our sin.

He died for us because he has always loved us. Therefore, we are forgiven in Him.

WHY?

Nevertheless he saved them for his name's sake, that he might make his mighty power to be known.
Psalm 106:8

And in very deed for this cause have I raised thee up, for to shew in thee my power; and that my name may be declared throughout all the earth
Exodus 9:16

It is evident that the majority of religionists will go to any extreme to rob God of his power and glory, especially in the salvation of sinners and the damnation of the wicked. This they do by placing man's eternal destiny in the hands of man. Free will works religion makes the power of God and the person and work of Christ nothing more than an instrument in the hands of the fallen creature to use as he will. Every false Gospel and false preacher perverts the Word of God to present God and his Christ to be less than the Scriptures declare them to be, and man to be more than he is.

The context of the two passages above never wavers throughout the Bible. It is God in Christ that saves sinners with an everlasting salvation according to his own will and purpose for his own glory, without the aid or assistance of the sinner. From election to glorification, the mighty power and glory of God is revealed. This is not just a point of doctrine; this is the heart and soul of the Gospel and our only hope.

WHY DOES GOD SAVE SINNERS? HE *saved them for his name's sake,* to the praise of the glory of his eternal power and sovereign love, mercy, and grace which was given us in Christ Jesus before the world began. *Who hath saved us, and called us with an holy calling, not according to our works, but according to his own purpose and grace, which was given us in Christ Jesus before the world began* (2 Tm 1:9).

WHY DOES GOD PUNISH THE WICKED? The power and glory of God is revealed in the judgment and condemnation of the unbelieving, as well as in the salvation of his elect. God's holy character and divine nature necessitates his hatred for and condemnation of sin. *God is ANGRY with the wicked every day* (Ps 7:11). *The foolish shall not stand in thy sight: thou HATEST all workers of iniquity* (Ps 5:5). His name, glory, person and being is holy and righteous, therefore for his great name's sake and honor he must by no means clear the guilty, that his NAME might be declared throughout all the earth.

The revelation of God's power in love, mercy, and grace in Christ, and the revelation of his hatred and wrath upon sin, is equally vital to his honor and glory.

GOD IS GOOD!!

Oh that men would praise the LORD for his goodness, and for his wonderful works to the children of men! For he satisfieth the longing soul, and filleth the hungry soul with goodness.
Psalm 107:8-9

God is essentially good. All the time, in every way, God is good. The goodness which is ascribed unto God is peculiar only to Him; *There is none good but one, that is, God* (Mk 10:18).

There is no being, created or uncreated, that is even close to being good compared to our God. As a matter of fact, we mere mortals have no idea of what this adjective means, when used to describe he who alone is good. Even those who have been quickened by his Spirit, have very little comprehension of the goodness of God.

We see and experience his goodness more clearly as he satisfies our longing soul and fills us with his goodness. But we believe he is good all the time, because he says he is good. To the unregenerate, God is believed to be good only when they are well and prospering in this world. When *good things* come their way, then they say, "God is good." When the child of God is afflicted, suffering, and stripped of all his earthly possessions, he bows his heart before the throne of mercy and worships God, and glories in his GOOD GOD. Our flesh may be ordained to suffer greatly while we are in this world, but our longing and hungry soul is ordained to be satisfied and filled with the goodness of God.

Truly God is good to Israel (Ps 73: 1).

MY HEART IS FIXED

O God, my heart is fixed; I will sing and give praise, even with my glory. Awake, psaltery and harp: I myself will awake early. I will praise thee, O LORD, among the people: and I will sing praises unto thee among the nations. For thy mercy is great above the heavens: and thy truth reacheth unto the clouds. Be thou exalted, O God, above the heavens: and thy glory above all the earth;

Psalm 108: 1-5

These verses are the same as (Ps 57:7-11). These are the words of Messiah, CHRISTOS, the Anointed of God. The word *fixed* here means PREPARED. It also means that his heart will not be changed or altered from present convictions. With perpetual determination, his heart is set upon the accomplishment of his Father's will and purpose in the establishment of an everlasting righteousness for his elect, whereby his truth is upheld, and his mercy and grace is manifested in their salvation, in which his Father is glorified.

In love, our Redeemer's heart was prepared for and fixed upon fulfilling God's holy law to perfection for every one of his people from the least to the greatest. No matter what the cost, no matter what the demands, no matter what the suffering, he would endure temptation, trials, and testings, and please his Father in all things as our substitute. In all his life he sinned not, yea, he even conquered every enemy of the soul. Thereby, he wrought an everlasting righteousness for his people.

That is not all! His heart was fixed upon putting away sin forever for those he loved. His people are a sinful race and their sin must be punished. The only punishment for sin is death. His heart was as much fixed upon, and prepared for, being made sin (which he actually was), and dying under the wrath of God (which he actually did), as it was to live a holy and righteous life. He said (in respect to his life and death as our substitute), *I delight to do thy will O God*—And—*Now is my soul troubled; and what shall I say? Father, save me from this hour:* BUT FOR THIS CAUSE CAME *I* UNTO THIS HOUR (Jn 12:27).

Our Lord's heart was fixed upon making his people acceptable to God by making them righteous, putting away their sin, and in doing so, glorifying his Father in every respect. And that he did!

And now, because his heart was fixed, our heart is fixed upon him, We say, *Awake up, my glory; awake, psaltery and harp: I myself will awake early. I will praise thee, O Lord, among the people: I will sing unto thee among the nations. For thy mercy is great unto the heavens, and thy truth unto the clouds. Be thou exalted, O God, above the heavens: let thy glory be above all the earth.*

GRACE AND MERCY

He hath made his wonderful works to be remembered: the LORD *is gracious and full of compassion*
Psalm 111:4

Every day the elect of God lives upon this earth is an illustrious display of God's sovereign mercy and grace. Whatever comes our way is from his loving hand of compassion and pity. No matter what it is that we experience, joy and gladness or pain and suffering, it is good because our good God has purposed it to be good for us, and that it will be. Every thing that is a blessing to the child of God is a curse to the unbelieving.

Every spiritual blessing—*Blessed be the God and Father of our Lord Jesus Christ, who hath blessed us with all spiritual blessings in heavenly places in Christ* (Eph 1:3), and every temporal blessing—*In every thing give thanks: for this is the will of God in Christ Jesus concerning you* (1 Thes 5:18), comes to his people through and by the person and work of our Redeemer, the Lord Jesus Christ. The physical bread that we enjoy, as well as the spiritual Bread that we feast upon, is from his hand. The making of the clothes for our backs, as well as the everlasting righteousness by and in which we are accepted before God, is all his doing. Therefore, *I will praise thee, O Lord my God, with all my heart: and I will glorify thy name for evermore* (Ps 86:12).

DO WE NEED TO TALK?

Psalm 115:3

I s the God you worship more holy, more just, more sovereign, more infinite, more majestic, and more glorious than the God I worship?

Let me know. We need to talk!

My God is in the heavens: he hath done whatsoever he hath pleased (Ps 115:3).

THE EMOTIONS OF A DEAD MAN

The dead praise not the LORD, neither any that go down into silence.

Psalm 115:17

The great work of redemption accomplished by Christ Jesus our Lord is his work alone. The sovereign work of God the Spirit in regeneration is likewise. The persevering faith and spiritual life of the child of God is solely owing to the triune God as well. The whole work of salvation from election to glorification, is preformed by someone outside our self. However, this great work preformed in us is not without effect. In the experience of grace, those who were spiritually dead toward God before, are now alive.

Where and when life exists there is feeling or emotion. We are not saved by feelings, and neither is our feelings the object of faith. However, life without feeling would be somewhat abstract. This is not the case of those who are alive in Christ. The spiritual virtues of *Christ in you* insist upon lively benefits of his grace which in themselves are not composed of man. And they bring and maintain that which we need and enjoy as believers. BELIEVING (faith) is the first and foundation of all that God gives, from which flows love, hope, confidence, assurance, consolation, comfort, peace, joy, and rejoicing in Christ Jesus our Lord.

A dead man has no love or praise for Christ and his truth. He finds, experiences, and feels no need for the things of God.

The affections of those who remain dead are upon things that are dead. The desires of the heart are revealed in the course of our life.

For those believers who struggle with emotions and shrink back from feelings for fear of misplaced faith, may I suggest reading these passages? *Now the God of hope fill you with all joy and peace in believing, that ye may abound in hope, through the power of the Holy Ghost* (Rom 15:13), and *Mary said, my soul doth magnify the Lord, And my spirit hath rejoiced in God my Saviour* (Lk 1:46). I am full of *joy and peace*—but I should not and do not feel it?

The presence of feelings is not always a denial of faith.

GOD'S THOUGHTS CONCERNING JUSTIFICATION

For ever, O LORD, Thy word is settled in heaven.
Psalm 119:89

Following are God's thoughts concerning substitution and justification. This is the context of all Scriptures. This is the good news from God to his people whom he has chosen in Christ before the world was. All who know him and preach his Gospel wholeheartedly agree.

FOR HE HATH MADE HIM TO BE SIN FOR US, *who knew no sin; that we might be made the righteousness of God in him* (2 Cor 5:21).

CHRIST HATH REDEEMED US FROM THE CURSE OF THE LAW, being made a curse for us: for it is written, Cursed is every one that hangeth on a tree (Gal 3:13).

WHO HIS OWN SELF BARE OUR SINS IN HIS OWN BODY ON THE TREE, that we, being dead to sins, should live unto righteousness: by whose stripes ye were healed (1 Pt 2:24).

Yet it pleased the LORD to bruise Him; he hath put him to grief: when THOU SHALT MAKE HIS SOUL AN OFFERING FOR SIN, he shall see his seed, he shall prolong his days, and the pleasure of the LORD shall prosper in his hand (Is 53:10).

Much more then, being now JUSTIFIED BY HIS BLOOD, we shall be saved from wrath through him (Rom 5:9).

But THIS MAN, AFTER HE HAD OFFERED ONE SACRIFICE FOR SINS FOR EVER, SAT DOWN ON THE RIGHT HAND OF GOD (Heb 10:12).

Knowing that A MAN IS NOT JUSTIFIED BY THE WORKS OF THE LAW, but by the faith of Jesus Christ, even we have believed in Jesus Christ, that we might be justified by the faith of Christ, and not by the works of the law: for BY THE WORKS OF THE LAW SHALL NO FLESH BE JUSTIFIED (Gal 2:16).

That being JUSTIFIED BY HIS GRACE, we should be made heirs according to the hope of eternal life (Ti 3:7).

REFORMED OR DEFORMED?

For ever, O LORD, thy word is settled in heaven.
Psalm 119:89

QUOTE: "We never want to focus on MORE NARROW ASPECTS OF REFORMED THEOLOGY to the neglect of TRUTHS THAT ARE CENTRAL, and that we share with MANY OTHER CHRISTIANS."— C.J. Mahaney, Sovereign Grace Ministries.

At the heart of all doctrinal error is the denial of particular redemption, most often in a subtle (cleverly indirect) manner. Such as Satan, who said, *thou shalt not surely die* (Gn 3:4). *Now the serpent was more SUBTLE than any BEAST of the field which the LORD God had made. And he said unto the woman, Yea, hath God said, Ye shall not eat of every tree of the garden?* (Gn 3:1).

The above quote from a reformed preacher who claims to believe the doctrine of God's sovereign grace, reveals what he (along with a multitude of others) really believes. He cleverly and deceitfully states that TOTAL DEPRAVITY, UNCONDITIONAL ELECTION, LIMITED ATONEMENT (PARTICULAR REDEMPTION), IRRESISTIBLE GRACE, AND THE PERSEVERANCE OF THE SAINTS, are not vital and central to the Gospel. He calls them "more narrow ASPECTS," and further states they are not "truths that are central."

To appease and embrace those who hate and deny the very truths that ARE CENTRAL (NOT JUST ASPECTS) AND VITAL to the glory of God, the Gospel of Christ, and the salvation of the elect, he further states there are "many other Christians" who do not believe the truth. Such charismatic rhetoric reduces and pollutes the blessed Gospel of Christ in his redemptive work to nothing more than just another doctrine for rebels to accept or reject. In their acceptance they are none-the-better, and God is blasphemed.

The reformed movement of our day is nothing more than an attempt to bridge the gulf between Calvinism and Arminianism at the expense of the truth for personal gain and self-glory. To make the truth palatable to all men is impossible without perversion and compromise. Those who do so shall be rewarded for their efforts. All the TRUTHS of God are CENTRAL, NARROW, and the FOCUS of the true Gospel and every believer in Christ.

EVERLASTING RIGHTEOUSNESS

Thy righteousness is an everlasting righteousness, and thy law is the truth.

Psalm 119:142

The righteousness that is ours by imputation and impartation is the righteousness of one who is infinitely and immutably righteous—The Lord Jesus Christ. Even when our sin was imputed to him, he remained righteous because he was God, and God cannot be anything less than righteous. When he was made sin for us, it was not his transgression, but ours for which he suffered death as a man. In this great transaction there is a great mystery of which we can only comprehend in part. Two great truths (many more than two) are revealed in the substitutionary death of our Lord.

IN HIS DEATH HE WAS MADE SIN—*For he HATH MADE HIM [to be] SIN FOR US, who knew no sin; that we might be made the righteousness of God in him* (2 Cor 5:21).

IN HIS DEATH HE DID NOT SIN—*And being found in fashion as a man, he humbled himself, and became OBEDIENT unto death, even the death of the cross* (Phil 2:8).

The Lord Jesus Christ died justly because he was made our sin (our sin became His)—*For Christ also hath once suffered for sins, the just for the unjust, that he might bring us to God, being put to death in the flesh, but quickened by the Spirit* (1 Pt 3:18). He died righteously because he did no sin, had no sin of his own (*WHO KNEW NO SIN*) and was obedient to the will and law of God. Therefore, it is as equally true that he *knew no sin,* as it is that he *was made sin*. If Christ our Lord be the same yesterday, today, and forever—If he be indeed God in the flesh—Then indeed his righteousness is an everlasting righteousness, and all those to whom his righteousness is imputed has an everlasting righteousness as well.

These great truths in no way contradict each other, but rather reveal the manifold wisdom of God in the great work of redemption. Some things revealed in the Scriptures are to be believed and declared rather than explained.

Thank God the Scriptures clearly reveal the substitutionary work of Christ and the imputed righteousness of Christ, as one and the same. It is the work of God and not man, otherwise it would not be everlasting and we would have no hope of salvation.

THE CHURCH OF THE LIVING GOD

The LORD hath chosen Zion; he hath desired it for his habitation. This is my rest for ever: here will I dwell; for I have desired it.
Psalm 132: 13-14

The church of the living God is not an organization founded by man and inhabited by those who choose to join its ranks. God's church on earth (and in Heaven) is the spiritual body of the Lord Jesus Christ, consisting of those whom he has chosen for himself before the foundation of the world. Christ himself is the Head. Zion (His church) is the result of his desire, and he dwells in her forever. Although the masses claim its name and fame, only those whom he has redeemed by his blood, sanctified by his Spirit, and called by his grace are members of his glorious body.

Only those in whom Christ the Lord dwells live and enjoy the blessings of his grace. It is in Zion that he reveals himself, and is worshipped and praised. The very existence of Zion is the evidence of God's sovereign grace and mercy. It is Impossible for the world to comprehend the glory of Christ in Zion and appreciate her beauty. They try to mimic it with form and ceremony and are a reproach to God. The true church of God is but little esteemed by man, yea, even scorned by religion. Yet, it is indeed desired and chosen by God and there will he rest forever.

I pray for them: I pray not for the world, but for them which thou hast given Me; for they are thine. And all mine are thine, and thine are mine; and I am glorified in them (Jn 17:9-10).

HIS MERCY ENDURETH FOR EVER

O give thanks unto the God of heaven: for his mercy endureth for ever.

Psalm 136:26

We are reminded no less than forty one times in the Bible that God's mercy is everlasting—*His mercy endureth for ever,* and that because he is good. All men in this world, no matter what their status, live under God's good providence. But God said of his mercy, *I will make all my goodness pass before thee, and I will proclaim the name of the LORD before thee; and will be gracious to whom I will be gracious, and will shew mercy on whom I will shew mercy* (Ex 33:19).

Grace and mercy are inseparable and always sovereignly directed toward the elect of God, and only comes through the glorious person and redemptive work of the Lord Jesus Christ. Outside of Christ there is no mercy for sinful man. But thanks be unto God, in Christ there is mercy for evermore. As long as the Lamb is in the midst of the throne of God, reigning over us—as long as he who obtained our eternal redemption loves and makes intercession for us, there will be everlasting mercy even for the chief of sinners.

O GIVE THANKS UNTO THE GOD OF HEAVEN!

TWO HEART ISSUES

Keep thy heart with all diligence; for out of it are the issues of life.

Proverbs 4:23

The heart in holy writ always makes reference to the inward man, the real man. The heart is the seat, the origin of all emotions, which prompt the actions of the outward man. The life of mankind is the heart. This is the spirit of man. Life issues or springs forth from it. The natural heart of man is dead toward the things of God as the result of the fall, rendering only that which is desirable and satisfying to the flesh.

According to God by the prophet Jeremiah, *the heart is deceitful above all things and desperately wicked.* Unregenerate man is void of any thing good and righteous, *As it is written, There is none righteous, no, not one: there is none that doeth good, no, not one* (Rom 3:10 & 12). Only the things of this natural life, this world (whatever it might be), stir the emotions of the DEAD HEART. In essence, man is in bondage to himself by virtue of a deceitful and wicked heart. God almighty's commentary of the fallen race of the Anti-deluvian world still stands today; *GOD saw that the wickedness of man was great in the earth, and that every imagination of the thoughts of his heart was only evil continually* (Gn 6:5). But thanks be unto God, in the regenerating work of God the Spirit, we are given a new heart. We are given a new life, a new Spirit, a new nature. We are given the life of Christ.

However, the old man is still present with us and will remain with us until death. The new heart is captive of the Lord Jesus Christ, and from it issues love and desire for him, and the things that are not of this world, rather the things of God. Thus, being partakers of the divine nature, a constant warfare is raging—*I find then a law, that, when I would do good, evil is present with me* (Rom 7:21). That *evil* is natural self, *For the flesh lusteth against the Spirit, and the Spirit against the flesh: and these are contrary the one to the other* (Gal 5:17). To deny the two natures is to glorify the natural man and deny the existence of the new man.

PRECIOUS MEMORIES

We will be glad and rejoice in thee . . . we will remember thy love more than wine.
Song of Solomon 1:4

We all have pleasant and precious memories of times and people in our life that brought great joy and happiness. Often we are caught up in the nostalgia of yesteryear. Sometimes it is almost as if we were there again. Eventually we are awakened to the reality those days are gone and we can never go back, and can only relive them in our memories. As precious as those memories are, they cannot be compared to the preciousness of Christ's ever-present love for us, his people.

The Gospel stirs our minds to remember he loves us with an everlasting love, and how that love was manifest for us. It was his sovereign, unchanging love that sent him to this world. It was his love that made him a man of sorrows and acquainted with grief as he lived a sinless life for us. It was his loved that moved him to suffer untold agonies of soul and body as he was willingly made sin for us, and died on the tree. And now upon the throne of his glory, he reigns in his office of High Priest, in love, making intercession for us!

These living memories do not cause us to look back with sadness, but rather to look forward to when we shall see him who loved us, face to face. Until then—*We will be glad and rejoice in thee—we will remember thy love more than wine.*

JEALOUSY

Jealousy is cruel as the grave: the coals thereof are coals of fire, which hath a most vehement flame.
Song of Solomon 8:6

Jealousy of one person to another is the offspring of a proud and insecure heart of unbelief. There is no scriptural foundation for a child of God to be jealous of anyone or anything in this world. The believer knows that God has provided all he is and has, according to his own good pleasure and will, whether it be talents, abilities or possessions. Jealousy causes ill-will, greed, covetousness, a holier-than-thou attitude, and hurtful divisions. The jealous heart is in bondage to self-righteousness and spiritually impaired. If jealousy goes unchecked, it will consume the man. Jealousy is not a fruit of the Spirit and can never be the tenor of a believer's life. Where there is jealousy, there is no humility, no repentance, no submission to God, no love for the brethren, and no worship of Christ.

But there is a Godly jealousy, which every believer has. The child of God is jealous over Christ and his Gospel. This jealousy is the same as DESIRE. This is not a selfish, fleshly passion. The child of God wants Christ and all that he is and has for himself. He wants it for others as well. The believer is possessed and consumed with the Gospel and the things of God, as the unbeliever is possessed and consumed with self and the things of the world.

I SAW THE LORD

In the year that king Uzziah died I saw also the Lord sitting upon a throne, high and lifted up, and his train filled the temple.
Isaiah 6:1

To see the Lord Jesus Christ in a vision as Isaiah did, surely would be a wonder to behold. The vision refers to the exaltation of Christ, after his humiliation here on earth. Although we do not see him in a vision, we see him exactly as Isaiah did; On the throne of his glory, high and lifted up, worshipped by the innumerable company of saints being accompanied by the host of heaven.

We see him by faith in his glorious reign, as he is revealed in his Word by the preaching of the Gospel. For the child of God to SEE HIM AS HE IS, initiates worship and adoration. Peace and comfort flows from him to us like a river, because we see ourselves gathered there with him. His love, mercy, grace, and omnipotence presides over all his loved ones to their good, to the destruction of every foe, and to his glory. Because he is there and we are there with him, everything will be all right. Every one of his sheep sees him exactly the same, because he is the same— *Jesus Christ the same yesterday, and to day, and for ever* (Heb 13:8).

We see him having accomplished eternal redemption for us, having purchased us with his own blood, having put away our sin by the sacrifice of himself, having raised from the dead proving our justification, having ascended to the throne of his glory ever living to make intercession for us. The sight of him there assures our hearts before him here.

The believer's desire is to see the Lord, and he has promised to give us the desire of our heart. *One thing have I desired of the LORD, that will I seek after; that I may dwell in the house of the LORD all the days of my life, to behold the beauty of the LORD, and to enquire in his temple* (Ps 27:4). Of all the wonders there are to behold there is nothing that compares to beholding the Lamb in the midst of the throne. How do you see the Lord?

HERE AM I

Also I heard the voice of the Lord, saying, whom shall I send, and who will go for us? Then said I, HERE AM I; send me.
Isaiah 6:8

There is no doubt that God knows where we are geographically. And he knows where we are spiritually as well. This *Here am I* in the verse before us is exactly the same place where our Heavenly Father eventually brings all his children. He brings us to the place of willingness before his Majesty—*Thy people shall be willing in the day of thy power, in the beauties of holiness from the womb of the morning: thou hast the dew of thy youth* (Ps 110:3). When our Lord confronted the Apostle Paul, he said; *Lord, what wilt thou have me to do?* (Acts 9:6). When God brings us to *HERE AM I*, he has brought us unto submission to Him. This is a condition of the new heart, which delights to do his will.

Our Lord brings us (and keeps bringing us) to absolute reverential worship and acquiescence to his holy character and virtues. This place where he brings us is to the end of our self and to his feet. This we do willingly, because he makes us love to be willing. When we can truly say *HERE AM I*, we are saying *not my will be done—Your will be done—*DO WITH ME WHAT SEEMS GOOD IN YOUR SIGHT. Where are those who have been chosen by the Father, redeemed by the Son, and regenerated by the Spirit? They are precisely where God has placed them, and they are glad to be there! *HERE AM I* is simply giving our selves up to God's sovereign purpose and good providence. Until we can say in our hearts *HERE AM I,* we are yet in rebellion and unbelief.

TRUTHFUL ERROR

To the law and to the testimony: if they speak not according to this word, it is because there is no light in them.
Isaiah 8:20

The Word of God admonishes us to *be no more children, tossed to and fro, and carried about with every wind of doctrine, by the sleight of men, and cunning craftiness, whereby they lie in wait to deceive* (Eph 4:14). Every doctrinal error is hedged about with many truths. It is like a beautiful, tasty apple pie laced with arsenic—when consumed it is fatal. The main and active ingredient is a paradox. The absence of the central truth is the deadly poison. An example of this is to use correct doctrinal terminology, and conveniently leave the application of these truths to the disposal of man.

Many are so mesmerized by intellectual genius, oratorical skill, and personal charisma, they can never see what is missing. When the glorious truths of the Gospel are made subject to the supposed exercise of man's free will, Christ is rendered an instrument in the hands of sinners, rather than the substance and cause of salvation in the hand of God.

Universal redemption (nonexistent) made particular and effectual by the exercise of faith is not the eternal redemption obtained for the elect of God by the sacrifice of Christ our Lord. The universal love of God (nonexistent) that embraces all of mankind is not the love of God manifested in the death of his Son for his bride. Preachers and teachers may cleverly use all the

Biblical and Calvinistic terminology they choose. However, until they clearly and distinctly proclaim, without apology, that God Almighty only, forever, and in every sense, loves his chosen ones in Christ alone; that God's Lamb died for them alone, and no one else; that they had nothing to do in it or with it, I am convinced they are purposely and premeditatedly omitting the heart of the Gospel. They preach a lie for personal gain and for the praise of man.

Particular and effectual redemption accomplished by Jesus Christ alone is the theme of all holy writ. It is the heart and soul of the Gospel of God. When this essential truth is veiled or omitted, there is poison in the pie (See also 2 Kings 4:40). Don't consume it!

WHAT DO I BELIEVE AND PREACH?

To the law and to the testimony: if they speak not according to this word, it is because there is no light in them.
Isaiah 8:20

Man's opinion, when it comes to the things of God, is of no consequence or profit to the glory of God, or to the salvation of sinful man. There must be a scriptural foundation, or it is nothing more than heresy and a false Gospel. *To the law and to the testimony: if they speak not according to this word, [it is] because [there is] no light in them* (Is 8:20). I do not have all understanding, nor do I have all the answers. However, God in grace and mercy, has made me to know that only that message which gives God ALL the glory, sets forth God the Son as its sum and substance, declaring God the Spirit as the divine revealer of the truth of God, is the heart and soul of the true Gospel of Christ. The Gospel, when made effectual by God's Spirit does not rehabilitate, reform or put man on probation—It gives life to spiritually dead men. *SALVATION IS OF THE LORD!* Concerning this Gospel, here is a brief summery of what I believe and preach.

1). THE GOD OF THE BIBLE IS ABSOLUTELY SOVEREIGN! This means that God reigns over all his creation in all time, and in every place, especially in salvation. See Is 52:7; 1 Chr 16:31; Ps 47:8; Ps 93:1; Ps 96:10; Ps 97:1; Ps 99:1; Rv 19:6.

2). ALL OF ADAM'S POSTERITY IS SPIRITUALLY DEAD. All are guilty of sin before God, none is good, none is righteous, none has faith, and none has either the desire or ability to come to Christ, apart from God's irresistible, sovereign grace. See Ps 110:3; Is 53:1-12; Jn 5:40; Jn 6:44; Rom 3:9-23; Eph. 2:1-10.

3). GOD CHOSE HIS PEOPLE IN CHRIST BEFORE THE WORLD BEGAN. See Jn 15:16; Jn 15:19; Acts 22:14; Rom 8:28-39; 1 Cor 1:27-28; Eph 1:4; 2 Thes 2:13; 1 Pt 1:2; 1 Pt 2:9-10; RV 17:14

4). ALL FOR WHOM CHRIST DIED SHALL BE SAVED, JUSTIFIED, AND MADE RIGHTEOUS.

This is the purpose of God's grace in Christ toward his people. See Mt 1:21; Mt 18:11; Jn 10:11; Jn 10:15; Jn 6:37; Acts 2:47; Acts 13:48; 2 Cor 5:21; 1 Tm 1:15. Not one for whom Christ died will be lost. See Jn 6:39; Jn 10:28; Jn 17:2

5). GOD'S GRACE IS POWERFUL AND EFFECTUAL IN CALLING HIS PEOPLE AND GIVING THEM LIFE. See Rom 9:14-24; Eph 1:3-7; Eph 2:8-9; Gal 1:15 ; Phil 1:6; Ti 3:5.

6). THOSE WHOM GOD HAS CALLED UNTO HIMSELF, AND SAVED WITH AN EVERLASTING SALVATION, SHALL PERSEVERE (CONTINUE) IN HIS GRACE UNTO THE END. See Jn 6:39; Phil 1:6; 1 Pt 1:3-5

7). THE PREACHING OF THE GOSPEL IS THE MEANS WHEREBY GOD, BY HIS SPIRIT, REVEALS CHRIST TO THE SAVING OF OUR SOULS. See Rom 10:14-15; 1 Cor 1:21; Eph 1:13

All the Scriptures point us to Christ. The Gospel message reveals our sin, our degradation, and Christ as the poor sinners only hope. Salvation is in his hands, not ours. May God in mercy reveal Christ to our hearts.

A GREAT LIGHT

The people that walked in darkness have seen a great Light: they that dwell in the land of the shadow of death, upon them hath the Light shined.

Isaiah 9:2

In this and the previous chapter, God the Spirit reveals a beautiful picture of Christ's deliverance of those whom God the Father has given to Him. They are a wonder of God's sovereign grace, manifested in the appearing and redemptive work of Christ Jesus our Lord. God's elect, who have all their life walked in spiritual darkness, dwelling in the land of the shadow of death, have now by the power and revelation of God, by the preaching of the Gospel of Christ, seen a great Light—*For God, who commanded the Light to shine out of darkness, hath shined in our hearts, to give the light of the knowledge of the glory of God in the face of Jesus Christ* (2 Cor 4:6).

The Lord Jesus Christ is that GREAT LIGHT, and in him is life, truth, peace, and assurance. It is now said of those upon whom that Light has shined, *Ye are all the children of light, and the children of the day: we are not of the night, nor of darkness* (1 Thes 5:5). When God effectually reveals Christ to a sheep who walks in darkness, there is a radical change; a change that is compared to the difference in darkness and light.

Our Lord gives us an example in Saul's (Paul's) conversion—*And it came to pass, that, as I made my journey, and was come nigh unto Damascus about noon, suddenly there shone from heaven a great light round about me* (Acts 22:6). Thereafter, Paul's life was never the same. Others saw that light, but not with discernment, just as many see and hear the truth, without faith and only with natural understanding. That great Light is a wonder and amazement only to those upon whom the Son of Righteousness has shined.

WORSHIP

And in that day shall ye say, praise the LORD, call upon his name, declare his doings among the people, make mention that his name is exalted.
Isaiah 12:4

It has always been the honor and privilege of the church of the living God, in every dispensation, to worship him whose name is above every name. This verse speaks particularly of the Lord Jesus Christ and his church, after his humiliation and exaltation. There can never be any thing added to private or public worship. If there is, it is not of God. He alone is to be praised, whether in song or word.

His doings—His great work of redemption, is the sum and substance of the Gospel, and his great name is therein exalted among his people. His church calls upon him in prayer and supplication in worship and devotion. Although contemporary religion has devised and invented many things, calling it worship, the Scriptures are clear that when the church comes together in his name, we are to worship him in SPIRIT and in TRUTH. Believers sing the Gospel, pray the Gospel and preach the Gospel.

O LORD, HAVE WE WAITED FOR THEE!

Yea, in the way of thy judgments, O LORD, have we waited for thee; the desire of our soul is to thy name, and to the remembrance of thee.
Isaiah 26:8

In the place where God's Word is proclaimed; where the Lord Jesus Christ manifests himself in the preaching of the Gospel, the desire of the souls of the children of God is—WAITING WITH ANTICIPATION OF HEARING OF HIM. The hearing of the Gospel brings him to remembrance and stirs our souls to worship. This the child of God diligently, joyfully seeks—*I was glad when they said unto me, Let us go into the house of the LORD* (Ps 122:1).

The nominal, casual professor has no real heart or craving for Christ, and finds every excuse that he can to justify absenting himself from the public worship of God. He tries to blame providence or lays the blame at someone else's door. The fact is, everyone does pretty much what they want (except when providence does indeed make it impossible) as the means and opportunity is provided. We are found at the dinner table when it is time for the evening meal. So, those that hunger and thirst after Christ are found gathered together feasting upon Christ, when it is time to hear the Gospel.

I fear many have arrived at the doctrines of Christ and yet never come to Christ. As God has given every living thing a desire for food, he has given all of his people a desire for the bread from heaven. We know the food is delicious, because of who it is that beckons us to come and sit at his table. *JESUS saith unto them, Come and dine* (Jn 21:12).

The Psalmist spoke for every awakened sinner when he said, *One thing have I desired of the LORD, that will I seek after; that I may dwell in the house of the LORD all the days of my life, to behold the beauty of the LORD, and to enquire in his temple* (Ps 74:4).

For the believer, the most pleasant, peaceful, satisfying place on this earth is with other believers worshipping Christ their Lord, in the preaching and hearing of the Gospel. May God in grace and mercy give us an insatiable, perpetual hunger for Christ and his Gospel!

THE LIVING DEAD

Thy dead men shall live, together with my dead body shall they arise. Awake and sing, ye that dwell in dust: for thy dew is as the dew of herbs, and the earth shall cast out the dead.
Isaiah 26:19

Natural life and corporal death are a present and evident phenomena of which we know little, and understand less by carnal reasoning. The Bible is a spiritual book, and therefore is a book of miracles as we perceive it by the revelation of God the Spirit. The book of God sets forth death, as well as life, as a wondrous miracle of God as executed by and revealed in Christ. Only by living faith in the experience of grace, can we believe or comprehend the incomprehensible, and conceive the inconceivable. We who were spiritually dead shall awake, live, and sing together with him who was dead and is now alive forevermore. That can only be conceived by the spiritually minded, and experienced by almighty grace.

The verse before us reveals God's promise of everlasting life to his chosen, and their bodily resurrection as well. Both are, and will be, made effectual by our Lord's death and resurrection. For the child of God, this natural life is a life of death. However, *I am crucified with Christ: nevertheless I live; yet not I, but Christ liveth in me: and the life which I now live in the flesh I live by the faith of the Son of God, who loved me, and gave himself for me* (Gal 2:20).

This natural man is as good as dead because of the inevitable—*As it is appointed unto men once to die* (Heb 9:27). It is just as certain that those for whom Christ died, those who WERE dead, shall never die! *Whosoever liveth and believeth in me shall never die. Believest thou this?* (Jn 11:26). One day soon this natural body will succumb to death, *So when this corruptible shall have put on incorruption, and this mortal shall have put on immortality, then shall be brought to pass the saying that is written, Death is swallowed up in victory* (1 Cor 15:54).

A SURE FOUNDATION

Therefore thus saith the Lord GOD, Behold, I lay in Zion for a foundation a Stone, a tried Stone, a precious corner Stone, a sure Foundation: he that believeth shall not make haste.
Isaiah 28:16

The passage before is not speaking of a creed, a doctrine, or a system of religion (traditional or contemporary). Without minimizing the necessity of sound doctrine clearly setting forth the Lord Jesus Christ, it is evident throughout Scripture that the foundation of our salvation is much more than agreement with doctrinal truth. One may embrace the fundamental truths of the Gospel and never rest upon that SURE FOUNDATION, which is none other than the blessed Son of God.

The person of the Lord Jesus Christ is the NECESSARY LIFE of the believing child of God—*He that hath the Son hath life; and he that hath not the Son of God hath not life* (1 Jn 5:12). Without question, myriads of professing Christians have only a religious experience for the foundation of their salvation, and always incorporate something they have done or know into the mix. There is only ONE sure foundation, and that is Christ. One may believe THE GOSPEL, hold and believe the DOCTRINES OF GRACE, ably argue and debate with convincing accuracy the points of sound doctrine, and never be vitally living upon and in the Lord Jesus Christ.

I understand there are some who would disagree with this truth, but those that do, stumble upon the Foundation Stone, who is Jesus Christ our Lord, the Rock of our salvation. He who truly believes upon Christ, believes because the life of Christ has been imparted to him in regeneration—*Verily, verily, I say unto you, The hour is coming, and now is, when the dead shall hear the voice of the Son of God: and they that hear shall live* (Jn 5:25). This truth is critical and necessary to be set forth because of the element of truth which is involved, and in which one is prone to find false security in the knowledge thereof.

What we know is vital, but WHO we know is MOST VITAL! *And this is life eternal, that they might know thee the only true God, and Jesus Christ, whom thou hast sent* (Jn 17:3). Believe what you will, call it what you please, but this I know for a certainty—*For other Foundation can no man lay than that is laid, which is Jesus Christ* (1 Cor 3:11). He is a LIVING, REIGNING, PERSON whom I must know, or else I must perish!

COMMITMENT

Isaiah 29:13

The only reason a child of God has need or desire for commitment and faithfulness to Christ, his Gospel and his church, is the Revelation of Christ and his faithfulness and commitment to us. Nothing else will work as pertaining to the heart. Faithfulness and commitment (or lack thereof) can often be seen, but not always. Negligence, carelessness, casual indifference, inconsistency, and downright disengagement and separation can clearly be seen.

However, it is possible and very likely, that many appear to be faithful by their profession and performance, yet are not. The Scripture says, *Wherefore the Lord said, Forasmuch as this people draw near me with their mouth, and with their lips do honour me, but have removed their heart far from me, and their fear toward me is taught by the precept of men* (Is 29:13). The child of God is taught of Christ by God the Spirit—*Take my yoke upon you, and learn of Me; for I am meek and lowly in heart: and ye shall find rest unto your souls* (Mt 11:29).

It is in Christ we learn commitment and faithfulness. His meekness and lowliness of heart reveals his commitment to our cause. A heart for Christ originates from his heart for us—*We love Him, because he first loved us* (1 Jn 4:19). Many have a heart for his good blessings, such as solving their problems, good health, prosperity, and a good heaven to go to when they die. They are very happy that he is committed to them (so they think). Yet they see no need for commitment to him, and have no heart desire for Him.

What law constrains us in commitment to Christ? The law of love!

ASSURANCE FOREVER

And the work of righteousness shall be peace; and the effect of righteousness quietness and assurance for ever.
Isaiah 32:17

There is no peace between God and man, or peace in the heart of man, in trying to keep the law of God. Those that do so have not submitted themselves to the righteousness of God in Christ. They are going about *to establish their own righteousness* (Rom 10:3). There is only ONE who fulfilled all righteousness and brought in an everlasting righteousness for sinners—CHRIST JESUS THE LORD. That work of righteousness, which our substitute wrought, pleased God because it was perfect, and therefore it is a work of peace. God's law demanded a perfect work! Christ provided it! Now the law of God is satisfied on behalf of those to whom it is imputed.

The effect of Christ's righteousness imputed is peace as well—*quietness and assurance for ever.* For the child of God there is an inward peace that comes with believing in Christ. He is THE LORD OUR RIGHTEOUSNESS. The faith God gives to HIS people produces a quiet, calm assurance in the heart and conscience, removing quilt, and yields a tranquility and serenity of mind. The effect is as sure as the work! God purposed both, and both are the work of Christ.

But after that the kindness and love of God our Saviour toward man appeared, Not by works of righteousness which we have done, but according to his mercy he saved us, by the washing of regeneration, and renewing of the Holy Ghost; Which he shed on us abundantly through Jesus Christ our Saviour; That being justified by his grace, we should be made heirs according to the hope of eternal life (Ti 3:4-7).

THE DOUBLE CURE

*Speak ye comfortably to Jerusalem, and cry unto her, that her
warfare is accomplished, that her iniquity is pardoned: for she
hath received of the LORD's hand double for all her sins.*
Isaiah 40:2

When the Lord Jesus Christ put away his people's sin, he
put away ALL their sin—Perfect sacrifice—Perfect
Forgiveness! This he accomplished by himself. This is the
comfortable, joyful, good news of the Gospel of God's saving
grace. This message is the herald from the throne of grace. The
church's warfare is accomplished, because her iniquity is
pardoned through the sacrifice of the Lamb of God, which taketh
away the sin of the world.

Not only is her warfare accomplished and iniquity
pardoned, she is adorned with the perfect, imputed righteousness
of Christ. So perfect is her garment, she enjoys full and complete
acceptance before the thrice-holy God. Not only did God
Incarnate bear his people's sin, he worked out an everlasting
righteousness for them, and freely gave it to them. What a
transaction! For our sins and iniquity, we have received pardon,
and the perfect righteousness of the Lord Jesus Christ!

"Rock of Ages, cleft for me,
Let me hide myself in thee;
Let the water and the blood,
From thy wounded side which flowed,
Be of sin the double cure,
Save from wrath and make me pure."

THE GLORY OF GOD

The glory of the Lord shall be revealed.
Isaiah 40:5

The glory of God is his infinite perfections and attributes. *Who [is] like unto thee, O LORD, among the gods? who [is] like thee, glorious in holiness, fearful [in] praises, doing wonders?* (Ex 15:11).

The essential glory of God is idiosyncratic to him alone. He is the uncaused being. All that he is he never acquired. He forever remains the same. All that can be known of him is that which he is pleased to reveal. This is that glory which he has revealed of himself in the incarnation and redemptive work of Christ. This is the context of the passage before us.

This glory is spoken of throughout the Scriptures in both the Old and New Testament. In Exodus 33:18-19 we see his sovereign mercy in Christ, and in 2 Corinthians 4:6 we see his sovereign grace in the face of the Lord Jesus Christ. The glory of God in the salvation of all the elect shall be and is revealed to them—*for the mouth of the LORD hath spoken it.* In Ephesians 1:3-12 we see the glory of God in Christ from election to glorification. Those to whom Christ has been revealed give him all the glory for all things, especially the salvation of their souls.

THE GLORY OF GOD REVEALED

The glory of the LORD shall be revealed, and all flesh shall see it together: for the mouth of the LORD hath spoken it.
Isaiah 40:5

This passage of Scripture is prophetic. It is concerning the coming of our great God and Saviour, the Lord Jesus Christ, the Messiah. It also concerns the Gospel dispensation from the incarnation of Christ until the end of all things.

The glory of the Lord is none other than the Lord Jesus Christ, and the salvation of his elect in and by Him. This glory we now see and enjoy by faith, as he is revealed by his Spirit through the preaching of the Gospel, is the same glory in which we will rejoice in heaven, throughout eternity.

The infinite God resides everlastingly in the Lord Jesus Christ, in all his glorious attributes—*For in him dwelleth all the fulness of the Godhead bodily* (Col 2:9). Although the effect of his attributes are seen in innumerable ways, his full glory is personified and revealed only in the Lord Jesus Christ—*I and my Father are one* (Jn 10:30). He *that hath seen me hath seen the Father* (Jn 14:9).

In infinite grace and mercy, God the Father is pleased to reveal himself to his people in the person of his glorious Son. We see his glory in his being made flesh—*And the word was made flesh, and dwelt among us, (and we beheld his glory, the glory as of the only begotten of the Father,) full of grace and truth* (Jn 1:14). We behold his glory in his fulfillment of the law and establishing an everlasting righteousness for us—*to finish the transgression, and to make an end of sins, and to make reconciliation for iniquity, and to bring in everlasting righteousness* (Dn 9:24); and in his death, as our substitute and sacrifice—*I have glorified thee on the earth: I have finished the work which thou gavest me to do* (Jn 17:4). We see his glory in his exalted position as our Prophet, Priest and King. The Lord Jesus Christ, having glorified the Father here on this earth, is now seated on the throne of his glory in majesty and splendor, upholding all things by the word of his power.

This is he of whom the prophets spoke. This is he who did indeed appear to put away sin by the sacrifice of himself. This is he who is even now our Great High Priest and intercessor. This is he whom we preach in all his glory!

HE SHALL NOT FAIL

Behold my Servant, whom I uphold; mine elect, in whom my soul delighteth; I have put my Spirit upon Him: he shall bring forth judgment to the Gentiles.
Isaiah 42:1

This prophecy is concerning the coming of the Messiah, the emphasis being upon the person and work of Christ. The Father speaks of him who is to come in highest regard and affection. The Lord Jesus Christ is seen in his incarnation glorifying his Father, and accomplishing everlasting salvation for his elect. God the Father upholds and delights in him, because of who he is and the perfect work which he performs. In great measure, his people behold him as the Father beholds him, and delights in him for the same reason as well.

We uphold and delight in him, in our hearts, by faith. He is the singular object of our faith as we see his eternal power, Godhead, and perfect work in his sinless humanity. He alone is the object of our worship, the Redeemer of our souls, the delight of our hearts. His people behold him, as he is revealed in his glorious person and perfect work, as our substitute. He shall not fail his Father, nor did he fail his people. We dare not look, nor desire to look, to any one other than who God commands and invites us to behold—THE LORD JESUS CHRIST!

THE PURPOSE OF HIS PEOPLE

This people have I formed for myself; they shall shew forth my praise.

Isaiah 43:21

This passage of Scripture is a beautiful picture of God's everlasting salvation and good providence for his people. This one verse reveals the eternal purpose of grace in Christ Jesus, his blessed Son. God's purpose is to save his people for his glory. Their purpose is to show forth his glory. In this twofold purpose it is all the work of God. The singular purpose for the sheep of Christ to remain on this earth is to glorify the Father and the Son. The singular purpose for the saints to inhabit heaven is the same, to glorify God. The church, the body of Christ, shows forth his praise in three ways, which are inseparable, and of one purpose:

BY BELIEVING ON CHRIST. Faith in Christ alone, for all our salvation, from start to finish, honors and glorifies the God of purpose, and the purpose of God in Christ our Redeemer. Believing on Christ for who he is (God Incarnate) and what he has done (redeemed his people), shows forth the praises of the Everlasting Father and the Everlasting Son, in whom all fulness dwells. *For God, who commanded the light to shine out of darkness, hath shined in our hearts, to [give] the light of the knowledge of the glory of God in the face of Jesus Christ* (2 Cor 4:6); he *that believeth on the Son of God hath the witness in himself: he that believeth not God hath made him a liar; because he believeth not the record that God gave of his Son* (1 Jn 5:10).

BY BEING IDENTIFIED WITH CHRIST, HIS GOSPEL AND HIS PEOPLE IN THIS WORLD. Contrary to popular opinion, which is— ALL PEOPLE OF ALL RELIGIONS WORSHIP THE SAME GOD AND ARE GOING TO THE SAME HEAVEN, there is but one God, one Lord Jesus Christ, and one Gospel. This one Gospel gives all glory and honor to Christ. This one people believes this Gospel, giving it their allegiance, and will be identified with none other. *But ye are a chosen generation, a royal priesthood, an holy nation, a peculiar people; that ye should shew forth the praises of him who hath called you out of darkness into his marvelous light* (1 Pt 2:9).

BY FAITHFULNESS AND COMMITMENT TO CHRIST, HIS GOSPEL, AND TO EACH OTHER. This is a work of God as well. *For it is God which worketh in you both to will and to do of his good pleasure* (Phil 2:13). *Let your light so shine before men, that they may see your good works, and glorify your Father which is in heaven* (Mt 5:16).

LOOK UNTO ME

Look unto me, and be ye saved, all the ends of the earth: for I am God, and there is none else.

Isaiah 45:22

There is but ONE to whom we must look for salvation. There is but ONE to whom we must look for forgiveness of sin. There is but ONE to whom we must come for eternal life. This ONE is none other than the GOD-MAN—the Lord Jesus Christ—*A just God and a Saviour; there is none else!*

Man in his fallen, dead, ignorant condition will do anything except what God says to do. He will come to anyone except to WHOM God says to come, believe anyone, anything and everything except the Word of God. He will do so until God in grace and mercy effectually calls, regenerates and reveals the Lord Jesus Christ to the heart, by his Spirit through the preaching of the Gospel. *For after that in the wisdom of God the world by wisdom knew not God, it pleased God by the foolishness of preaching to save them that believe* (1 Cor 1:21).

When God effectually calls elect sinners to himself, they come! *All that the Father giveth me shall come to Me; and him that cometh to me I will in no wise cast out* (Jn 6:37). They come gladly, joyfully, willingly, by faith that he has given. *For by grace are ye saved through faith; and that not of yourselves: it is the gift of God* (Eph 2:8). They come looking unto him only. When one truly sees Christ by faith, as he is revealed in the Gospel, he is overwhelmed and stands in awe of his glorious person. The sinner who truly sees Christ as his salvation is nauseated with his own supposed righteousness, which he trusted in before. *I have heard of thee by the hearing of the ear: but now mine eye seeth thee. Wherefore I abhor myself, and repent in dust and ashes* (Jb 42:5-6).

We look unto Christ alone, who is all our salvation and desire. There is no salvation in any other—*Neither is there salvation in any other: for there is none other name under heaven given among men, whereby we must be saved* (Acts 4:12). Away with our GOOD WORKS, away with our credentials, away with our traditions, away with our false gods! It is him alone that shines as a beacon before us to light the way to glory. He is THE WAY, THE TRUTH and THE LIFE. And NO MAN can come to the Father but by HIM! *Jesus saith unto him, I am the way, the truth, and the life: no man cometh unto the Father, but by me* (Jn 14:6).

DIVINE SOVEREIGNTY

Isaiah 46:9-11

The blessed truth of God's sovereignty arouses the two strongest emotions in man. When the doctrine of the sovereignty of God is declared, as it is set forth in the Bible, men either love it or hate it. There is no middle ground. There is no middle view. God is either absolutely sovereign or he is not sovereign at all. The meaning of the word SOVEREIGN allows no degrees of power or authority. Since Adam expressed his desire to be like God and rebelled against God's authority over him, all men by fallen nature hate the sovereign God. Since man could not be as God, man has invented himself a god to be as himself—IMPOTENT!

Christians love the sovereign God. He is our God, and we are his people. We as equally hate the imaginary god of false religion. To love the ONE is to hate the other. To hate the ONE is to love the other. We who know the TRUE and LIVING GOD believe HIM, bow to HIM, and worship HIM upon the THRONE of HIS GLORY. We believe his declaration. *Remember the former things of old—for I am God, and there is none else; I am God, and there is none like me, Declaring the end from the beginning, and from ancient times the things that are not yet done, saying, my counsel shall stand, and I will do all my pleasure.– Calling a ravenous bird from the east, the man that executeth my counsel from afar country: yea, I have spoken it, I will also bring it to pass, I have purposed it, I will also do it* (Isaiah 46:9-11).

Not believing in the sovereign God of the Bible is the heart of idolatry. *The workman made it; therefore it is not God: but the calf of Samaria shall be broken in pieces* (Hos 8:6).

AS FOR OUR REDEEMER

As for our REDEEMER, the LORD OF HOSTS is his name, The HOLY ONE OF ISRAEL.

Isaiah 47:4

In this short sentence God the Spirit has given us no less than three names of our Lord, revealing his glorious person and wondrous work. Throughout the Bible, in both the Old and New Testament, he reveals himself as the sovereign Redeemer of spiritual Israel.

As he declares himself, so Israel identifies Him—*AS FOR OUR REDEEMER, the LORD OF HOSTS is his name, the HOLY ONE OF ISRAEL.* Never does one to whom he has revealed himself think or speak of him in any other way. We speak of him as the one *who hath saved us, and called us with an holy calling, not according to our works, but according to his own purpose and grace, which was given us in Christ Jesus before the world began* (2 Tm 1:9).

He is the one who *is the faithful witness, and the first begotten of the dead, and the Prince of the kings of the earth. Unto him that loved us, and washed us from our sins in his own blood, And hath made us kings and priests unto God and his Father; to him be glory and dominion for ever and ever* (Rv 1:5-6). Our Redeemer is not the paper king of the free will, works religionist, who tried, and was revealed to be a pathetic failure in that his blood is insufficient and his will is powerless to execute his desire. Our Redeemer *shall not fail nor be discouraged* (Is 42:4).

Our Redeemer redeems! He didn't TRY to redeem. Our Redeemer is the Lord OF HOSTS! He is THE SOVEREIGN over the armies of heaven and over the inhabitants of the earth. We see our Redeemer high and lifted up, and *gladly Give unto the LORD the glory due unto his name* for our everlasting salvation which he alone accomplished. And we desire to *worship the LORD in the beauty of [His] holiness* (Ps 29:2).

While the free-willers fear they will not give man enough glory and Christ too much, the child of grace claims only the blood and righteousness of OUR REDEEMER.

OUR REDEEMER

As for our Redeemer, the LORD of hosts is his name, the Holy One of Israel.

Isaiah 47:4

We often use the terms "particular redemption" and "limited atonement" as we preach the Gospel of Christ. If we indeed use these terms scripturally, we are saying, "All for who Christ died shall be saved, no more—no less. The Word of God sets forth this grand and glorious truth from beginning to end.

However, living faith, the faith that God Almighty gives in regeneration, is not in this doctrinal point, or in any doctrinal point. Saving faith has for its object the Redeemer, rather than any work that he wrought. There is a difference. The Bible does not say, "Believe in particular redemption and thou shalt be saved." The Bible says, *Believe on the Lord Jesus Christ and thou shalt be saved.* We often hear folks say, "I came to the doctrines of grace." Our Redeemer says, *Come unto me.*

What I am saying is this: the Lord Jesus Christ alone is our Redeemer. In him alone is all truth revealed. We trust the one who redeemed, he who made eternal redemption efficacious. Those who know Christ, believe on Christ, look to Christ and trust Christ for all their salvation. They believe he accomplished eternal redemption for them, and all for whom he died. But, as for our Redeemer, the Lord of Hosts is his name, the Holy One of Israel. We labor to preach Christ and all truth in Him. It is he that adorns all truth with his glorious person.

We desire to point sinners to Christ, in whom alone is life. I fear that many may find a false security in some doctrinal truth rather than having a living faith in a LIVING person, the Lord Jesus Christ. I realize that some will disagree with me. However, salvation is not in what we know and believe, salvation is in *the Lamb of God which taketh away the sin of the world.* As for me, there is no argument or debate; Christ Jesus is my Redeemer. *For I know that my Redeemer liveth, and that he shall stand at the latter day upon the earth* (Jb 19:25).

THE PROSPERITY OF THE SEED

Yet it pleased the LORD to bruise Him; he hath put him to grief: when thou shalt make his soul an offering for sin, he shall see his seed, he shall prolong his days, and the pleasure of the LORD shall prosper in his hand.
Isaiah 53:10

The Word of God makes it remarkably evident that the work accomplished is solely his work. The Lord is positively referenced no less than a dozen times in this one verse. We also see the eternality of God's purpose of grace in the redemptive work of Christ as the past, present and future is dissolved or fulfilled in the prosperity of the Seed (Christ) as to his pleasure accomplished. The purpose of God is wonderfully certain and successful in Christ's hand as he cannot fail or be discouraged (Is 42:4). The certainty of the salvation of God's loved ones revealed in this verse is undeniable. From the suffering, death and resurrection of Christ there springs forth from death and ever exists a multitude of redeemed ones which is innumerable. *After this I beheld, and, lo, a great multitude, which no man could number, of all nations, and kindreds, and people, and tongues, stood before the throne, and before the Lamb, clothed with white robes, and palms in their hands; And cried with a loud voice, saying, Salvation to our God which sitteth upon the throne, and unto the Lamb* (Rv 7:9-10).

The church of the living God is secure and prosperous as promised by our Lord himself. *And I say also unto thee, That thou art Peter, and upon this Rock (Christ is this Rock) I will build my church; and the gates of hell shall not prevail against it* (Mt 16:18). Contrary to popular opinion, the prosperity or success of Christ and his church does not depend in any way, shape form or fashion upon man, his will or his inventions. The visible contemporary church seems to be desperate and competitive in its quest to make converts, while being completely oblivious to the glory of God in Christ in calling his elect to himself by the preaching of the Gospel; but *the pleasure of the LORD shall prosper in his hand.*

Come Unto Me

Ho, every one that thirsteth, come ye to the waters, and he that hath no money; come ye, buy, and eat; yea, come, buy wine and milk without money and without price. Wherefore do ye spend money for that which is not bread? and your labour for that which satisfieth not? hearken diligently unto me, and eat ye that which is good, and let your soul delight itself in fatness. Incline your ear, and come unto me: hear, and your soul shall live; and I will make an everlasting covenant with you, even the sure mercies of David. Behold, I have given him for a witness to the people, a leader and commander to the people. Behold, thou shalt call a nation that thou knowest not, and nations that knew not thee shall run unto thee because of the LORD thy God, and for the Holy One of Israel; for he hath glorified thee.
Isaiah 55:1-5

It is God's decree and purpose that all those whom he has chosen in Christ will, without fail, come to him by faith that he has freely given; they will persevere in his grace unto eternal glory and forever be in his presence. All the elect, without fail, will hear his voice and obey his gracious summons and loving invitation to bow and worship before him in humble submission and admiration.

There are no IFS or MAYBES concerning God's purpose of grace in Christ Jesus our Lord. Neither is there any conditions prefixed to his call in electing grace— *Come unto me.* All that God the Father required and demanded of his people has been answered and fulfilled in Christ, our substitute. So, when he

108

effectually calls, THEY COME! There is no obstacle or barrier to prevent those he calls from coming to Him, not even sin, because Christ has redeemed us from the curse of the law, being made a curse for us. We have no sin! In him we are complete— no sin,— righteous— accepted— glorified in Christ!

The godless religion of our day insists upon man's worth, works and free will as the moving cause of salvation. This is a lie, that glorifies the flesh and renders God powerless. Free will doctrine makes the blood of Christ ineffectual and makes God's call *Come unto me* nothing more than a pitiful plea to proud, arrogant, self-exalted, and self-righteous men.

Not only is it our privilege, pleasure, and calling to preach the unsearchable riches of Christ, it is our burden of duty in so doing to expose all enemies of the cross of our Lord. When Christ is set forth in his glorious person and perfect work, error is exposed.

REJOICE AND BE JOYFUL

I will greatly rejoice in the LORD, my soul shall be joyful in my God.

Isaiah 61:10

The body of Christ, the church of the living God, has every reason to rejoice and be joyful. God is for his people, always has been and always will be. He has revealed his love, mercy and grace toward his people in the Lord Jesus Christ. Our Lord lived for us, died for us, and is now reigning in his High Priestly office for his redeemed in power and great glory. The eternal security of the child of God rests in the person and work of Jesus Christ.

Therein do we greatly rejoice and have joy. We rejoice and our soul is joyful in his incarnation. He became flesh and dwelt among us, and we behold his glory—*the only begotten of the Father, full of grace and truth*—full of truth to reveal God, and full of grace to redeem man. Abraham rejoiced to see his day and was glad; so do we rejoice! Christ Jesus came into the world to save sinners. In him all saved sinners rejoice and are joyful.

We greatly rejoice in Christ's righteousness. As a man, he fulfilled the law for his people to God the Father's complete satisfaction. He wrought a righteousness for all the elect that makes us acceptable to God, and clothed us with it so we are found not having our own righteousness but His. Therefore, thereby, and therein, he presents us to God not having any spot or blemish or any such thing.

We greatly rejoice in Christ and joy in our God in his death. The Lord Jesus Christ put away all our sin by the sacrifice of himself. He bore our sin in his own body on the tree. He put our sin so far away that God the Father remembers it against us no more. In the sacrificial death of Jesus Christ, every sin was atoned for forever for all his sheep. All our sins and transgressions were charged to our substitute and he willingly, gladly, and lovingly took them for his own and died in our place.

We rejoice in the Lord in his resurrection. He was raised for our justification. He not only lived for us and died for us, now he ever lives for us. Because he lives, we live. He rose from the dead having conquered every enemy that was against his people. He so vitally joined himself to us that when he died, we died; when he arose we arose, and now we live in Him. The Lord Jesus Christ ever lives to make intercession for us.

We rejoice in his providence. Our Lord rules and reigns for us in heaven and on earth. He is sovereign over all things and events. All things are ours and all things are for our good.

I will greatly rejoice in the LORD, my soul shall be joyful in my God; for he hath clothed me with the garments of salvation, he hath covered me with the robe of righteousness.

THE LORD DELIGHTETH IN THEE

Thou shalt no more be termed forsaken; neither shall thy land any more be termed desolate: but thou shalt be called Hephzibah, and thy land Beulah: for the LORD delighteth in thee, and thy land shall be married.
Isaiah 62:4

To "delight in someone" is to find and derive pleasure and joy from knowing him or her in pleasant, sweet relationship and fellowship. It is no great mystery that God the Father and God the Son abide in perpetual delight with each other, being in perfect union and agreement in all holiness and righteousness. *Behold my Servant, whom I uphold; mine elect, in whom my soul delighteth* (Is 42:1).

However, in our text verse, God the Spirit makes the astounding declaration and promise of God's love, delight and perpetual union to those who were by situation and identity Forsaken and Desolate. This wonderful, unmerited, eternal promise and favor of grace and mercy is surely the best word from God that one of such circumstance has ever, or will ever, experience! This is truly a marvel of God's redeeming grace in Christ Jesus our Lord. God has never changed his affection for his people as we are from everlasting viewed and accepted by him in Christ. He has always delighted in his children, *for the* LORD *delighteth in thee.*

He manifested his delight in us in the life and death of his blessed Son. Our sin and depravity was no hindrance to Him. *He is gracious unto him, and saith, Deliver him from going down to the pit: I have found a ransom* (Jb 33:24). Furthermore, he delights in his people as we by faith come to Christ and worship him in Spirit and in truth. We delight in him as the direct and effectual result of his delight in Christ and we in Him.

Our Lord has identified himself with his people and made known his delight in us; accordingly, we are no longer termed and called Forsaken. We are called Hephzibah—*My delight is in her.* Neither do we abide in a land of Desolation, we live in Beulah—MARRIED—in a land favored and blessed of the Lord, united to him who loves, and has given himself for, his bride.

COMPLETE RECOVERY – A GREAT PHYSICIAN

Is there no balm in Gilead; is there no physician there? why then is not the health of the daughter of my people recovered?
Jeremiah 8:22

The verse before us proposes three Gospel questions. The answers to these questions reveal the inherent and willing idolatrous heart of all men, especially the elect of God before conversion. This verse reveals the recovery of the same as well. We find these truths revealed not only in this verse and context but throughout the Scriptures.

Although the glorious Gospel of God's free and sovereign grace is proclaimed, men will not believe it and receive it. Although Christ is evidently set forth as the only propitiation for sin, men will not come to Him. Lost, idolatrous mankind will not, yea cannot, come to Christ of their own will because they are in bondage to the idol of sinful self. *And ye will not come to me, that ye might have life* (Jn 5:40); *Therefore said I unto you, that no man can come unto me, except it were given unto him of my Father* (Jn 6:65).

Left unattended by the grace of God, men will continue to grovel before their false god in the darkness of spiritual death until God says, *Let there be light!* There is a balm! There is a physician! Man CANNOT recover himself from his damned condition, but Jehovah-Rapha can and will recover his people from their deadly disease. *With his stripes we are healed* (Is 53:5). The Great Physician has guaranteed the complete, eternal recovery of all the spiritual infirmities of all his sheep, even death. He is the believer's balm.

He applies himself to us in love, mercy and grace. *Bless the LORD, O my soul: and all that is within me, bless his holy name. Bless the LORD, O my soul, and forget not all his benefits: who forgiveth all thine iniquities; who healeth all thy diseases who redeemeth thy life from destruction; who crowneth thee with lovingkindness and tender mercies; who satisfieth thy mouth with good things; so that thy youth is renewed like the eagle's* (Ps 103:1).

HOW WILT THOU DO IN THE SWELLING OF JORDAN?

If thou hast run with the footmen, and they have wearied thee, then how canst thou contend with horses? and if in the land of peace, wherein thou trustedst, they wearied thee, then how wilt thou do in the swelling of Jordan?
Jeremiah 12:5

The child of God does not run the race that is set before him in the strength of the flesh, but rather by the strength, grace and faith of the Almighty. It is Christ that shall not fail or be discouraged. Because the Lord Jesus Christ is the strength and object of our faith, we shall not be wearied and discouraged to the point of abandoning all hope and assurance in him and turning to the world. When the slightest temptations continually allure and draw us away from the things of God, and adversity continually and repeatedly drives us to try to find rest and peace in the world and the things of the world, there is great scriptural reason for alarm.

If running with the footmen in the land of peace (that is a false peace wherein we trusted) is too much for us, how will it be in the swelling of Jordan, when great and mighty temptations assault and then death comes? The Lord Jesus Christ is not in competition with the world. Neither is the believer. The unbeliever and the world are in competition with God. The man without true faith in Christ will become weary with the things of God and ultimately fail.

The child of God perseveres in faith, continually leaving the world behind. True, the believer has troubles on every side; without are fightings and within are fears. True, the child of God is tempted, tried and tested, and in his own estimation falls many a time. However, at the end of the day it will be revealed that the faithfulness of the Redeemer has caused each child of God to endure to the end in commitment to him and his Gospel.

"Fade, fade, each earthly joy, Jesus is mine!
Break every tender tie, Jesus is mine!
Dark is the wilderness, Earth has no resting place,
Jesus alone can bless, Jesus is mine!"

SALVATION; A HEART-WORK

And I will give them an heart to know me, that I am the LORD: and they shall be my people, and I will be their God: for they shall return unto me with their whole heart.
Jeremiah 24:7

No one by natural birth has a heart for the true and living God. One may be religious and even come into agreement, superficially, with Biblical doctrine, yet never embrace and love Christ and his Gospel. Those that have no heart for Christ take great comfort and assurance in WHAT they know. *He answered and said unto them, Well hath Esaias prophesied of you hypocrites, as it is written, This people honoureth me with their lips, but their heart is far from me* (Mk 7:6). Those that love Christ find their only comfort and hope in HIM who has given them a heart to know him. *I know whom I have believed, and am persuaded that he is able to keep that which I have committed unto him against that day* (2 Tm 1:12).

In order for anyone to embrace Christ with love and desire, and to be committed to Christ and his Gospel, God, in sovereign grace and mercy, must give that individual a new heart. Sound doctrine is vital; yet, the true doctrine of God will never be known and embraced apart from a living, vital union with Christ. The natural heart is so full of self and so deceitful that it will continue to go on in unbelief even in the face of truth unless halted by omnipotence. *The heart is deceitful above all things, and desperately wicked: who can know it?* (Jer 17:9).

Being unable to have sufficient desire to have a desire to be faithful and committed to Christ and his Gospel is reason to be alarmed. When the cares of this life begin to hinder, and the comforts and pleasures of this life bring more satisfaction than the beauty and joy of the worship of Christ in the Gospel, we are in trouble. Salvation is a heart work of God, and a work in the heart wrought by God. May God give us a heart to love Him!

When thou saidst, Seek ye my face; my heart said unto thee, thy face, LORD, will I seek (Ps 27:8).

I HAVE LOVED THEE

The LORD hath appeared of old unto me, saying, Yea, I have loved thee with an everlasting love: therefore with lovingkindness have I drawn thee.

Jeremiah 31:3

The love of God, in Christ Jesus our Lord, is the foundation of all things concerned with the accomplishment of the salvation of his elect. In fact, it is his love for us that is the cause

116

of our love for Him. *We love him,* BECAUSE *he first loved us* (1 Jn 4:19). The union of Christ and his sheep is a union of love. It is not just a judicial agreement between the Father, Son, and Spirit. Although the law must be satisfied, love is the motive and moving cause.

When love is absent, all that is left is a legalistic system of works, both with God and with man. Christ's love for his sheep is revealed in God's eternal covenant of grace, in the person and work of Christ, and in the glorification of his elect. The love of God grips the hearts of all to whom he reveals himself. The union of the love of the blessed Trinity is amazing, yet conceivable. But the love of the blessed God for sinful man is incomprehensible. The only way that we can comprehend the love of God for us, to any degree, is that he died for us. *Hereby perceive we the love of God, because he laid down his life for us* (1 Jn 3:16).

IN LOVE, GOD SENT CHRIST INTO THE WORLD—*In this was manifested the love of God toward us, because that God sent his only begotten Son into the world, that we might live through him* (1 Jn 4:9).

IN LOVE CHRIST LIVED FOR US—fulfilling the law, thereby he worked out a righteousness for us. Not only do we see God's justice satisfied in the cross-death of the Lord Jesus Christ, we see his LOVE displayed and fulfilled. *God commendeth his LOVE toward us, in that, while we were yet sinners, Christ died for us* (Rom 5:8).

If it be not Christ's love for us that captivates us and Christ's love in us that motivates us in religious privileges and duties, then it is all in vain. It is nothing more than self-righteous works of the flesh and will condemn us in that great day of judgment.

That Christ may dwell in your hearts by faith; that ye, being ROOTED AND GROUNDED IN LOVE, *May be able to comprehend with all saints what is the breadth, and length, and depth, and height; And to* KNOW THE LOVE OF CHRIST, *which passeth knowledge, that ye might be filled with all the fulness of God* (Eph 3:17-19).

THE INCURABLE CURED

Behold, I will bring it health and cure, and I will cure them, and will reveal unto them the abundance of peace and truth.
Jeremiah 33:6

There is nothing more hopeless and helpless than sinful man. He is alone with himself in utter darkness and death, and ignorant thereof. The light that is in man is darkness, and how great is that darkness! Man, left to himself, is doomed to the eternal woes of separation from the presence of all that is good. The wounds of the fall are deadly, and incurable by anything short of a miracle of God's sovereign grace in Christ Jesus our Lord. Thanks be unto God; he opened a fountain for the healing of that deadly wound, whereby life, peace and truth flows freely to poor creatures of the dust, raising them up and sitting them among the princes of the Most High God.

We spend all our life to make ourselves better and are the worse for it. Our Redeemer gave his life once in the end of the world to cure all his sheep's deadly ills, and we are forever healed! Darkness and death are no match for the life-giving efficacy of the blood of the Lamb! The deadly ravages of our sin cannot contend with the balm of God's sovereign, infinite love executed in and by our Great Physician!

Speak ye comfortably to Jerusalem, and cry unto her, that her warfare is accomplished, that her iniquity is pardoned: for she hath received of the LORD's hand double for all her sins (Is 40:2).

ISRAEL'S CURE

Behold, I will bring it health and cure, and I will cure them, and will reveal unto them the abundance of peace and truth.
Jeremiah 33:6

The hand of God duly issued the corporal afflictions of old Israel upon them. However, in the execution of his wrath and fury against the idolatrous nation, there remained an infinite love. It was a love that was effectual in the preservation of these elect in which he would joy and be glorified. This great deliverance of his earthly people is but a picture of a greater deliverance. God the Spirit reveals to us the great and wondrous person and work of Messiah. God's Word of promise (*I will*) to Jeremiah concerning Israel is his covenant promise to spiritual Israel, the church of the living God.

This promise is according to his purpose of grace originating in the infinite Godhead before the worlds. To put this properly, there was never another purpose for his chosen ones. Spiritual Israel's health and cure is revealed and executed in the anointed, beloved, and incarnate Redeemer, Christ Jesus our Lord. The disease of sin and death ravaged the souls of all the elect of God without recovery by themselves. The Deliverer, and the deliverance of his elect from their plight, being predestinated by divine omnipotence was, and is revealed, in the abundance of peace and truth. *For the law was given by Moses, [but] grace and truth came by Jesus Christ* (Jn 1:17).

The putting away and forgiveness of their sin, the imparting of The Lord our Righteousness, and the imputing of his wrought-out righteousness, is the sovereign exercise of the love, mercy and grace of Jehovah-Jireh—Jehovah-Rapha (The Lord that provideth healing). Make no mistake, nothing can be added to or taken away from his justifying work. *I know that, whatsoever God doeth, it shall be for ever: nothing can be put to it, nor any thing taken from it: and God doeth it, that men should fear before him* (Eccl 3:14). The only cure for the sin-sick soul is the blood of the Lamb of God.

A NEW HEART AND A NEW SPIRIT

A new heart also will I give you, and a new spirit will I put within you: and I will take away the stony heart out of your flesh, and I will give you an heart of flesh.
Ezekiel 36:26

One of the undeniable evidences of regeneration is that God, by his sovereign grace, and by his Spirit, has given all those who know Christ, a new heart and a new Spirit. Where there is life in Christ, there is a believing heart and the Spirit of the living God. Before regeneration, there is only a heart of unbelief and the spirit of the natural man, which is a proud spirit of rebellion against God. This is not to say that sin is eradicated, and that we do not have the natural faculties and ability to sin any more. This is saying that the new man, who is created in Christ Jesus, has preeminence and dominion over the old man of sin. *For sin shall not have dominion over you: for ye are not under the law, but under grace* (Rom 6:14), because it is the *Spirit of God that dwelleth in you.*

THE NEW HEART BELIEVES GOD. The new heart, without question, unreservedly believes the Word of God—all of the Word of God. The new heart believes the record that God has given us concerning his Son and salvation in Him. *These are written, that ye might believe that Jesus is the Christ, the Son of God; and that believing ye might have life through his name* (Jn 20:31). The new heart believes the Gospel of God's free and sovereign grace in Christ alone.

THE NEW HEART RENOUNCES AND ABHORS ALL FALSE GODS AND RELIGIONS. The new heart is in no wise sympathetic with, or in agreement with, nor will have any fellowship with the free will, false gods of darkness and deceit. *For they themselves shew of us what manner of entering in we had unto you, and how ye turned to God from idols to serve the living and true God* (1 Thes 1:9). The new heart hates every false way and loves that which honours and glorifies God and his Word. There is no exception.

THE NEW HEART LOVES GOD. The new heart and new Spirit embraces God, his Christ, his Word, and his people with affection and desire, not just in a theological and doctrinal sense. *Whosoever believeth that Jesus is the Christ is born of God: and every one that loveth him that begat loveth him also that is begotten of him* (1 Jn 5:1).

The new heart and new Spirit is no less than *Christ in you, the hope of glory.* God has promised this new heart and new spirit, and he will give the same to all his chosen, from the least to the greatest.

A NEW HEART

A new heart also will I give you, and a new spirit will I put within you.

Ezekiel 36:26

The natural heart of man is concerned only with natural, temporal things. The desires of the flesh and mind are by natural origin self-centered. Man is a habitual, self-serving creature. He may be at times (especially when in the presence of the Gospel) consciously aware of this, but finds it impossible to change because this is his love. *Men shall be lovers of their own selves—lovers of pleasures more than lovers of God* (2 Tm 3:2 & 4).

He may reform outwardly for a while and try to adjust his priorities, and even strive to think differently; but alas, he is like the dog and its vomit, and the sow and its muck. He has not a heart for Christ, his Gospel, or his church. This is not his love. This is not his desire. He has only a desire for the vomit and the muck (2 Pt 2:22). The only way one will ever have a heart for the things of God will be if God gives him a new heart and a new Spirit. God's promise to his people is *A new heart also will I give you, and a new spirit will I put within you.*

The new heart which God gives has preeminence over the old one. Oh yes, the old heart is still there to aggravate and even temporarily distract us. However, *Ye are of God, little children, and have overcome them: because greater is he that is in you, than he that is in the world* (1 Jn 4:4). The new heart is one of faith, love and commitment. The new heart embraces Christ, his

Gospel and his church. This comes as natural to the new heart as embracing self and the things of the world comes to the old heart.

If we have not a new heart and Spirit when temptation comes, when cares come, or when it is time for self-denial, then we will take the low road to fulfilling the desires of the flesh and mind. It will be revealed that we are yet the servants of self rather than the servants of God. We will be, in our heart, true to what we treasure most. *For where your treasure is, there will your heart be also* (Mt 6:21).

WHATEVER WILL BE, WILL BE

All the inhabitants of the earth are reputed as nothing: and he doeth according to his will in the army of heaven, and among the inhabitants of the earth: and none can stay his hand, or say unto Him, What doest thou?

Daniel 4:35

An Armenian preacher once accused me of preaching "A WHATEVER WILL BE, WILL BE Gospel." my answer was, "I preach a WHATEVER GOD WILLS TO BE, WILL BE Gospel." I would be a fool to believe WHATEVER WILL NOT BE, WILL BE. However, it is a greater fool to believe WHATEVER GOD WILLS TO BE, WILL NOT BE. I make my argument, not solely upon human logic, but wholly upon the declaration of God himself.

The position of all religious men by nature is one of exalting the imaginary free will of man and the bringing into bondage the free will of God. The position of all those who know God is the opposite. *He doeth according to his will in the army of heaven, and among the inhabitants of the earth.* A god who is not sovereign over ALL is NO GOD.

Man's will is in bondage to sin and self, and is governed and overruled by divine omnipotence. God's will is consistent with himself in virtue and character, and is the essence and revelation of divine omnipotence. The Bible plainly declares our Lord Jesus Christ, *in whom dwells all the fullness of the Godhead bodily* has *all power in heaven and in earth.* The perfect, complete will of God will be accomplished by one Lord Jesus Christ in past, present, and future history to the praise of the glory of his Majesty.

God works all things to the end that all those whom he loves shall be saved with an everlasting salvation in Christ Jesus, and all those who believe not shall be damned unto everlasting torment. His will is as himself—unchangeable. *None can stay his hand, or say unto Him, What doest thou.* Yes, I believe "WHATEVER WILL BE WILL BE" because every minute "WHATEVER" is in the hand of the infinite true and living God.

IN WRATH REMEMBER MERCY

O LORD, I have heard thy speech, and was afraid: O LORD, revive thy work in the midst of the years, in the midst of the years make known; in wrath remember mercy.
Habakkuk 3:2

A lmighty God, having revealed unto Habakkuk his great work in the latter days when righteousness and judgment would meet in Messiah, moved the prophet to prayer and supplication for a greater revelation of his tender mercies; mercies which would be unaltered by the execution of his wrath upon sin, but would rather be confirmed, as promised in the eternal covenant of grace, in the salvation and comfort of his people. Nowhere is God's wrath and mercy more clearly revealed than at Calvary. The judgment and wrath of God executed upon our Lord as he was made sin, and bore our sin in his own body on the tree, initiates an incomprehensible, reverential fear, and an unspeakable peace and comfort to the heart of the awakened sinner.

O Lord, make known unto us your immeasurable hatred for sin and your infinite love, mercy and grace personified and executed in our dying substitute! Little is known in our generation of the wrath and mercy of God, especially as executed in Christ, because today's contemporary ministry and religion is silent upon the character and virtues of Almighty God and the perfections and accomplishments of the God-man, Christ Jesus our Lord. However, there are a few to whom the Lord has spoken and made known his work and they are fearfully and prayerfully proclaiming his wrath and mercy as revealed in the center and circumference of all truth. *Behold, The Lamb of God.* And a few shall hear!

Although the fig tree shall not blossom, neither shall fruit be in the vines; the labour of the olive shall fail, and the fields shall yield no meat; the flock shall be cut off from the fold, and there shall be no herd in the stalls: Yet I will rejoice in the LORD, I will joy in the God of my salvation (Hb 3:17-18).

A SURE SALVATION

And the LORD their God shall save them in that day as the flock of his people: for they shall be as the stones of a crown, lifted up as an ensign upon his land.
Zechariah 9:16

The heart and design of all false religion is the promotion of man's self-righteousness and imagined free will in opposition to the glorious righteousness of Christ and God's sovereign free will. The righteousness and free will of man is non-existent in the justification of sinners before God. The works and will of man is certain damnation for those who trust therein. The Lord Jesus Christ and his redemptive work is the only ground for justifying righteousness before the holy God.

The Bible only knows and reveals a full, free and sure salvation wrought by the one *whom God hath set forth to be a propitiation through faith in his blood, to declare his righteousness for the remission of sins that are past, through the forbearance of God* (Rom 3:25), and he *is the propitiation for our sins* (1 Jn 2:2). The salvation of God in Christ is certain, sure and everlasting because it is his salvation, wrought by him and dispensed by Him. I fall and fail ten thousand times a day, but he never has and never will fail, yea, CANNOT fail! He *shall not fail nor be discouraged* (Is 42:4). The salvation of God's elect children is as sure as the majestic throne of his glory, eternal in the heavens.

The earth shall burn and crumble, the sun will refuse to shine, the stars will fall like rain, and death and hell shall be cast into the lake of fire; but the Great Shepherd and his sheep shall dwell safely together on the Mountain of the Lord in the Land of Promise and *they shall be as the stones of a crown, lifted up as an ensign upon his land.*

When our Lord said, *It is finished,* it was finished! PERIOD! Our surety sealed all covenant promises with his everlasting, efficacious blood. Away with all fancies and notions contrived in the hearts of fallen, unregenerate mankind concerning salvation. May we ever raise the banner of God's free, sovereign, and everlasting grace in Christ Jesus our Lord!

HE SHALL

For he shall save his people from their sins
Matthew 1:21

The statement in the passage above is a declaration from the throne of God. There is nothing indefinite about the purpose of the Lord Jesus Christ in accomplishing and executing the salvation of God's elect people. The salvation of those whom God loved from all eternity is certain and sure. Particular redemption is that great work of our Redeemer, that gives God all the glory from alpha to omega. Preachers may say a lot of GOOD THINGS concerning Jesus and God and heaven, but if they are not crystal clear on this truth they are GOD-ROBBERS.

All for whom Christ died shall be saved with an everlasting salvation. *Israel shall be saved in the LORD with an everlasting salvation: ye shall not be ashamed nor confounded world without end* (Is 45:17). And that Israel spoken of is spiritual Israel—the chosen of God. If only one for whom Christ died will not be saved, then he failed, and no one has any hope. The truth of the efficacy of Christ's atoning sacrifice is the GOOD NEWS of the Gospel. *This is a faithful saying, and worthy of all acceptation, that Christ Jesus came into the world to save sinners; of whom I am chief* (1 Tm 1:15).

Our hope as believers is in the Lord Jesus Christ. He came into the world and successfully worked out a righteousness for us, actually took our sin upon himself and was punished for it by death. Therefore having satisfied God's justice in our place, he arose from the dead and is now making intercession for us as our Great High Priest. There is nothing that rejoices the hearts of the children of God more than knowing Christ was, and is, successful in all that he did and is doing. The result of his perfect work is the impartation of his divine nature and the imputation of his blessed righteousness to all those he came to save.

The announcement was, he *shall save his people.* The proof is that he arose from the dead *Having obtained eternal redemption for us. Neither by the blood of goats and calves, but by his own blood he entered in once into the holy place, having obtained eternal redemption for us* (Heb 9:12).

THE HEART'S TREASURE

Where your treasure is, there will your heart be also.
Matthew 6:21

The treasure of one's heart will consume his or her life without premeditation. It is a natural thing. That which we love and cherish is that with which we will occupy our thoughts and actions to the satisfaction of our desires. Therefore it is evident that *Where your treasure is, there will your heart be also* (Mt 6:21). Is our treasure Christ, his Gospel, and his church?

THE TREASURE OF OUR HEART

Where your treasure is, there will your heart be also.
Matthew 6:21

I have been in religion since I was a child. I have been a believer for a few years now. Since God has revealed Christ to my heart I have observed many things that were previously of no concern to me.

One of the things that is now a great concern to me is the faithfulness (or unfaithfulness) of those that profess to know God, and love his Son and his Gospel. I know that God will be faithful to save his people, and they will have a desire to be faithful to him. This is the life of a child of God. God has made it so. I understand that one can appear to be faithful outwardly and yet not have their heart in it. On the other hand, those who are unfaithful outwardly, evidently have no consistent desire for the things of God. Every true believer has a desire for the salvation of others, especially family and friends. It hurts and concerns us when we see those who profess to know Christ, deliberately, without conscience, choose anything and everything above the worship of our Lord.

I understand that being faithful saves no one, but what about love and desire? Is this not the seed that springs up from within the new heart that worships the Lamb of God and constrains us to be faithful? This is not an appeal to men to start doing something they don't want to do. This is an appeal to examine ourselves, by the grace of God. I find by experience, that we do pretty much what we desire to do as much as we have the means. The question is WHY DO I DO IT? or NOT DO IT? I am certain every believer weeps and repents over his unfaithfulness.

I am equally certain that every unbeliever could care less. One might say, "You have no scriptural foundation for this conclusion." Here is one: *For where your treasure is, there will your heart be also* (Mt 6:21). And where our heart is, there we will be, if at all possible..

THE GREAT DARKNESS OF LIGHT

But if thine eye be evil, thy whole body shall be full of darkness. If therefore the light that is in thee be darkness, how great is that darkness!

Matthew 6:23

The eye that cannot see is in bondage to that which is within. Someone that has never had the gift of sight has no visual concept of anything outside himself. Therefore there is nothing but darkness. This condition is so natural and fixed that this is the way of life for him. There is no hope for anything different except for a miracle. And even then, this must be wrought by a power other than his own.

This is the case of all mankind spiritually. How great is that darkness? Complete! No light at all! The spiritual light that is in man by virtue of our fallen nature is great and is total darkness. Newton described it this way, "I once was lost, but now am found; Was blind, but now I see." This great darkness can only be attributed to blindness. The only way that this horrible condition can be reversed is by a miracle of God's grace. AMAZING GRACE!

Those who live and remain in darkness cannot see the light of the glorious Gospel of Jesus Christ. They cannot see the truth of God. They cannot see Christ crucified. They cannot see themselves in the light of God's Word.

Spiritual blindness is far greater and worse than physical blindness. Those who are spiritually blind would have it no other way. They love it! *This is the condemnation, that light is come into the world, and men loved darkness rather than light, because their deeds were evil* (Jn 3:19). A sight of the Lord Jesus Christ is the last thing they want. But, thanks be unto God; if and when Christ reveals himself to them, he is all they want! A sight of HIM makes all the difference between great darkness and great light. How great is THAT LIGHT? *For God, who commanded the light to shine out of darkness, hath shined in our hearts, to give the light of the knowledge of the glory of God in the face of Jesus Christ* (2 Cor 4:6). GREATER THAN THE DARKNESS!

THE END OF TWO THOUSAND ARMINIANS

The whole herd of swine ran violently down a steep place into the sea, and perished in the waters.
Matthew 8:32

Once the devils entered the swine it would be impossible to distinguish them from the swine. The reason being, and the truth of the matter is, the swine and the devils are now one. The will and desire of the swine (the Lord now giving them leave to act upon the same and they supposed their will now to be free), was to flee from the presence of Christ and feast upon the mountain of their own self-righteousness.

However, being blind and violent in their own pursuits, having no sense of direction, they ended up perishing in the waters of condemnation which is the just desert for all who are not found in Christ Jesus and who trust in their own righteousness. The truth is, their will was not free at all but rather bound by their own foolish nature and desires. Oh how natural man loves and adores his FREE WILL! Oh how natural man hates and is violent against the Lord Jesus Christ and his sovereign grace! Free-willers put their fingers in their ears and scream *we will not have this man rule over us*! They call those whom the Lord has clothed and given life, heretics.

These representatives of self-righteous, free will religionists (the devil-possessed swine) would rather die therein than be in the presence of Christ and be clothed with his righteousness (freewillism and self-righteousness are one and the same). This is how we all are from birth until death, unless the Lord in sovereign grace and mercy comes where we are to clothe us with his righteousness and dwell in us giving us spiritual life and sanity.

Arminianism is insanity and certain death to all who embrace it. All those who cling to their will and righteousness will not come to Christ that they might have life. *And ye will not come to me, that ye might have life* (Jn 5:40). The whole herd of free will preachers and all their disciples will come to the same end as portrayed by the swine. *And the devil that deceived them was cast into the lake of fire and brimstone, where the beast and the false prophet are, and shall be tormented day and night for ever and ever* (Rv 20:10).

SOUL REST

Take my yoke upon you, and learn of Me; for I am meek and lowly in heart: and ye shall find rest unto your souls.
Matthew 11:29

There is no real and lasting rest for the unbelieving soul. He seeks rest and satisfaction in things that are perishing. He can never look beyond the mortal and corruptible. The yoke of the faithless is the heavy burden of sin and the sentence of death. He looks to the law for help but is only condemned for his efforts. However, those who are taught of Christ by God the Spirit find sweet and lasting rest in his person and work.

The accomplishment of Christ for his people is complete satisfaction to God. The only rest for the soul is God-given faith in Christ through the preaching of the Gospel. Christ our Lord was made sin and suffered our punishment for us, His elect, and now ever reigns for us in glory. Looking to him we find peace, comfort and rest in trials and adversity, as well in times of prosperity and peace.

IN VAIN DO THEY WORSHIP ME

This people draweth nigh unto me with their mouth, and honoureth me with their lips; but their heart is far from Me.
Matthew 15:8

This was our Lord's commentary concerning the professing Pharisee. Their outward form of worship was in vain because of their unbelief. They had his name upon their lips but no love for him in their hearts. I fear this is the case of many in the visible churches today. Although the Lord knows what is in man then and now, it is more evident now than then for all to see. The Pharisee of his day was devoted and committed to the external motions of ceremonial religion. The average church-going Pharisee of our day holds to a profession of doctrine with little or no devotion or commitment in any form.

Sad to say, this is not only the case in rank Arminian assemblies, it is the case in many assemblies where the sovereign grace of God is preached faithfully. Many would fight and argue over the five points of Calvinism and their profession of faith, but they don't have a heart of love and commitment to Christ and his church. Even many in the ministry seem to believe that if they can convert men from Arminianism to Calvinism their salvation is certain and the ministry is successful.

I am convinced by the Word of God and by experience that those whom God the Spirit has efficaciously called to faith in Christ Jesus our Lord will have a new heart that is near to Christ in love, devotion and commitment. God's preachers will not be cheerleaders and babysitters. They will preach Christ and him crucified to sinners. Do we have a head for doctrine without a heart for Christ? There could be no more sorrowful edict from Jesus Christ than, *I never knew you: depart from me, ye that work iniquity.*

PERFORMING THE IMPOSSIBLE

Matthew 19:26

The ability to see, hear, understand, and especially to believe the things of God is not possible with unregenerate man. *Jesus beheld [them], and said unto them, With men this is impossible; but with God all things are possible* (Mt 19:26). No matter how intelligent one is in worldly things, he is blind, deaf, ignorant and unbelieving when it comes to spiritual matters. This is true of all of us because of our depraved human nature.

We are spiritually dead. *And you [hath he quickened], who were DEAD in trespasses and sins* (Eph 2:1), not just slightly impaired. Man, apart from a work of grace, has as much ability in spiritual things as some one or some thing that does not exist. The carnal mind and unbelieving heart is in fact mad at God and has no desire for truth. *Because the carnal mind is enmity against God: for it is not subject to the law of God, neither indeed can be* (Rom 8:7).

For one of Adam's race to see, hear, understand, believe and love God and his Christ, and his Gospel is an absolute miracle of God's sovereign grace! Here falls the demon of freewillism and self-righteousness at the foot of redeeming love and sovereign mercy. *Lord, if thou wilt, thou canst make me clean.* The undeniable truths of man's depravity and God's sovereignty sheds remarkable light upon why there are so many casual, uncommitted, and unfaithful so-called Christians. These truths reveal as well how it is that a few depraved worthless worms love Christ and his Gospel and desire the truth, and longs to be committed and faithful to him who loves them and gave himself for them.

NOT KNOWING THE SCRIPTURES

Jesus answered and said unto them, Ye do err, not knowing the scriptures, nor the power of God.
Matthew 22:29

The former is a result of the latter. There is no saving knowledge of God and his Christ apart from the Word of God revealed. Although one may read the Scriptures and hear the Gospel preached, Christ is only known by divine revelation. All error springs from *not knowing the scriptures, nor the power of God.* The Lord Jesus Christ, who is the *power of God, and the wisdom of God* (1 Cor 1:24), is the sum and substance of all Scripture. *Search the scriptures; for in them ye think ye have eternal life: and they are they which testify of me* (Jn 5:39). The first words of Scripture, *In the beginning God,* and the last words of the Bible, *The grace of our Lord Jesus Christ be with you all,* speak of Him.

The preaching of Christ *is the power of God unto salvation to everyone that believeth* and *these are written, that ye might believe that Jesus is the Christ, the Son of God; and that believing ye might have life through his name* (Jn 20:31). There must be spiritual life to KNOW the Word of God and the power of God because *the natural man receiveth not the things of the Spirit of God: for they are foolishness unto him: neither can he know [them], because they are spiritually discerned* (1 Cor 2:14). Spiritual ignorance of not knowing the Scriptures always results in error and in a theoretical or abstract conception of Christ. There can be no faith in Christ without knowing Him; there can be no knowing him apart from the Scriptures. There can be no knowing the Scriptures without spiritual life, and there can be no life apart from a work of almighty grace.

"HOW OFTEN..."

O Jerusalem, Jerusalem, thou that killest the prophets, and stonest them which are sent unto thee, how often would I have gathered thy children together, even as a hen gathereth her chickens under her wings, and ye would not!
Matthew 23:37

The words of our Lord to Jerusalem not only condemn those who show despite to Him, but they also reveal his willingness to save. These words leave men without excuse. How often have many turned a deaf ear to the Gospel, the very Word of God? How often have many who profess to know and love him excused themselves from attending the Gospel for some petty, selfish, carnal motive? Many delude themselves into believing that all is well, even though there is no heart love for Christ, his Gospel or the brethren.

Israel believed in God, participated in the ceremony of worship, yet had no affection for the Lord Jesus Christ or those that loved Him. How often our Lord preached to the multitude (Jews included), yet they *would not*. How often is the Gospel preached in this place, yet many WILL NOT! When the Gospel is declared and men choose not to hear (for whatever reason if not providential), they are left without excuse before God. The very presence of the Gospel in a community reveals Christ's willingness to save. The presence of a Gospel church in our community is a work of God and it is our responsibility as believers to be faithful to his work and an example to those who dwell with us.

SOME THINGS ARE EVIDENT

Matthew 23:27

L ast week, during a consultation with a physician that I had not met before, I made the statement, "I am not in your hands, I am in his hands." he came back with the remark, "Yes, you are in HIS OR HER hands." his remark made it evident to me that he did not give any credibility to the Scriptures and that he did not believe in the true and living God. This was an outstanding, brazen denial of the truth, which revealed his unbelief. But this is not always the case. There are some, according to the Scriptures, that know and say the right things, yet their lives prove otherwise. *Woe unto you, scribes and Pharisees, hypocrites! for ye are like unto whited sepulchres, which indeed appear beautiful outward, but are within full of dead men's bones, and of all uncleanness* (Mt 23:27).

No matter what men profess to believe, if there is NO HEART LOVE FOR CHRIST, his Gospel and his church, there is no life. And, believe it or not, eventually this will be revealed in men's lives, in God's time. Most of the time, if not every time, it will have something to do with attitude and the lack of the Spirit of love. Read 1 Corinthians 13. There is yet another evidence of unbelief among those who falsely profess to know Christ, and that is BEING COMFORTABLE IN THEIR PROFESSION WHILE NOT COMMITTED TO CHRIST AND HIS CHURCH. Inconsistency, negligence, unfaithfulness, and lack of interest in the privilege of the public worship of God and the care and welfare of the church is an undeniable evidence of a lack of love and passion for Christ. Hence, there is no life. Although every believer feels that he, or she, comes up short, and we do, nevertheless the desire of a child of God in this world is a life of love for Christ and commitment to Him. Read Luke 14:26, 27 & 33.

CHRIST SANG A HYMN

The only record of our Lord singing during his life on this earth is recorded by Matthew and Mark and is worded exactly the same by both—And when they had sung an hymn, they went out into the mount of Olives.
Matthew 26:30 & Mark 14:26

This hymn that he sang with his disciples is thought to be the same as was sung on the eve of the Passover, the HALLELL, which is a hymn or SONG OF PRAISE (Ps 113—118). It should be no surprise that the Son of God would praise God his Father for the work that he would soon accomplish and that he would sing his praises with those whom he had chosen for his own and would redeem with his own blood. It would do us good to remember that we not only worship Christ, we worship with Christ as well. If he is not present, there is no true worship of

God. In the reading of his Word, the preaching of his Gospel, approaching the throne of his grace, singing praises unto Him, he must be with us else we worship in vain.

We must be as exacting of the songs we sing as the message we preach. The Gospel of Christ renders him all the glory and praise, so must the hymns that we sing. When the saints of God gather together in his name, may he meet with us in Spirit and in truth directing our hearts to him in song, prayer and in his Word. It is recorded that he will sing unto us of God his Father as we worship him by faith. *I will declare thy name unto my brethren, in the midst of the church will I sing praise unto thee* (Heb 2:12).

This promise of God the Son to God the Father not only makes reference to those with him on the eve of his crucifixion, it is to all those for whom he was sacrificed. Neither do I think it is presumptuous to anticipate hearing his voice in heavenly chorus with the redeemed through eternity. We shall see him as he is and shall hear him say, *Come, ye blessed of my Father, inherit the kingdom prepared for you from the foundation of the world.*

RESPONSIBILITY

The time is fulfilled, and the kingdom of God is at hand: repent ye, and believe the gospel.
Mark 1:15

"Responsibility" has nothing to do with "ability." The words are not even spelled alike (ibility—ability). Man is responsible for his sin but has not the ability to change what he is: a sinner. Nor can he UN-COMMIT the sin he has committed.

Responsibility in the context of our fallen nature suggests BLAME, or to be at FAULT, or GUILTY before God.

We must, and do, bear the blame for our sin. Otherwise God would not be just in legal condemnation, especially in the death of Christ. If we are not responsible, then we are a victim of God, and the death of Christ would be essentially to justify God rather than the sinner and correct a mistake he has made. Every sinner that comes before God seeking mercy and forgiveness, confesses and owns his RESPONSIBILITY AND his INABILITY to render God payment for it. David, by the inspiration of God makes this very clear. *Against thee, thee only, have I SINNED, and done this evil in thy sight: that thou mightest be justified when thou speakest, and be clear when thou judgest* (Ps 51:4). The Lord Jesus Christ in his suffering and death assumed the responsibility of his sheep's sin, taking the blame, being made sin for them as their substitute. That is one thing. Furthermore, he was, and is, able in the accomplishment of the same to satisfy the just demands of God as he has commanded. We are responsible but have naught to pay. Thank God Christ did; He paid with HIS PRECIOUS BLOOD! *Wherefore he is able also to save them to the uttermost that come unto God by him, seeing he ever liveth to make intercession for them* (Heb 7:25). Not only are we responsible for our sin, we are responsible to repent to God and believe on the Lord Jesus Christ. We can do neither. We have not the ability. We are dead in our sin. We do the sinning; God in Christ does the saving. By his assuming the first, he accomplished the second. *For if, when we were enemies, we were reconciled to God by the death of his Son, much more, being reconciled, we shall be saved by his life* (Rom 5:10).

SOWN AMONG THORNS

And these are they which are sown among thorns.
Mark 4:18

We are exhorted to *take heed how we hear* the Word of God (Lk 8:18). Often the preached Word falls on unattending ears. The reason given for the Word not being regarded in the verse above is that *the cares of this world, and the deceitfulness of riches, and the lusts of other things entering in, choke the word.* It is evident that those among whom the Word was sown professed to believe, at least for a while, but eventually it was revealed that they had no real interest in Christ. God sends prosperity and poverty, sickness and health, trials and afflictions upon all men for a purpose. For a child of God, it is a trial of faith, which is precious.

For a false professor it is to reveal no faith. What God gives us or withholds from us reveals where our heart is. Our reaction is spontaneous and true to our nature. *For where your treasure is, there will your heart be also* (Mt 6:21). For example, often when one has little, he gives a lot; when he is increased, he gives little in proportion to his increase of whatever it might be. The *cares of this world* include anything and everything of self-interest. The cares of this world, riches and other things only become evil and damning when they keep men from Christ. It is a sad thing to see those who profess to love Christ being swallowed up by themselves and the world.

O Lord, if I am such a one, empty me of myself and fill me with love for Christ and his church.

THEY CAME TO JESUS AND FOUND THE MAN

Then THEY *went out to see what was done; and* CAME TO JESUS, AND FOUND THE MAN, *out of whom the devils were departed, sitting at the feet of Jesus, clothed, and in his right mind: and they were afraid.*

Luke 8:35

The focus of those who fed the swine and those who came from the city was to see the one out of whom the devils were cast. But where would they find the man? Where will the one be found in whom God has wrought a work of grace, of which this miracle is a beautiful illustration? Where will this one desire to be? Where will the ONE that wrought the miracle of grace be found? We find the answer to these questions in both the spiritual and literal context of our passage of Scripture. *THEY CAME TO JESUS AND FOUND THE MAN.* Our Lord is always with his people because he has joined himself to us and therefore we are one with Him. *That they all may be one; as thou, Father, art in me, and I in thee, that they also may be one in Us: that the world may believe that thou hast sent me* (Jn 17:21), &, *I will dwell in them, and walk in them; and I will be their God, and they shall be my people* (2 Cor 6:16). Paul's desire was that he would *be found in Him, not having mine own righteousness, which is of the law, but that which is through the faith of Christ, the righteousness which is of God by faith* (Phil 3:9). Not only is the believer found in and with Christ before God, but as the result of being one with Christ in regeneration, we will be found worshipping him in his Word as he reveals himself to us in the preaching and hearing of his Gospel. *For where two or three are gathered together in my name, THERE AM I in the midst of them* (Mt 18:20). Where will the child of grace be found when the preaching of Christ is accessible? He will be found sitting at the feet of his Redeemer, desiring to hear a word from Him—just happy to be there. *I was glad when they said unto me, Let us go into the house of the LORD* (Ps 122:1). Where will others be found? Doing what they esteem to be more important, enjoyable and entertaining.

THAT GOOD PART

One thing is needful: and Mary hath chosen THAT GOOD PART, which shall not be taken away from her.
Luke 10:42

The things Martha was concerned with were the things that our natural life consists of and all of mankind is concerned with. Those things are a part of our lives and cannot be neglected, but they will soon be taken away from us. However, she was cumbered, troubled, and anxious with these things to the neglect of the one most wonderful and needful part of life in which one can be employed here on this earth and in the world to come—sitting at the feet of Christ Jesus in worship and adoration.

While the world is singularly occupied with the world and its cares and seeks to be gratified and made whole with its temporal pleasures, the child of grace is made willing to gladly put the world aside and choose that good part which has become his greatest need. Mary chose that good part because God had chosen to reveal the beauty of her Redeemer unto her, that beauty and glory which transcends all of the pleasures and desires of this temporal life. By God's grace she *esteemed the words of his mouth more than* (her) *necessary food.* In light of being in his presence and learning of him, everything else was of little or no importance.

How rude and unprofitable it would be for her to cumber herself with the things of worldly nature when she had the God given opportunity to sit at the feet of her Savior and worship Him. How rude, disrespectful and ungrateful it is to refuse the feast of the Lord when he has bidden, *Come and dine!* So it is with those who refuse the Gospel. They have no appetite for *that good part,* and choose the world over Christ.

And the lord said unto the servant, Go out into the highways and hedges, and compel them to come in, that my house may be filled. For I say unto you, That none of those men which were bidden shall taste of my supper (Lk 14:23-24).

"SEEK YE THE KINGDOM OF GOD"

But rather seek ye the kingdom of God; and all these things shall be added unto you.

Luke 12:31

In the context of this passage of Scripture our Lord warns, yea, rather forbids, his people to be possessed of the things of this world. He reminds us that we will possess the things that he provides for us according to his good providence. He is not saying that we should not work or possess anything; rather he is saying that THINGS should not POSSESS us to the point that this is where our heart is and what we live for. The world seeks after these things. *For all that is in the world, the lust of the flesh, and the lust of the eyes, and the pride of life, is not of the Father, but is of the world* (1 Jn 2:16). The child of God seeks after the things of God and the kingdom of God. The love of the heart is manifest in the conversation (walk or life) of the man. *Love not the world, neither the things that are in the world. If any man love the world, the love of the Father is not in him* (1 Jn 2:15).

Our jobs and possessions are not sinful until one's love for and commitment to them infringe upon our worship of and commitment to Christ and his Gospel. As a matter of truth, the believer knows that all we have, both spiritually and materially, comes from his hand and therefore gladly commits it all to Him. The child of God diligently seeks the glory of God and lives and works toward that end. In Christ and in his Gospel, the believer finds his portion, his desire, his life, his rest, his comfort, fulfillment and joy. This is his treasure and this is where his heart is. The propensity of the professor who does not have a love for the things of God is to seek to fulfill his desire for the things of the world first, and then if there is any thought, time, resources or energy left, he appeases and seeks to gratify his conscience by offering these leftovers to God along with his excuses.

Seeking the Kingdom of God is a continual slaughtering of the flesh and a resurrection of the new man created in Christ Jesus, who walks not after the flesh, but after the Spirit and reckons that Godliness with contentment is great gain.

Often prosperity and success, as well as poverty and failure, is sent to reveal one's point of rebellion as well as one's faith. Can each of us, before God, truthfully say, *I am crucified with Christ: nevertheless I live; yet not I, but Christ liveth in me: and the life which I now live in the flesh I live by the faith of the Son of God, who loved me, and gave himself for me* (Gal 2:20).

PROFESSORS: TRUE AND FALSE

For where your treasure is, there will your heart be also.
Luke 12:34

There is a distinguishing difference between a true child of God and a false professor. The Bible is filled with illustrations of this truth:Mt 7:22-23; Mt 23:27; Mt 25:32; Jn 14:21; 1 Jn 3:14. This discernable difference is characterized from an inward principle of the indwelling Spirit of God which is produced and manifested by the love of God in the true believer, and is absent in the false professor. The child of God, by his grace, loves God, loves his Son, loves his Gospel, loves the brethren, and loves his work. Although this inward principle can be IMITATED outwardly to some degree for a while by the false professor, it can never be counterfeited in the heart.

What a person loves and gives himself to is, at some point, revealed in his life. *For where your treasure is, there will your heart be also* (Lk 12:34). There are those who profess their allegiance and love to Christ and his church, yet can never bring themselves to commitment to the same. They remain their own person, not Christ's. The true children of God have a new nature, the divine nature, which continually causes them to give themselves to the things of God. The truth is that the distinguishing difference is LIFE and DEATH.

To those who know Him, he is their life. Those who only profess to know Him, their life consists of themselves, which is death. It is of a truth that the true believer's life revolves around Christ, and that to the false professor Christ revolves around his life. It is comforting to know that God has a people in this world of falseness and deception, and that they, having the divine nature, live for his glory. No, they are not perfect in themselves! But they are perfect in him and seek to honor him and his cause by his distinguishing grace. WHICH ONE OF THESE PROFESSORS ARE WE?

DESPICABLE INGRATITUDE

And they all with one consent began to make excuse
Luke 14:18

The excuses given by those who had opportunity and invitation and chose not to attend the feast prepared, were ridiculous, and revealed many things about them. This is an example of those who have no heart for the Gospel, although professors of religion. The first thing revealed about them was, they had no appetite for the food prepared, which is Christ. They had no taste for the Gospel, having never really eaten of his flesh nor having drunk of his blood, they had no life in them for Christ. Another thing revealed about them was their priorities. Their hearts were fixed upon the things of the world—the flesh. Their first love was the satisfaction and gratification of their lust of the flesh, the eye, and pride in themselves and their possessions.

Even though they were bade to come to this delightful banquet and feast with the Master, their carnal cravings made earthly things more important to them and forbade them to come. Their words and actions revealed their love for the world was greater than their love for God. *Love not the world, neither the things that are in the world. If any man love the world, the love of the Father is not in him* (1 Jn 2:15). Their stupid, ridiculous excuses reveal an ungrateful, unthankful, hard, cold, calloused heart toward one who is worthy of all love, respect, honour, praise and glory. All those who casually esteem the glorious Gospel of Christ and classify it somewhere below the top of their list of priorities in the attending of it will inevitably *with one consent begin to make excuse.* I would be remiss if I did not direct our attention to the Master of the feast and his feelings in this matter. *Then the master of the house being angry. He* here distinguishes those who dine with him from those who don't. *For I say unto you, That none of those men which were bidden shall taste of my supper* (verse 24). And *If any man come to me, and hate not his father, and mother, and wife, and children, and brethren, and sisters, yea, and his own life also, he cannot be my disciple* (Lk 14:26).

THE BEST ROBE

The father said to his servants, Bring forth the best robe, and put it on him.
Luke 15:22

The position, circumstance and attire of the younger son (now in the presence of his father) is remarkable and vitally significant because of his former condition and situation. His self-confessed unworthiness and his father's unreserved acceptance of him unveils to us the heart-love and infinitely-free and sovereign grace and mercy of God our Saviour in vivid beauty and wondrous detail. The Holy Ghost has conspicuously placed the first visible and most worthy (yet undeserved) imputed gift (i.e., the best robe) upon the son which merits all other blessings. The best robe, which renders all other robes worthless, is the covering of the righteousness of Christ, which he wrought for his loved ones while here on earth. Our utter nakedness before God necessitates the best covering before the strict justice of God.

God himself has provided and covered us with this robe. With the best robe on, divine justice can only see the righteousness of Christ. One of the wonders of this best robe is that those who are adorned with it are not only covered but have no sin at all! It is only those who have no sin that qualify for this beautiful apparel. Our blessed Redeemer, having wrought our righteousness for us, put away our sin as well by his own bloody sacrifice on the tree. In essence, viewing the best robe inside AND from the outside, we see Christ in his sinless perfection, embracing worthless chosen sinners so closely that they are one with him and he one with them. *Who his own self bare our sins in his own body on the tree* (1 Pt 2:24) and *For he hath made him to be sin for us, who knew no sin; that we might be made the righteousness of God in him* (2 Cor 5:21).

Only the best robe will do for the worst of sinners. In regeneration, the worthless sinner receives the imparted righteous Christ and the imputed righteousness of Christ. There is nothing better than the best!

EXALTED HUMILITY

And he spake this parable unto certain which trusted in themselves that they were righteous, and despised others.
Luke 18:9

There is one conclusive evidence of inherent sinfulness and depravity peculiar to all false professors of Christianity that stands head and shoulders above all else; that is the obstinate pursuit of self-worth. Prideful man will not willingly let it go. We will, by virtue of our fallen nature, trust in and cling to our own supposed righteousness. Or by the omnipotent grace of the living God, we will flee from and abhor our obnoxious self-unworthiness and trust in and cling to Christ and his intrinsic perfection. The false preacher and professor in his inward parts gloats and unreservedly basks in the light of his darkness.

He is so proud of his cloak of humility! This pompous parasite proudly parades himself up and down every street, alley and concourse of every religion and denomination on the topside of the earth, even as a wolf in sheep's clothing hiding among the sheep. I am thinking that this prating pretender of humility clothed in an outward garment of intellectual doctrinal truth is the most dangerous and deceptive of all. The combination of intellectualism, charisma and the superficial display of humility is a magnet and overwhelming to the natural man and often engenders a great following. The danger and deception of this procession is that men are following men rather than Christ. It cannot be the man and his visible attributes and Christ both.

May God humble us before Him, his Gospel and each other as he reveals Christ to us! I pray he gives us respect for those whom he has called to preach Christ to us. May we render appropriate honor to all the brethren as we abide in Christ. On the other hand may God save us from trusting in or glorying in ourselves or following any other because of the way WE or HE appears to be. Sadly to say, too often when the Gospel is preached, more glory is poured on the head of the preacher than on the head of THE PRIEST. RESERVEDLY, in reverence to God, compliment the preacher. UNRESERVEDLY worship the King of kings and Lord of Lords. Who we worship reveals who and what we trust in.

WHY DO GOOD MEN GO TO HELL?

I tell you, this man went down to his house justified rather than the other: for every one that exalteth himself shall be abased; and he that humbleth himself shall be exalted.

Luke 18:14

The thinking of natural man concerning Christ, salvation, and himself is in complete opposition to the Word of God. This parable reveals a vivid picture of all men's depraved conception of salvation when left to themselves. The Pharisee believed that he was good enough to be justified before the holy God. This Pharisaical principle originated in the fall of our natural father Adam and is passed on to all of his posterity.

Self-justification is the first and most clearly revealed product of unbelief. This damning virtue of fallen man flows like a river through all false doctrine. The object of all falseness is to glorify man and abase the glory of Christ. This is the heart and soul of all free will, Armenian doctrine. Christ Jesus came into the world to save sinners, not good folks. He came to call sinners to repentance, not righteous people.

The first thing a sinner will confess concerning himself when Christ is revealed to him is that he has no goodness and cannot justify himself before God. *The publican, standing afar off, would not lift up so much as his eyes unto heaven, but smote upon his breast, saying, God be merciful to me a sinner* (Lk 18:13). It is amazing how poor sinful creatures suppose themselves to be good when Christ himself said, *there is none good but one, that is, God* (Mk 10:18). And again, *there is none that doeth good, no, not one* (Rom 3:12).

Man is so much in darkness and wrapped up in his own righteousness that unless God in grace and mercy calls him from the cold, dark tundra of spiritual death, he will perish in his own filth. There is no way that a sinner can be justified before God and enter the kingdom of heaven by his own works because God requires perfection. *I say unto you, That except your righteousness shall exceed the righteousness of the scribes and Pharisees, ye shall in no case enter into the kingdom of heaven* (Mt 5:20). To be clothed with the righteousness of Christ is our only justification and acceptance before God (Phil 3:9; 2 Cor 5:21).

WHO THEN CAN BE SAVED?

Luke 18:26

The false religionists, which are many and prosperous in the work of deception, are crying to their hearers—ANY ONE CAN BE SAVED, AT ANY TIME; IT IS UP TO YOU! SALVATION IS IN YOUR HANDS! JUST EXERCISE YOUR FREE WILL. Nothing could be further from the truth. Salvation is impossible with man. But with God salvation is sure and certain. *This is a faithful saying, and worthy of all acceptation, that Christ Jesus came into the world to save sinners* (1 Tm 1:15). If God is not pleased to reveal Christ to spiritually dead sinners, they will perish.

All those to whom he will reveal Christ will be saved with an everlasting salvation. Salvation is by God's free will, not man's supposed free will. Who then can be saved? Those whom God will save!

Those whom God will save are those whom he loved and chose in Christ before the world began. *Who hath saved us, and called us with an holy calling, not according to our works, but according to his own purpose and grace, which was given us in Christ Jesus before the world began* (2 Tm 1:9).

Those whom God will save are those whom the Lord Jesus Christ wrought a righteousness for in the days of his flesh here on this earth.

Those who will be saved are those for whom Christ offered himself up to God, being their substitute and sacrifice for sin. *Much more then, being now justified by his blood, we shall be saved from wrath through him* (Rom 5:9).

Those who will be saved are those for whom Christ now intercedes at the right hand of the Majesty on high. *Wherefore he is able also to save them to the uttermost that come unto God by Him, seeing he ever liveth to make intercession for them* (Heb 7:25).

Those who then will be saved are those that God, in his time, effectually calls by his sovereign grace, by the preaching of the Gospel of God's free and sovereign grace in Christ Jesus. He thereby imparts to them his divine nature and imputs to them Christ's perfect righteousness. Therefore, those who were dead in trespasses and sins are now alive unto God.

Those who will be saved are those that persevere by God-given faith in Christ, believing the Gospel, committed to the Gospel, trusting in Christ, looking to Christ, bowing to Christ, and worshipping Christ. *And ye shall be hated of all men for my name's sake: but he that endureth* (continues) *to the end shall be saved* (Mt 10:22). Who then can be saved? *All that the Father giveth me shall come to Me; and him that cometh to me I will in no wise cast out* (Jn 6:37).

I FIND NO FAULT IN HIM

Then said Pilate to the chief priests and to the people, I find no fault in this man.

Luke 23:4

Although this statement was made by the cowardly, compromising Pilate, it is the glorious truth acknowledged by all who know the Lord Jesus Christ. He is the essence of perfection as God and as man. He is the embodiment of truth, holiness, righteousness and justice. There is none with whom he can be compared. His glory is his perfection, and his perfection is his glory. His faultlessness sets him apart from all others. The glorious person of the Lord Jesus Christ makes all he does radiate with his wondrous perfections and beauty.

As a matter of fact, it is this virtue that captivates the hearts of all who behold him as he is! *One generation shall praise thy works to another, and shall declare thy mighty* acts. *I will speak of the glorious honour of thy majesty, and of thy wondrous works* (Ps 145:4-5)! The Lord Jesus Christ is faultless in his person and his work. His work in the glorification of the Father and the redemption of his people reveal to us the impeccable virtues of his holy character. His children look upon him in wonder and amazement as we behold his perfect salvation.

He worked out a perfect righteousness for us and perfectly put away our sin as he became sin for us. *For he hath made him to be sin for us, who knew no sin; that we might be made the righteousness of God in him* (2 Cor 5:21). Therefore, his elect is clothed with his perfections as we abide in him and are accepted in him by God the Father. As there is no fault found in Him, there is no fault found in those who are in Him. To him be all honour, all glory and all praise. *Unto him be glory in the church by Christ Jesus throughout all ages, world without end. Amen* (Eph 3:21).

A SINNER LEARNS CHRIST

And he said unto Jesus, Lord, remember me when thou comest into thy kingdom.
Luke 23:42

I said in a message a few weeks ago, "The redeemed thief didn't know a lot as far as quantity, but he knew the Lord." I recant on this statement. I was wrong. I believe God the Spirit teaches us in this experience that Christ taught this sinner upon regeneration what every saved sinner is taught in the Gospel of Christ. In all probability he had heard of our Lord in all things concerning Him which led to his crucifixion. This was not done in secret or in a corner. However, the thief knew him not in his glorious person until this divinely appointed, wondrous moment on his vertical deathbed. By God's sovereign quickening grace, the once spiritually dead, physically dying thief beheld the LAMB OF GOD in the midst of the throne with God-given faith!

Thank God for his sovereign love, mercy and grace given to his people in Christ Jesus! Our dying Redeemer was in command of this poor sinner's eternal life by his own vicarious death! What did this brother learn in this short hour? He learned he was an utterly helpless guilty sinner in the presence of the Lord of Glory. He learned if he were to be saved, Christ must save Him. He learned the Lord was sovereign in all things, especially in bringing him into his presence. And, thanks be unto God, he learned in a brief moment he would be with Christ in Paradise.

Whereof may this justified, glorified sinner glory? In NOTHING of his own—in CHRIST ALONE! HIS recognizing and calling upon the Lord was not of his doing. It was all of Christ's pleasure, power and glory. *All things are delivered to me of my Father: and no man knoweth who the Son is, but the Father; and who the Father is, but the Son, and he to whom the Son will reveal him* (Lk 10:22). The blessed truths of the Gospel are not doctrinal points to learn, argue, and debate, and cram down people's religious digestive systems. These blessed truths are only revealed, received and lovingly embraced in Christ by sinners whom God the Father has looked upon in our time of his everlasting love. *The hour is coming, and now is, when the dead shall hear the voice of the Son of God: and they that hear shall live* (Jn 5:25).

IN THE BEGINNING

John 1:1

All things begin with God. *IN THE BEGINNING was the Word, and the Word was with God, and the Word was God. The Same was in the beginning with God. ALL THINGS WERE MADE BY HIM; and without him was not any thing made that was made* (Jn 1:1). All things that follow stream from his eternal purpose, which will ultimately be accomplished. Our Lord Jesus Christ did not just enter into the scheme of things in time; he is the eternal Son of God from everlasting which was manifest in the flesh, in time. Neither God nor his Son has a beginning, yet all things have their beginning in the Godhead. This Biblical truth is the quintessence of all truth. If this be not so, then Divinity has no real meaning, value or merit. I believe that is why, by divine inspiration, holy writ begins thusly—*In the beginning God.*

In respect to this revelation of God in Christ, the child of God has great interest, primarily because in him who is the beginning of all things our salvation originates or has its beginning. *But OF HIM* (God) *are ye in Christ Jesus, who OF GOD is made unto us wisdom, and righteousness, and sanctification, and redemption* (1 Cor 1:30). If it be so that the beginning of our salvation is Christ, and is in Christ who is the Alpha, then all our salvation, to the end, is in him who is the Omega as well. Not only was he in the beginning, he is the Beginning! And he never changes! *Jesus Christ THE SAME yesterday, and to day, and for ever* (Heb 13:8). The word *Beginning* is strictly to accommodate us mere mortals because with God all things are in the eternal present. The way we, by faith, see this great and wonderful mystery revealed is that *in the beginning,* before the foundation of the world, God the Father chose his people in Christ unto salvation. In time the Son of God was manifest in the flesh to begin and accomplish eternal redemption for us. In time the Lord Jesus Christ, in the person of his blessed Spirit, begun a good work in us and will perform it unto perfection. Dear reader, what we experience now, and will experience in the future, as the children of God, is a work finished from *THE BEGINNING. For we which have believed do enter into rest, as he said, As I have sworn in my wrath, if they shall enter into my rest: although the WORKS WERE FINISHED FROM THE FOUNDATION OF THE WORLD* (Heb 4:3). In this context our great comfort is twofold:

(1.) God never begins anything that he doesn't finish.

(2.) All that he does for his people is in Christ, who is *the Beginning.*

158

You agnostics perish with your vain thoughts. You who know Christ rejoice with great joy that all things are in Him.

THE WILL OF THE FLESH

Which were born, not of blood, nor of the will of the flesh, nor of the will of man, but of God.
John 1:13

The so-called FREE WILL of man being the determining cause of regeneration is at the heart of all false doctrine. The supremacy of the natural WILL is the delusional dream of the demented mind of depravity. There is not one verse or context of holy writ that even suggests man is empowered with an ability to move himself to spiritual life or has a natural desire for the true and living God. The will of the flesh is the god of the flesh. Man's natural ungodly will is concerned with and in bondage to self in three areas, which constitute the whole man. *For all that is in the world, the* (1.) *LUST OF THE FLESH, and the* (2.) *LUST OF THE EYES, and the* (3.) *PRIDE OF LIFE, is not of the Father, but is of the world* (1 Jn 2:16).

Man's will is only functional in the realm in which it is in captivity, and that is the realm of spiritual death and darkness. Man's spiritual demise forbids him to move to the Light and to life. *And this is the condemnation, that light is come into the world, and men loved darkness rather than light, because their deeds were evil* (Jn 3:19); *And ye will not come to me, that ye might have life* (Jn 5:40). Spiritual birth, or regeneration, is *not of blood, nor of the will of the flesh, nor of the will of man, but of God.*

What part does man have in regeneration? NONE! Here is the determining, sufficient and efficient cause of a once dead sinner being alive unto God. *No man can come to me, except the Father which hath sent me draw him: and I WILL raise him up at the last day* (Jn 6:44); *And I GIVE UNTO THEM ETERNAL LIFE; and they shall never perish, neither shall any man pluck them out of my hand* (Jn 10:28).

Any message that is not clear as to God's free will in the salvation of the elect and the bondage of man's will to sin and self is blasphemous in content and damning in consequence. Thy *people shall be willing in the day of thy power, in the beauties of holiness from the womb of the morning: thou hast the dew of thy youth* (Ps 110:3). This is the work of God!

GRACE AND TRUTH

John 1:17

The whole of the work of salvation is a work of God the Father, God the Son, and God the Spirit. While man never ceases to attempt to take part in the glorious work of redemption, he will continually fail. Fallen man never has and never will accomplish what Christ accomplished for his people. Sinful, religious man tries to find hope, peace and comfort, and eternal life in his own supposed righteousness, while the child of God, by God's grace, finds all he desires in the person and work of Christ. To the believer the benefits of God's saving grace is wonderful and glorious, but the substance of God's grace is most excellent of all, which is the Lord Jesus Christ himself!

The child of God's great joy and satisfaction is not in the SYSTEMATIC doctrine of salvation by grace or works of righteousness which he has done (which is really unrighteousness), but in Christ in whom all true doctrine is found. In Christ we see the love, mercy, and grace of God freely given to sinful man. In him we rest, knowing that the great work of salvation is finished in perfection and entirety without our aid or assistance. As not to minimize the importance of sound doctrine, we must conclude that one may know sound doctrine and yet never know Christ. On the other hand, all who know Christ know and believe the truth because grace and truth is revealed in him alone.

For the law was given by Moses, but grace and truth came by Jesus Christ (Jn 1:17).

A NEW CREATURE

Jesus answered and said unto him, Verily, verily, I say unto thee, Except a man be born again, he cannot see the kingdom of God.
John 3:3

Something so dreadful happened in the fall of man that it is almost incomprehensible. As a matter of fact only those to whom God has given of his Spirit have any understanding of it at all. Man died spiritually, alienating himself from God. This woeful condition is passed down from generation to generation. Except for a work of the sovereign Spirit of the grace of God, man will remain dead. Anything short of a spiritual understanding of this truth only leaves man with the supposed, damning theory of free will as to his recovery from the fall. One can only enter life by birth, which is the impartation of life where once there was no life. This is a work of almighty grace.

Religion says I CAN DO IT! God says, *Except a man be born again,* (born from above) *he cannot see the kingdom of God.* The new birth is a receiving of the divine nature (2 Pt 1:3-4). Although the old carnal nature lives, there is a new nature within those whom God has given spiritual life.

This life is not just new principles to live by, it is the life and Spirit of the Lord Jesus Christ. *To whom God would make known what is the riches of the glory of this mystery among the Gentiles; which is Christ in you, the hope of glory* (Col 1:27).

The new man believes on the Lord Jesus Christ for all his salvation. He loves him WHO loves him. The new man looks by faith, which God has given, upon him who is his salvation, because he knows Him. *And this is life eternal, that they might know thee the only true God, and Jesus Christ, whom thou hast sent* (Jn 17:3).

The new birth is not a reformation of the old; it is a new life, a new nature, a new beginning. Once we did not live unto God, now we do. Once we did not see the Lord Jesus Christ by faith, now we do. Once we did not hear the Word of God, now we do. Once we did not understand the truth of God, now we do. And here, I believe, is the vital, undeniable evidence of spiritual life: a God-given love for Christ, his Gospel, and his church. *We love him because he first loved us* (1 Jn 4:19). Therefore, the absence of love for him is an undeniable evidence of the absence of spiritual life. *He that loveth not knoweth not God; for God is love* (1 Jn 4:8).

The sheep's love for Christ is the unalterable result of Christ's love for the sheep.

BORN: THEN BORN AGAIN

John 3:6

The Bible speaks of two births: every man's natural or fleshly birth; and his people's supernatural or spiritual birth (*That which is born of the flesh is flesh; and that which is born of the Spirit is spirit* (Jn 3:6). The verb "is" in our Lord's statement to Nicodemus reveals to us that we will remain as we are born until death. The truth and realization of this concerning the first birth is discouraging and depressing. It means that we will be prone to, and subject to sin and all its afflictions and hindrances as long as we live. Thank God for his throne of grace where-upon sits our intercessor and advocate! But, alas, the evidence of our sinful nativity will follow us to the grave. And worse, those who are not born again spiritually will live in eternity as they are here: without Christ and with sin and it's consequences, eternal death.

The second birth, or spiritual birth, our Lord speaks of is from above (not fleshly, but of God). Those who are born of this birth will remain the same—ETERNALLY! This truth gives us much comfort and joy. What we are here as the people of God, we will remain so for ever. For those who do not know Christ here, eternity will be worse. But for those who have been born again, eternity will be indescribably better for we shall see him as he is, and we will be totally dead to the first birth, which is sin (1 Cor 15:54).

TRUE WORSHIP

But the hour cometh, and now is, when the true worshippers shall worship the Father in spirit and in truth: for the Father seeketh such to worship him.

John 4:23

"Worship" means to adore, reverence, love, respect, devote one's self to, submit to, to esteem and acknowledge a person or thing above all else.

Worship of any one or any thing other than the true and living God is idolatry. *It is written, thou shalt worship the Lord thy God, and him only shalt thou serve* (Lk 4:8).

Man is a worshipper and as a result of his fallen nature, is an idolater. We see this in the Scriptures from the fall of Adam even to our own selves. Man's false god is the last thing to go in coming to Christ, and is the unbeliever's point of rebellion.

True worshippers worship the true and living God. *And we know that the Son of God is come, and hath given us an understanding, that we may know him that is true, and we are in him that is true, even in his Son Jesus Christ. THIS IS THE TRUE GOD, and eternal life* (1 Jn 5:20).

True worship has one singular object, that is God in Christ. *There is no God else beside Me; a just God and a Saviour; there is none beside me* (Is 45:21).

In order for there to be true worship, there must be a new heart, a new Spirit and a new mind, and these God must give. *A NEW HEART also will I give you, and a NEW SPIRIT will I put within you: and I will take away the stony heart out of your flesh, and I will give you an heart of flesh* (Ez 36:26).

The truth is essential to true worship as well; the truth as it is in God's Word, the truth as it is in Christ. True worship requires the truth concerning who God is, who Christ is and what he accomplished, and where he is now. True worship requires the truth concerning salvation for his people in Christ alone and all that pertains thereunto. The Lord Jesus Christ said, *I am the way,* THE TRUTH, *and the life: no man cometh unto the Father, but by me* (Jn 14:6).

True worship is not in form, ritual or ceremony. It is from the hearts of those to whom God has revealed himself. True worship is born of God and is toward God. For sinners to worship the true and living God, we must come with the accepted sacrifice, and that sacrifice is the Lamb of God, Christ our Lord.

IS IT WHAT, HOW, WHEN, WHERE, OR WHO?

Search the scriptures; for in them ye think ye have eternal life: and they are they which testify of Me.
John 5:39

The substance of all Biblical doctrine is the Lord Jesus Christ, the Son of the living God. The message of the Gospel of God is the Lord Jesus Christ. The object of God given faith is the Lord Jesus Christ. The essence of eternal life is the Lord Jesus Christ.

What, how, when, where, or any thing else means nothing when severed or omitted from the glorious, wonderful, beautiful person of my Redeemer. To be doctrinally correct is essential. However, it is an impossibility to be doctrinally correct when he who is truth is set aside to prove a point. The center, the heart and soul of all true doctrine, of all Gospel preaching and teaching is Jesus Christ and him crucified.

Dear friends, we may know intellectually all that can be known of doctrinal truth and yet perish. However, not one single person to whom the Lord Jesus Christ has been revealed will believe a lie or come into condemnation. Church, let men argue, fuss, fight and debate over what they will. We, by God's grace, have one two-fold objective, and purpose: to declare the glorious person of Christ Jesus, and to know him and be found in Him.

Much knowledge without Christ only leads to pride, arrogance and self-righteousness. Much Christ with knowledge leads to repentance, humility and peace. The wonder and beauty of Gospel preaching is not how well doctrine is expounded, it is when Christ and all truth in him is preached. I want someone to tell me of a successful Redeemer. The only way I will learn what redemption really means is to know the Redeemer. What I am saying is this: all truth is revealed in Christ, and only revealed in Christ. If we do not preach Christ, we have not preached the Gospel. Salvation is by God-given faith in Christ, not in what we know. Because we preach some truth and believe some truth does not necessarily mean that we know Christ. Do we know Christ?

And this is life eternal, that they might know thee the only true God, and Jesus Christ, whom thou hast sent (Jn 17:3).

COMING TO CHRIST

All that the Father giveth me shall come to me; and him that cometh to me I will in no wise cast out.

John 6:37

Coming to Christ is not a decision that sinners make by the exercise of their so-called free will. It is only he who has been and is being called by God's sovereign, discriminating, efficacious grace that comes to Him. It is an absolute absurdity to even think that man's will is sovereign over God's will.

Coming to Christ is believing upon him with a new heart as he is revealed in the Scriptures by the Spirit of God in regeneration. When Christ is revealed in the hear,t the sinner renounces all his righteousness, strength, ability and even himself. The elect of God come to Christ because they are loved and chosen of God, and because they are redeemed by the precious blood of Christ. They come because, in time, they heard the Word of truth (the Gospel of their salvation) and are given faith to believe on Him. Those to whom Christ is revealed continue to believe in him, and therefore will never perish because he will in no wise cast them out. The child of God is kept by the power of God through faith.

NO MAN CAN COME TO ME, EXCEPT . . .

No man can come to me, except the Father which hath sent me draw him: and I will raise him up at the last day.
John 6:44

All that the Father giveth me shall come to Me; and him that cometh to me I will in no wise cast out.
John 6:37

MAN CAN NOT—GOD SHALL! *The things which are impossible with men are possible with God* (Lk 18:27). Those that come to Christ are identified in the Scriptures as THE ELECT, THE CHOSEN, THE SAINTS, THE REDEEMED, THE CALLED, THE SHEEP, THE CHILDREN OF GOD, just to mention a few. There is one thing very noticeably common to each one; it is the Lord that gives them these titles. With each title is the revelation of the truth that salvation is a work of God, not of man. We can see as well that the great work of salvation is a complete and everlasting work. Therefore, even our coming to Christ is the result of God bringing us to Christ, otherwise we would not come. *No man can come to me, except the Father which hath sent me draw him: and I will raise him up at the last day* (Jn 6:44).

Coming to Christ is simply believing on Him, bowing to Him, trusting him and committing ourselves to him for time and eternity. Where faith, submission, trust and commitment is not everpresent in the heart, there is no coming to Christ. All of the above is given to us of God in regeneration. Now, there is one ingredient upon which everything in salvation is dependent upon and is born of—LOVE! *The LORD hath appeared of old unto me, [saying], Yea, I have loved thee with an everlasting love: therefore with lovingkindness have I drawn thee* (Jer 31:3). *We love Him, because he first loved us* (1 Jn 4:19).

The child of God keeps coming to Christ because he loves him, loves his Word, and loves his people, those who are the body of Christ.

THE BREAD OF LIFE

I am that bread of life.
John 6:48

There could be no clearer Gospel declaration than this singular statement of our Lord. Religious men today love to complicate the truth of God with many words and raise many questions in an effort to cast doubt upon both the living Word of God and the written Word of God. This attitude is no different than the attitude of the unbelieving Jews whom our Lord confronts in this text. The heart of Christ's message is very simple, too simple for the proud intellect of unbelieving man.

The singular, vital truth of his message is THERE IS NO SPIRITUAL LIFE ANYWHERE, FOR ANY MAN, IN ANY GENERATION, APART FROM BEING ONE WITH THE LORD JESUS CHRIST. There is no spiritual life in man, or in the doings of man. Man is spiritually dead and will remain dead unless and until God, in sovereign grace and power, reveals Christ to him in vital union. The Lord Jesus Christ is the bread of life, PERIOD! Plus nothing and minus nothing!

*This is that bread which came down from heaven: not as
your fathers did eat manna, and are dead: he that eateth of this
bread shall live for ever* (Jn 6:58).

DEPRAVITY

*Then Jesus said unto them, Verily, verily, I say unto you, Except
ye eat the flesh of the Son of man, and drink his blood, ye have
NO LIFE in you.*

John 6:53

Contrary to all false religions, mankind, apart from the
impartation of the divine nature of the Lord Jesus Christ by
the sovereign Spirit of Almighty God, is completely and
absolutely spiritually dead. Not one man, the best or worst, has
one spark of spiritual life in him until God, in sovereign grace
and mercy, gives him life. Therefore this is God's call, not man's
call. Any preacher or any message that gives man something to
do as a prerequisite to salvation is false. A dead man cannot do
anything. It is only those to whom God has given life that believe
on, look to, and trust in the person and work of the Lord Jesus
Christ. The depraved human heart is a heart of darkness and
unbelief, void of understanding and faith. *There is none that
understandeth, there is none that seeketh after God* (Rom 3:11).

Man cannot give himself life. *NO MAN CAN COME TO ME,
except the Father which hath sent me draw him: and I will raise
him up at the last day* (Jn 6:44), and no one will come to Christ
and the truth by his own will and volition. *And ye will not come
to me, that ye might have life* (Jn 5:40). Man is dead in trespasses
and sin. He will remain justly so, and justly perish in his sin and

unbelief if he is passed by, by the true and living God that will by no means (other than by substitution) clear the guilty.

What I am saying is this: salvation, necessarily and completely, is in the sovereign purpose and will of Almighty God in the person and work of the ONLY Savior, the Lord Jesus Christ. *Neither is there salvation in any other: for there is none other name under heaven given among men, whereby we must be saved* (Acts 4:12). A misunderstanding of the depravity of the human heart will always lead to a perverted view of Christ and his accomplishment in the redemption of sinners. A misunderstanding of the depravity of man will always lead to self-righteousness.

The preacher and so-called Gospel that gives the sinner his own will and ability in regeneration is cursed by God and is no Gospel at all. *But though we, or an angel from heaven, preach any other gospel unto you than that which we have preached unto you, let him be accursed* (Gal 1:8). Our only hope is this—*I will have mercy upon her that had not obtained mercy; and I will say to them which were not my people, thou art my people; and they shall say, thou art my God.*

WILL YOU GO AWAY ALSO?

Lord, to whom shall we go? thou hast the words of eternal life.
John 6:68

Our Lord's assertion in the previous verses that he is indeed the bread of life was found to be offensive to many of those who followed him. As a matter of fact, they were so offended that they refused to be identified with him any longer and went their own way. However, those whom he had chosen and revealed himself to refused to follow any other than the Lord Jesus Christ. They were completely happy and satisfied to be identified with him and follow him who is life.

The child of God has no options. Neither does he desire to follow any other than the one who loves us and gave his life for us. Without exception, those to whom Christ is precious, desire communion and fellowship with him in his Gospel and with others *that have obtained like precious faith.* Eventually those who are offended by Christ and his doctrine will *go away also.*

I fear that some are gone away that are still with us, even as Judas. When they do completely go away, it will be revealed that *they went out from us, but they were not of us; for if they had been of us, they would no doubt have continued with us: but they went out, that they might be made manifest that they were not all of us* (1 Jn 2:19). The absence of love and desire will always be revealed by an offensive self-justifying, prideful attitude and the lack of an humble, sweet, submissive spirit toward the Gospel and toward others. This always leads to a lack of commitment and interest in the things of God. I am convinced that if our heart is not in what we profess to believe, we too will *go away also,* if we have not already gone away.

If we find our interest slowly dying, and are more and more committed to ourselves and the enjoyment of the things of this world than to Christ and his kingdom, and are not concerned about it, there is reason for alarm. The true child of God will endure whatever he must to sit at the Lord's table and eat the Bread of life. And certainly he will not be offended by the truth.

DAMNED SEEKERS

*Then said Jesus again unto them, I go my way, and ye shall seek
me, and shall die in your sins: whither I go, ye cannot come.*
John 8:21

This singular verdict of the Judge of all the earth carries with
it the death sentence for all those who remain in unbelief and
rebellion against God. Our Lord spake this *unto certain which
trusted in themselves that they were righteous* and had not
submitted themselves unto the righteousness of God. All men will
indeed seek the Lord, but not everyone will seek him *while he
may be found.*

Although those to whom he spake would one day seek
Him, they would yet die without Him. He left them with no IFS,
BUTS, or MAYBES. They were left absolutely and eternally to
themselves, in their sins, without a single ray of hope. The
judgment of God upon the impenitent is irreversible and precise.
This statement of our Lord to the Pharisees reveals two great and
vital Gospel truths.

THE ONLY PLACE SAFE FROM CONDEMNATION BEFORE GOD
IS IN THE LORD JESUS CHRIST. They would not have died in their
sins had they been with the Lord Jesus Christ. *And if I go and
prepare a place for you, I will come again, and receive you unto
Myself; that where I am, there ye may be also* (Jn 14:3). Almighty
God's wrath was exhausted in the vicarious death of Christ for
his chosen ones. God's elect will not die in their sins; they will
live in his righteousness!

SALVATION IS NOT IN THE HANDS OF SINNERS. No man shall ever seek the Lord for the right reason unless Christ has already sought the man. Man will trust in his own righteousness, seeking the Lord for preservation in it, and perish embracing it.

The execution of God's judgment upon sinful man is just and righteous in respect to, not only God's law, but in proportion to the person and work of Christ in the fulfillment of it. *I said therefore unto you, that ye shall die in your sins: for if ye believe not that I am He, ye shall die in your sins* (Jn 8:24).

SAVING FAITH

I said therefore unto you, that ye shall die in your sins: for if ye believe not that I am He, ye shall die in your sins.
John 8:24

One of the great wonders of salvation in Christ the Lord is the simplicity and singularity of faith in Him. All false religions, false faiths, and false gospels, always add to or take away from the simplicity of believing on the Lord Jesus Christ as he is declared in the Scriptures by the faith which he gives in regeneration. The faith that he gives always has one object: the Lord Jesus Christ. True saving faith is not faith in the work that is done, but in he who has done the work.

The work that is done—redemption, atonement, sanctification, justification, regeneration—is efficacious because of him who redeemed, atoned, sanctified, justified and has given us spiritual life. Saving faith is in the person of Christ, in him who did these wonderful things for us. Essentially, we cannot *separate* Christ from his work, yet faith makes a *distinction*. The *distinction* is this: Faith looks to, trusts in, and believes in the

LIVING PERSON CHRIST, and sees all things in salvation in Him. Saving faith embraces, not only the doctrine of Christ, but, first and foremost, embraces Christ in whom all truth is embodied and revealed. I fear that there are some, maybe many, who believe in the blessed doctrine of grace, but who do not have faith in the Christ of the doctrines.

Again I stress this scriptural truth. Anyone can embrace doctrinal truth, but it is only those whom God has effectually called to faith in Christ in regeneration that can and will embrace Christ himself, and live upon Him. *Then Jesus said unto them, Verily, verily, I say unto you, Except ye eat the flesh of the Son of man, and drink his blood, ye have no life in you* (Jn 6:53). Truth is declared, the Gospel is preached, and man may give assent to the truth; yet no one is saved until sinners are vitally joined to Christ in living union, which is the operation of the sovereign Spirit of the living God.

This is the simplicity of the Gospel. *We preach Christ crucified, unto the Jews a stumblingblock, and unto the Greeks foolishness; But unto them which are called, both Jews and Greeks, Christ the power of God, and the wisdom of God* (1 Cor 1:23-24). No matter what one knows, until he knows Christ, he has no saving interest in Christ or claim to eternal life. *And this is life eternal, that they might know thee the only true God, and Jesus Christ, whom thou hast sent* (Jn 17:3).

THE SHEPHERD

John 10

O ur Lord's title of "Shepherd" is most endearing to the heart of the believer. In this title we can see all that he is, has done, and is doing for his people.

THEY ARE HIS SHEEP, CHOSEN IN HIM. *I am the Good Shepherd, and know my sheep, and am known of mine* (Jn 10:14). *According as he hath chosen us in him before the foundation of the world* (Eph 1:4).

He PURCHASED THEM. HE GAVE HIS LIFE FOR THE SHEEP. *I am the good shepherd: the good shepherd giveth his life for the sheep* (Jn 10:11). *Take heed therefore unto yourselves, and to all the flock, over the which the Holy Ghost hath made you overseers, to feed the church of God, which he hath purchased with his own blood* (Acts 20:28).

He PROVIDES FOR THEM. *The LORD is my Shepherd; I shall not want* (Ps 23:1). *But my God shall supply all your need according to his riches in glory by Christ Jesus* (Phil 4:19).

He KEEPS AND PROTECTS THEM. *Yea, though I walk through the valley of the shadow of death, I will fear no evil: for thou art with me; thy rod and thy staff they comfort me* (Ps 23:4). *My sheep hear my voice, and I know them, and they follow Me: And I give unto them eternal life; and they shall never perish, neither shall any man pluck them out of my hand* (Jn 10:27-28).

HE LOVES THE SHEEP. *As the Father knoweth me, even so know I the Father: and I lay down my life for the sheep* (Jn 10:15).

Having loved his own which were in the world, he loved them unto the end (Jn 13:1).

THE BELIEVER'S SECURITY

I give unto them eternal life; and they shall never perish, neither shall any man pluck them out of my hand.
John 10:28

The security of the child of God is more than just an argument about how long one will be saved, or if one can lose his salvation. The salvation of God's elect is an eternal salvation because it is a work of God in Christ. Life eternal is in, and only in, union with the Lord Jesus Christ. *This is the record, that God hath given to us eternal life, and this life is in his Son* (1 Jn 5:11). The opposing position— that a child of God might lose their salvation— suggests that salvation is by our works rather than by the grace of God. Nothing could be further from the truth. The Lord Jesus Christ is our life. In him we live, by him we live, and our life is the very life of the Spirit of the living God. Therefore eternal life is measured in quality rather than in longevity.

The verse of Scripture before us (as well as hundreds of others) plainly, dogmatically, and simply declares that God gives unto his people eternal life in his Son; we shall never perish because we are in his hand. Our security is the person and work of our Redeemer. He accomplished eternal redemption for us. He provides an everlasting righteousness for us. We are kept by the power of God through faith that he has given to us. There is nothing uncertain with God, especially concerning the salvation of his people. *She SHALL bring forth a son, and thou SHALT call his name JESUS: for he SHALL save his people from their sins* (Mt

1:21). *ISRAEL SHALL BE SAVED IN THE LORD WITH AN EVERLASTING SALVATION: ye SHALL not be ashamed nor confounded world without end* (Is 45:17).

When the Lord Jesus ceases to be the Saviour of sinners, then will our salvation be ended. When God ceases to be God, then will we cease to be his people. Until then, his people have an anchor of the soul, both sure and steadfast, eternal in the heavens.

Which hope we have as an anchor of the soul, both sure and stedfast, and which entereth into that within the veil (Heb 6:19).

ETERNAL LIFE

John 17:3

The Scriptures emphatically declare the holy character and glorious attributes of Jehovah. Yet, the majority of religions insist that he is not as the Scriptures reveal him to be. I insist that this is a willing refusal to believe and bow to revealed truth. Any other god than the God described in the Scriptures is a false god, and the worship of a false god is idolatry. The Gospel of God, when preached, is met with in one of two ways: believed and embraced, or rejected and hated.

There seems to be a common ground upon which all false religions agree. It is that God can be any way you imagine him to be as long as you believe in Him, and that every one that believes in a god is going to heaven. NOT SO! Read Matthew 7:21. *This is life eternal, that they might know thee the only true God, and Jesus Christ, whom thou hast sent* (Jn 17:3). The Bible is dogmatic and clear concerning the character of God, and salvation being in Christ alone (Acts 4:12). False religion insists upon the free will of man; the Bible insists upon the free will of God (Is 46:10). False religion insists upon the person and work of Christ plus the works and cooperation of man. The Bible insists upon the person and work of Christ alone (Heb 9:12). False religion insists that there is good in every one. The Bible insists that there is none good except Christ (Mt 19:17; Mk 10:18). In short, what the Scriptures plainly declare is either ignored or perverted by false religion in order that depraved man may retain his pride and imagined sovereignty over God; therefore the truth is rejected and hated. Those that, by God's grace and power bow to and believe the truth, embrace Christ by faith that he gives by the preaching of the Gospel (Rom 10:17).

But we are bound to give thanks alway to God for you, brethren beloved of the Lord, because God hath from the beginning chosen you to salvation through sanctification of the Spirit and belief of the truth (2 Thes 2:13).

THE ACCOMPLISHMENT OF THE LORD JESUS CHRIST

I have glorified thee on the earth: I have finished the work which thou gavest me to do.

John 17:4

The JESUS of the Armenian-free-will-works-religionist accomplished precisely nothing for the glory of God, nor did he accomplish anything for sinful man. There could be nothing more dishonoring to the character of God the Father and the person and work of God the Son than the system of works religion which delegates the cause and accomplishment of salvation to the sinner. Neither does the self-acclaimed Calvinistic intellectual, who insists upon the mere doctrinal knowledge of revealed truth as the foundation of faith and hope of eternal life in Christ Jesus our Lord, honor God and his Son. They completely ignore the accomplishment of our Redeemer in the work of the Holy Spirit, in the execution of that which Christ has accomplished in regeneration—in the impartation of the righteousness of Christ, and spiritual life to the elect.

When our Lord said, *I have glorified thee on the earth: I have finished the work which thou gavest me to do,* he was speaking of every thing from election to glorification, even our calling and preservation in Christ. Everything that God the Father required, God the Son provided. He finished the work, even the giving of life to dead, chosen sinners. Any system of religion that hints that salvation is by anything the sinner knows or does, robs God and his Son of his glory, and is false. Doctrinal truth is revealed in Christ to those whom he has given life. That life includes faith, knowledge, and understanding. The life and faith of God's elect is the accomplishment of the Lord Jesus Christ as well as the righteousness he wrought for us and the death that he died to put away our sin. He completely, perfectly, and eternally finished all the work the Father gave him to do. Therefore, God is glorified in the Son, and those for whom he accomplished salvation are glorified in Him, and he is glorified in them. *All mine are thine, and thine are mine; and I am glorified in them* (Jn 17:10). The Lord Jesus Christ started my salvation, and HE FINISHED IT! WHAT AN ACCOMPLISHMENT!

"To God be the glory;
Great things he hath done!"

180

SALVATION BY WORKS

I have glorified thee on the earth: I have finished the work which thou gavest me to do.

John 17:4

In this prayer to his Father, our Lord speaks of the great work of redemption which he accomplished for his people. If there is one passage in all holy writ that should silence the WORKS religionists, it would be this one. The salvation of the elect is by works, but not by our works. The salvation of poor sinners is by the perfect work of our Redeemer, *Not by works of righteousness which we have done, but according to his mercy he saved us* (Ti 3:5).

The perfect work of Christ is the ONLY work that God Almighty will accept, and has already accepted it, from all eternity. Christ's perfect work guarantees the acceptance of all those for whom he performed it, by the Father. The work that our Lord is speaking of is the establishing of a perfect, justifying righteousness for the elect of God as their substitute. The Father's demand of perfect obedience to his holy, just, inflexible law from his people, Christ performed to the letter. Anything less is an abomination to the Father, slanders the blessed Son of God, and is a reproach to the Gospel of God's grace. The work that our Lord finished is the putting away of his people's sin. *Now once in the end of the world hath he appeared to put away sin by the sacrifice of himself* (Heb 9:26). Man can no more put away sin than he can establish righteousness. Man cannot, Christ can, and bless his name, HE DID! He said, *IT IS FINISHED, AND HE BOWED HIS HEAD AND GAVE UP THE GHOST.*

Therefore, there is absolutely nothing that can be attributed to man, or the works of man, in the great work of salvation. Yet many say that it is up to man to make his work effectual, by accepting Jesus in a SUPPOSED act of an IMAGINARY free will. Not according to God! This is the work of God as well, for *No man can come to me, except the Father which hath sent me draw him* (Jn 6:44).

Therefore said I unto you, that no man can come unto me, except it were given unto him of my Father (Jn 6:65). The call of God in regeneration to faith in Christ is not something we do, it is a work of the sovereign Spirit of the living God. It is the Spirit that gives life, not the letter of the law. *Christ in you* is the life of the believing sinner. Salvation is indeed by works, but not those of the sinner. SALVATION IS BY THE WORK OF THE SAVIOUR. *Thou shalt call his name JESUS: for he SHALL SAVE his people from their sins* (Mt 1:21).

IN CHRIST

That they all may be one; as thou, Father, art in me, and I in thee, that they also may be one in us: that the world may believe that thou hast sent me. And the glory which thou gavest me I have given them; that they may be one, even as We are one.
John 17: 21-22

The phrase *in Christ* appears over seventy times in the New Testament, not to mention similar phrases like those in the above verses. This term speaks of a vital union, oneness, a partaker of, in agreement with Christ, and all that pertains to our salvation in Him. Remove *in Christ* and *in him* and we would have nothing. Outside of Christ there is only death which is the wrath and judgment of God on sinners like ourselves. As those inside the ark, we who are in Christ are safe and secure. In Christ we have eternal life and rejoice in hope. In him we are righteous and accepted by God.

In Christ we have peace, which passes all understanding. In Christ we have fellowship with him and the Father. In Christ we have all the promises of God. All that the believer is and has is in Christ. As our holy and just God looks upon his Son and is well pleased, so he views Christ's people in him, and is well pleased. He smiles upon us. This truth—that we are in Christ—is the cure for all our ills in this life, and affords us the hope of glory in eternity. Whether it be the babe in Christ or the aged dying saint, to be in Christ is his great confidence and rest.

Lord, thou hast been our dwelling place in all generations (Ps 90:1).

THE SAME JESUS – JESUS THE SAME

Acts 2:36, Hebrews 13:8

These passages of Scripture speak of ONE that is separate and exclusive in his own right. The virtue, character and quality of this ONE can never be credited to another being. All creation is ultimately for HIS honor and glory. *Thou art worthy, O Lord, to receive glory and honour and power: for thou hast created all things, and for thy pleasure they are and were created* (Rv 4:11). All of holy writ's wondrous story and detail penned by Divinity, declares HIS majesty and excellence above all others. No matter when or where, in time or eternity, this ONE IS THE SAME JESUS—JESUS THE SAME. The Lord Jesus Christ is exactly that which his name declares him to be—Lord and Christ! He is immutably Lord, and there is no other Lord. He is the Father's anointed Lord and Savior. He is Lord and Savior yesterday, today and forever!

This same Jesus created all things, sovereignly rules over all things, changes what he is pleased to change, saves whom he is pleased to save, and destroys what he is pleased to destroy. All this in perfect holiness and righteousness. Yet HE NEVER CHANGES! *For I am the LORD, I CHANGE NOT; therefore ye sons of Jacob are not consumed* (Mi 3:6).

It is virtually impossible for creatures of dust to fathom the immutability of another, but this we must remember; he is not a creature. He IS THE CREATOR! By God's grace, we must view him as he is. THE SAME JESUS—JESUS THE SAME. Some day, those who know him by faith will *see him as he is* (1 Jn 3:2). *For the Lamb which is in the midst of the throne shall feed them, and shall lead them unto living fountains of waters: and God shall wipe away all tears from their eyes* (Rv 7:17). Until then the message of the Gospel is the SAME; *For we preach not ourselves, but CHRIST JESUS THE LORD; and ourselves your servants for Jesus' sake* (2 Cor 4:5).

With all of life's transitions, the children of God have an Anchor of the soul, both sure and steadfast, eternal in the heavens: THE SAME JESUS—JESUS THE SAME.

BELIEVING IN THE HEART

And as they went on their way, they came unto a certain water: and the eunuch said, See, here is water; what doth hinder me to be baptized? And Philip said, If thou BELIEVEST *with all thine heart, thou mayest. And he answered and said, I* BELIEVE *that Jesus Christ is the Son of God.*

Acts 8:36

The BELIEVING to which this passage refers is not a casual agreement with doctrinal truth. This conversation was much more than intelligent dialogue between two men. This was not a preacher persuading a sinner to make a decision for, or a commitment to Jesus. This is God Almighty saving a sinner by his sovereign irresistible grace, through the preaching of the Gospel of the Lord Jesus Christ. The BELIEVING is the FAITH that God gives in regeneration. This is a work of grace that God does in the heart, not just in the head! The message was JESUS CHRIST from Isaiah 53—not points of doctrine. What the eunuch believed was, *I* BELIEVE *that Jesus Christ is the Son of God.*

In the preaching of Christ, the wondrous doctrines of God's free grace are sovereignly unfolded and revealed by his Spirit to dead sinners. Believing on Christ is much more than an accumulation of doctrinal truth. Believing in the heart is KNOWING CHRIST, BOWING TO CHRIST, LOVING CHRIST, COMING TO CHRIST, AND WORSHIPPING CHRIST IN SPIRIT AND TRUTH. What he has done is glorious, but who he is, is more glorious. Who he is gives virtue to what he has done, and what he is doing.

Nowhere in the Scriptures are we commanded to believe on what he has done, it is always to BELIEVE ON THE SON OF GOD.

I am saying this: Believing on the Lord Jesus Christ is believing in a person with a new heart that God GIVES, a heart of faith. It is not just giving mental accent to some facts concerning this person. Believing with the heart only comes with the impartation of spiritual life, and this life is the indwelling of Christ by his Spirit—*He that hath the Son hath life; and he that hath not the Son of God hath not life* (1 Jn 5:12).

There is certainly no knowing Christ, or believing on him apart from doctrinal truth. Yet you can be certain, no one will ever know and believe TRUTH apart from knowing and believing on Christ. *Jesus saith unto him, I am the way, THE TRUTH, and the life: no man cometh unto the Father, but by me* (Jn 14:6). This TRUTH is always concerning HIM! May God help us who preach, to PREACH CHRIST and HIM CRUCIFIED! *For I determined not to know any thing among you, save Jesus Christ, and him crucified* (1 Cor 2:2).

BELIEVERS' BAPTISM

And now why tarriest thou? arise, and be baptized, and wash away thy sins, calling on the name of the Lord.

Acts 22:16

Baptism is not necessary to salvation. In other words, baptism does not secure or seal our union with Christ, or guarantee any special blessings to the believer. However, baptism is necessary to the child of God because it is taught in the Scriptures (Rom 6:1-11). Baptism, the burial of our bodies in water by immersion, is the believer's public confession of faith in Christ. It is the answer of a good conscience toward God, and a picture of salvation by our substitute (Acts 22:16; I Pet 3:21). It is publicly declaring our allegiance and commitment to Christ and his church.

Many of those professing salvation, hang their hopes of heaven upon church membership, baptism, and partaking of the Lord's supper. On the other hand, many who profess to know Christ refuse to submit to any of these, or they feel free to pick and choose which ones. Neither circumstance reflects the attitude of a believing heart. Baptism, the Lord's Supper, and uniting with a local assembly of believers identifies us with Christ and his Gospel; the greatest honor and privilege with which a child of God could be blessed on this earth.

AND BE CONTENT

Let your conversation be without covetousness; and be content with such things as ye have: for he hath said, I will never leave thee, nor forsake thee.
Hebrews 13:5

Contentment with God's providence is peculiar only to the child of God. The things we have, God has given us. The things we do not have, he has withheld. This truth he teaches us by experience *for I HAVE LEARNED, in whatsoever state I am, therewith to be content* (Phil 4:11).

By his grace we will learn he will never leave us or forsake us. He sends trials, afflictions, peace, contentment, good times, and bad times that we might trust him, and look to him for all things spiritual and temporal. It honors our Lord when we can say in our heart, and to the world, *The Lord is my helper, and I will not fear what man shall do unto me.* It dishonors him when we murmur and complain as if God were doing us an injustice. Happy is the man that is content. *Godliness with contentment is great gain. For we brought nothing into this world, and it is certain we can carry nothing out. And having food and raiment let us be therewith content* (1 Tm 6:6-8).

When he causes me to consider all of my spiritual blessings in Christ, and all he has provided in this world through Christ, I am humbled and shamed that I ever complained about anything. May God help us enjoy the blessings from our Lord's hand, and live our remaining days with contentment and peace in our hearts.

In every thing give thanks: for this is the will of God in Christ Jesus concerning you (1 Thes 5:18).

THE GOSPEL IN PERSON – THE DOCTRINE OF GOD

Paul, a servant of Jesus Christ, called to be an apostle, separated unto the gospel of God, (Which he had promised afore by his prophets in the holy scriptures,) Concerning his Son Jesus Christ our Lord.

Romans 1:1-3

B efore the coming of our Lord Jesus Christ in the flesh, the Gospel of God was in promise by oath, or covenant. Christ was, and remains the surety and substance of that promise—*Who hath saved us, and called us with an holy calling, not according to our works, but according to his own purpose and grace, which was given us in Christ Jesus before the world began* (2 Tm 1:9).

HE IS THE PROMISE OF THE GOSPEL. The Gospel and Christ are synonymous. He is the mystery of the Gospel revealed to his people. *We speak the wisdom of God in a mystery, even the hidden wisdom, which God ordained before the world unto our glory* (1 Cor 2:7). The preaching of the Gospel is the declaration of Christ, who has come into the world and effectually put away the sin of his people by the sacrifice of himself.

THE LORD JESUS CHRIST IS THE GOOD NEWS. Make no mistake, if the message that we preach is not saturated and permeated with the person of Christ, we have not preached THE GOSPEL. He is our doctrine! The Lord Jesus Christ is not revealed in the doctrine of God, the doctrine of God is revealed in HIM! If we preach the Lord Jesus Christ, as he is revealed in the Scriptures, our doctrine will be correct.

Confused? Let me simplify it. *We preach Christ crucified, unto the Jews a stumbling block, and unto the Greeks foolishness; But unto them which are called, both Jews and Greeks, Christ the power of God, and the wisdom of God* (1 Cor 1:23-24).

The Gospel concerns the Lord Jesus Christ, all he is, all he has done, and all he is doing. He has preeminence in all things. It is vital to be doctrinally correct. However, there is no correct doctrine apart from Christ our Lord. Whether one labels me a Calvinist or not, is of no concern to me. I pray that it may be said of all who hear me, he *determined not to know any thing among you, save Jesus Christ, and him crucified* (1 Cor 2:2).

THE CONCERN OF GOD

Paul, a servant of Jesus Christ, called to be an apostle, separated unto the gospel of God, concerning his Son Jesus Christ our Lord, which was made of the seed of David according to the flesh.

Romans 1:1&3

T he particular subject with which the Gospel of God is concerned is our Lord Jesus Christ, and redemption in Him. The GOOD NEWS is to chosen sinners, but it is not about them, it is about Him. All false religions make the concern of their message about themselves, not about Him. Identifying the substance of a message, will reveal it to be either true of false. The glory of the Gospel of God is the person and work of Jesus Christ, who is God manifest in the flesh. Every messenger that God almighty calls and sends, preaches THE GOSPEL OF GOD, CONCERNING HIS SON JESUS CHRIST OUR LORD.

Every true professor of faith in Christ will acknowledge Christ Jesus the Lord and his work, rather than themselves and their own work. The Gospel preacher's life is concerned with and consists of the Gospel of the Lord Jesus Christ. The life of those to whom Christ has effectually revealed himself in divine regeneration by his omnipotent Spirit, and the preaching of the Gospel, is concerned with and consists of the Gospel of the Lord Jesus Christ. This message of the Gospel, Jesus Christ, is the concern of every God called preacher as well as every saved sinner.

If this is not the case, there is no scriptural foundation to identify anyone as Gospel preachers or Christians. Likewise should this not be the case, any ministry and any profession is but a sham, a fake, and an imposter. As Christ embraces those whom he loves in the Gospel, so those who love him embrace him and his Gospel. They are his concern and he is their concern. *We love Him, because he first loved us* (1 Jn 4:19). That which we love will prove to be our greatest concern!

THE MEANS OF SALVATION

For I am not ashamed of the gospel of Christ: for IT IS THE POWER OF GOD UNTO SALVATION to every one that believeth; to the Jew first, and also to the Greek.
Romans 1:16

The Gospel of the Lord Jesus Christ, in the sovereign hand of God the Holy Spirit, is most powerful and the ONLY means of salvation for sinful man. Man with his religious inventions and gimmicks, in trying to entice sinners to become Christians, is useless and a mockery to the triune God. Nothing can improve or replace what God has ordained. Even when Christ is preached in truth, and only then, God must make his Word effectual to the heart, giving faith, life and understanding. The Gospel of Christ is not just part of a larger plan that God uses to save his people. It is the sum and substance of all that is revealed of God's salvation in Christ.

For I am not ashamed of the gospel of Christ: for IT IS THE POWER OF GOD UNTO SALVATION to every one that believeth; to the Jew first, and also to the Greek (Rom 1:16). *For the preaching of the cross is to them that perish foolishness; but unto us which are saved IT IS THE POWER OF GOD* (1 Cor 1:18).

There has never been, nor ever will be one sinner saved apart from the preaching of Christ and him crucified, because the GOSPEL OF CHRIST *is the power of God unto salvation.*

THE POWER OF THE GOSPEL

For I am not ashamed of the gospel of Christ: for IT IS THE POWER OF GOD unto salvation to every one that believeth; to the Jew first, and also to the Greek.
Romans 1:16

T he Gospel of the Lord Jesus Christ is not just a system of theology set for man to believe or not believe. It is not just points of doctrine for man to accept or reject—changing, adding and subtracting to fit his agenda. The Gospel concerns Christ, the Son of God, and his redemptive work in the salvation of the elect of God. The Gospel is the revelation of the Lord Jesus Christ and what he accomplished to the glory of God the Father, and the eternal good of his people.

The Gospel is powerful to save—God has made it so. There are many systems of religion that embrace what they call the Gospel; but there is only one Gospel that clearly sets forth the God-Man and what he has done. Anything else is *another gospel, which is not another,* and is cursed of God (Gal 1). The Gospel of the Lord Jesus Christ is made effectual by the power of God's Spirit, giving spiritual life to dead, chosen, sinners. Nothing else will work. Our text insists that there is no salvation apart from Christ and him crucified.

This message is always POWERFUL to accomplish that which God has purposed. The Gospel is POWERFUL because it is *the gospel of Christ.* The Gospel and Christ are synonymous.

The Gospel is POWERFUL because it is the Word of God! Christ is the living Word of God! *In the beginning was the Word, and the Word was with God, and the Word was God* (Jn 1:1).

The Gospel is POWERFUL to give life—*Being born again, not of corruptible seed, but of incorruptible, by the word of God, which liveth and abideth for ever* (1 Pt 1:23).

The Gospel is POWERFUL to give faith in Christ—*So then faith cometh by hearing, and hearing by the word of God* (Rom 10:17).

The Gospel is POWERFUL to provide that necessary Food for the soul, without which we would die—*And Jesus answered him, saying, It is written, That man shall not live by bread alone, but by every word of God* (Lk 4:4). The Lord Jesus is *that Bread of life* and it is he that is POWERFUL to save, to keep, and to provide.

We preach *the mystery which hath been hid from ages and from generations, but now is made manifest to his saints: To whom GOD WOULD MAKE KNOWN what is the riches of the glory of this mystery among the Gentiles; which is Christ in you, the hope of glory*—(Col 1:26-28).

RIGHTEOUSNESS REVEALED

I am not ashamed of the gospel of Christ . . . for therein is the
righteousness of God revealed.
Romans 1:16-17

The Gospel of the Lord Jesus Christ reveals the righteousness
of God in the justifying work of Christ, which he wrought
for the elect and credited to their account before God. It is
imputed to them and imparted in them, by the regenerating work
of his omnipotent Spirit. The Gospel exalts the righteousness of
Christ and condemns man's self-righteousness. Paul says, *I am*
not ashamed of the gospel of Christ, for therein is the
righteousness of God revealed. God Almighty is just and
righteous in accepting sinners clothed in the righteousness of
their appointed substitute.

The righteousness of God is not revealed by the light of
nature or by the works of man. Only the GOOD NEWS of the
Gospel of Christ reveals and declares this wondrous work and
transaction. Man has nothing to accomplish or perform; therefore,
we glory in Christ and him alone, and we are not ashamed *To*
declare, I say, at this time his righteousness: that he might be
just, and the justifier of him which believeth in Jesus (Rom 3:26).
The answer to the unanswerable question is in the Gospel of
Christ. *How should man be just with God?* (Jb 9:2).

His Spirit reveals to us, and in us, the glory of his
righteousness through the preaching of the Gospel, and will one
day be revealed openly and universally for all to behold and
wonder. *In those days shall Judah be saved, and Jerusalem shall*

dwell safely: and this is the name wherewith she shall be called, The LORD our righteousness (Jer 33:16). This is what the Gospel is all about—*He shall see of the travail of his soul, and shall be satisfied: by his knowledge shall my righteous servant justify many; for he shall bear their iniquities* (Is 53:11). We may rightfully be ashamed of any other so-called Gospel. Any messenger with any other message is accursed of God. *As we said before, so say I now again, If any man preach any other gospel unto you than that ye have received, let him be accursed* (Gal 1:9).

LIVING FAITH

For therein (the Gospel) *is the righteousness of God revealed from faith to faith: as it is written, The just shall live by faith.*
Romans 1:17

There is no way the importance of the Gospel and the preaching of it can be emphasized enough. Everything concerning the glory of God in the redemption of chosen sinners, by the person and work of Christ our Lord, is revealed therein. The faith of God's elect comes to us by his omnipotent Spirit in God's appointed means of preaching the Word. He imparts spiritual life and thereby gives them living faith in Christ. Those whom he has justified now live by faith in Christ Jesus, not trusting in their own works of righteousness, but rather in him. The Gospel is the life of the child of God, because it is the revelation of Christ and his righteousness, the means of faith. *So then faith cometh by hearing, and hearing by the word of God* (Rom 10:17).

The center of the believer's life in this world is comprised of, taken up with, involved with, and committed to Christ and his

Gospel. *I am crucified with Christ: nevertheless I live; yet not I, but Christ liveth in me: and the life which I now live in the flesh I live by the faith of the Son of God, who loved me, and gave himself for me* (Gal 2:20). The Gospel is the heartbeat and pulse of the believer's life. There is no life where there is no Christ. There is no Christ where there is no Gospel. He *that hath the Son hath life; and he that hath not the Son of God hath not life* (1 Jn 5:12).

A nominal professor of Christianity has no love for, no heart for, no commitment to the Gospel, and therefore no faith or life in Christ. *Then Jesus said unto them, Verily, verily, I say unto you, Except ye eat the flesh of the Son of man, and drink his blood, ye have no life in you* (Jn 6:53). We live upon Christ by faith as he is revealed in the Gospel. One can no more live spiritually without the Gospel than he can live physically without natural food. *The just SHALL live by faith.*

GOD GAVE THEM UP

When they knew God, they glorified him not as God, neither were thankful; but became vain in their imaginations, and their foolish heart was darkened.
Romans 1:21

The context of this passage seems to deal primarily with the reprobation of those who give themselves up to homosexuality. However, the warrant of Almighty God is against all those who having the light of God's creation, and the light of the Gospel, refused to reverence him in the knowledge he revealed to them. Therefore, he left them to themselves to do things which are not convenient, and without conscience. God gave them up to believe a lie, never to experience even the consideration of light again. *Their foolish heart was darkened.* Those whom God gives up are, and will forever be, deaf and blind to the living truth and life of the Gospel. They are untouched and unaffected by the preaching of the Gospel of Christ. They will never have a heart for the things of God and will continue to do as their foolish heart pleases to their own damnation.

It makes no difference what God says, they esteem themselves to be wiser than Him. They are unthankful and it is manifest by their irreverence, disrespect, disregard and rude attitude toward Him, his Word, and his church. Their refuge of lies will continually be reinforced. Their evil heart of unbelief will become more and more hardened and set in their own ways, which are *the ways of death. There is a way which seemeth right unto a man, but the end thereof are the ways of death* (Prv 14:12). This Biblical commentary of reprobation will never touch the heart of those whom God has given up. However, those to whom God has given *the light of the knowledge of the glory of God in the face of Jesus Christ* will flee to *the throne of grace, that we may obtain mercy, and find grace to help in time of need.* Those whom God has given up will one day soon hear him say, *I never knew you: depart from me, ye that work iniquity.*

THE JUDGMENT OF GOD IS ACCORDING TO TRUTH

But we are sure that the judgment of God is according to truth against them which commit such things.
Romans 2:2

The conclusion of all matters, concerning both the righteousness and unrighteousness of all men, and all the deeds preformed by them, is according to divine truth. The rendering of punishment or acquittal is according to divine justice. With the judicial system established among man is something called BEYOND REASONABLE DOUBT. This suggests there is a possibility of error in judgment. Therefore, we cannot compare the judgment of man with the judgment of Almighty God, which is according to infinite truth. With him there is NO DOUBT! Furthermore, the judgment of God perceives the motive of the heart. Man looks on the outward appearance, God looks on the heart. The verdict is forever settled in Heaven. *Now we know that what things soever the law saith, it saith to them who are under the law: that every mouth may be stopped, and all the world may become guilty before God* (Rom 3:1).

But with God there is justification for guilty sinners whereby God judges them in truth, perfectly innocent! This does not fit into man's religious thoughts of justice and judgment, and can in no wise be incorporated into the moral judgment of fallible man. The judgment according to God is a contradiction to the judgment according to man, in that the Lord Jesus Christ is his people's substitute. *For he hath made him to be sin for us, who knew no sin; that we might be made the righteousness of God in him* (2 Cor 5:21). Sinful man is judged and condemned by God according to truth. Those for whom Christ lived and died are judged by the Almighty God to be sinless, and therefore accepted by him in his Beloved—*To the praise of the glory of his grace, wherein he hath made us accepted in the Beloved* (Eph 1:6).

Those for whom Christ died, though guilty of every sin and transgression, have no guilt. Those who are judged by themselves and others to be innocent and righteous, are in truth judged guilty by God, and condemned to everlasting damnation. Christ makes the difference!

JUDGED BY CHRIST

In the day when God shall judge the secrets of men by Jesus Christ according to my gospel.
Romans 2:16

The Lord Jesus Christ did not replace the law of God in its demand for righteousness. He fulfilled the law, satisfying those demands of divine justice, for everyone whom God the Father predestinated to be conformed to the image of his Son. He provided them a righteousness fit for eternal glory. Hence, the righteousness of Christ is imputed, and in regeneration imparted, to all who believe.

God judges men's hearts as to faith in Christ and his righteousness. Jew or Gentile, no matter who we are, what we have done, or not done, if we do not have God given faith in Christ and continue to trust in our own righteousness, we shall perish without Christ. The Lord Jesus Christ is the righteous standard by which all men are and shall be judged.

The Gospel does not set forth the law of God for justification, but rather the Christ of God for righteousness and justification. The law can only condemn, because we all come short of the glory of God. Christ our Lord glorified the Father rendering perfect obedience in his flesh. The elect of God is not only judged by Christ's righteousness, we are judged IN Christ because he is THE LORD OUR RIGHTEOUSNESS! *And be found in Him, not having mine own righteousness, which is of the law, but that which is through the faith of Christ, the righteousness which is of God by faith* (Phil 3:9).

The believer's justification is traceable not only to faith, and not only to the cross, but even to the eternal council, decree, and purpose of God's predestinating grace, which is revealed in Christ and his accomplished redemptive work. The secrets of the heart are who we really are and why we do what we do.

True heart-faith in Christ or not, will be revealed.

A BREAKER OF THE LAW

For circumcision verily profiteth, if thou keep the law: but if thou be a breaker of the law, thy circumcision is made uncircumcision.
Romans 2:25

There is only one who kept the law of God, and that is Jesus Christ the Lord. All others who claim to do so are liars—*yea, let God be true, but every man a liar* (Rom 3:4). There is no merit or profit in man's claims of who he is, or professions of what he has done to justify himself before God. As a matter of fact, Almighty God has pronounced judgment upon those who say they are righteous and are not—*Behold, I will make them of the synagogue of Satan, which say they are Jews, and are not, but do lie; behold, I will make them to come and worship before thy feet, and to know that I have loved thee* (Rv 3:9). The Apostle Paul, by the inspiration of God, makes it crystal clear that we all, both Jew and Gentile, are lawbreakers. Even if we could obey the law outwardly, what about inwardly?

What about the motions of the evil heart and carnal mind? That is where God looks. That is where God demands perfection. If we could obey only one outward demand of God, would it be done in perfect love, by faith, and all for the glory of God and his blessed Son? Can we do this by the mere exercise of the will of the flesh? Or does God accept it because we are of a certain sect or believe a certain doctrine? There is only ONE HOPE for us lawbreakers, whom God has made to know our guilt. That hope is the ONE who kept the law for us, both inwardly and outwardly. *Herein is love, not that we loved God, but that he loved us, and sent his Son to be the propitiation for our sins* (1 Jn 4:10). Not only does a believer know and own his guilt, he knows and owns the Lord Jesus Christ as his justification before God.

For he hath made him [to be] sin for us, who knew no sin; that we might be made the righteousness of God in him (2 Cor 5:21).

A JEW INWARDLY

But he is a Jew, which is one inwardly; and circumcision is that of the heart, in the spirit, and not in the letter; whose praise is not of men, but of God.

Romans 2:29

The spiritual lineage of the children of God is traceable only to the Lion of the tribe of Judah—the Lord Jesus Christ—God The Son. The triune love of the eternal Godhead begat the infinite desire of divine purpose. God alone is to be praised for the supernatural indwelling of the mystical person of Christ in Spirit. Circumcision of the heart, the identifying and distinguishing mark of a child of God, is *the riches of the glory of this mystery among the Gentiles; which is Christ in you, the hope of glory* (Col 1:27). *Christ in you* separates the children of God from all other people and creatures.

The difference lies in heart and in Spirit, *A new heart also will I give you, and a new spirit will I put within you* (Ez 36:26). The Jews boasted in the law (outwardly); the Gentiles boasted without the law (outwardly). However God's Word declares, *circumcision verily profiteth, if thou keep the law: but if thou be a breaker of the law, thy circumcision is made uncircumcision* (Rom 2:25). The new heart and Spirit imparted to the children of God operates by love, produces an inward desire, spiritual obedience, faith, love, and devotion to Christ, and excludes boasting. This is not a servile obedience to the letter of the law which genders boasting. *For by grace are ye saved through faith;*

and that not of yourselves: it is the gift of God: Not of works, lest any man should boast (Eph 2:8).

Although one may make a fair show in the flesh, if he has not the Spirit of Christ and a heart for Christ, he cannot be truthfully called a child of God—*though I bestow all my goods to feed the poor, and though I give my body to be burned, and have not charity* (love for Christ), *it profiteth me nothing* (1 Cor 13:3). *It is the spirit that quickeneth; the flesh profiteth nothing: the words that I speak unto you, they are spirit, and they are life* (Jn 6:63).

NO FEAR OF GOD

There is no fear of God before their eyes.
Romans 3:18

The apostle, by the inspiration of God the Spirit, sumarily characterizes depraved mankind with this conclusion; THEY HAVE NO REVERENCE OR CONSIDERATION OF GOD. All of the foregoing charges brought against both Jew and Gentile in the previous verses, culminate in their irreverent hearts of self-justifying, self-righteous unbelief. There could be no better description of OUR religious generation found in all of the Scriptures: *There is no fear of God before their eyes.* The mass of SO-CALLED Christianity brazenly set up their self-gods without conscience or shame, and pridefully bow in adoration and worship of their own image. There is nothing more disrespectful to God and his Christ than the suggestion that man's will is sovereign over the will and purpose of God.

This is an affront to the very being and nature of Divinity. Those who do so in message, method, and profession indeed have *no fear of God before their eyes.* To ignore the person and justifying work of Jesus Christ, and to assert man's GOODNESS AND ABILITY, clearly reveals the epitome of irreverence. There is an unparalleled, universal, disrespect of God in our day, in every religious setting—both Arminian and Calvinistic. To enthrone our knowledge of a doctrine rather than the Christ of the doctrine is to take the things of God and say, "Look at me, see what knowledge I have acquired! Thereby, I am justified!" This too reveals an unconscionable reverence of self and an unmistakable irreverence of God. Those who fear God bow to Him, his Son, and his Gospel, as they find themselves condemned in themselves. We say as Thomas when he saw his risen Saviour, *my Lord and my God* (Jn 20:28).

RIGHTEOUSNESS REVEALED

But now the righteousness of God without the law is manifested, being witnessed by the law and the prophets.
Romans 3:21

The Word of God distinctly reveals the righteousness of God from Genesis through Malachi (then, being witnessed by the law and the prophets) and from Matthew through Revelation (now, without the law, or since the law). The righteousness which the law and prophets spoke of, is the same righteousness which is now manifested in the person and appearing of Messiah. The proclamation of the Gospel is *THE LORD OUR RIGHTEOUSNESS* (Jer 23:6). This is the GOOD NEWS manifested to God's children in every generation.

God the Son upheld and fulfilled every demand of divine justice to infinite satisfaction for his elect. God the Spirit, in revealing God's righteousness to them in regeneration, sets before them a person rather than just a mere judicial transaction as THE OBJECT of faith—*Even the righteousness of God which is by faith of Jesus Christ unto all and upon all them that believe* (Rom 3:22). True God-given faith is not in the *work* of Jesus Christ, but in JESUS CHRIST who did the work. This distinction can only be comprehended experimentally (based on substance and evidence) (Heb 11:1) in the experience of saving grace.

The believer views the righteousness of God with a single eye upon Christ Jesus The Lord because he is the how, where, and whom the fullness of all righteousness is wrought, embodied and revealed.

"He is all my righteousness,
I stand complete in him and worship Him,
He is all my righteousness,
I stand complete in him and worship Him."

"He is all my righteousness,
I stand complete in Him
And worship Christ the Lord,
Worship Him, Christ the Lord."

ABRAHAM BELIEVED GOD

For what saith the scripture? Abraham believed God, and it was counted unto him for righteousness.
Romans 4:3

Abraham, without tangible, physical evidence believed the WORD OF GOD. God Almighty promised him that which was conceivably impossible according to the reasoning of the natural, carnal intellect and overruled even the ordained laws of natural order. We must be careful not to glorify Abraham in this unnatural performance of believing the unbelievable. In the divine order of all things purpose foregoes proof and evidence. In God's promise is the infinite, *I will.* Abraham believed God because God said, *I will.* Faith in God comes from God—*So then faith cometh by hearing, and hearing by the Word of God* (Rom 10:17).

Omnipotent ordination initiates faith in those who are VOID of it. *When the Gentiles heard this, they were glad, and glorified the Word of the Lord: and as many as were ORDAINED to eternal life believed* (Acts 13:48). The idolatrous Abraham believing God at his Word was a miracle of sovereign grace. Does the Scriptures commend Abraham for the grace of faith? As Paul would say, *God forbid!* Neither do we. If we would, then we must commend him for his righteousness as well. What we have here, I believe, is faith and righteousness imparted and imputed.

The substance of God's promise to Abraham and his seed (those who would believe as he did) is the singular object of faith—JESUS CHRIST. All the promises of God to his children are bound up in the incarnate Lord Jesus Christ, and are certain—*For all the promises of God in him are yea, and in him Amen, unto the glory of God by us* (2 Cor 1:20). Our Lord said, *Your father Abraham rejoiced to see my day: and he saw it, and was glad* (Jn 8:56). In unison with Abraham, every believer confesses—*whom having not seen, we love; in whom, though now we see him not, YET BELIEVING, we rejoice with joy unspeakable and full of glory.*

THE SURE PROMISE

Therefore it is of faith, that it might be by grace; to the end the promise might be sure to all the seed; not to that only which is of the law, but to that also which is of the faith of Abraham.
Romans 4:16

The Promise of Almighty God to his elect church is essentially the Lord Jesus Christ. In him alone is justification and righteousness before God. By the grace of God through the gift of faith our justifying righteousness (Christ) is imputed, imparted and revealed to us in regeneration—*To whom God would make known what is the riches of the glory of this mystery among the Gentiles; which is CHRIST IN YOU, the hope of glory* (Col 1:27). The Lord Jesus Christ is the substance, surety, and promise of God's everlasting covenant of grace to his children. *Fear not, Abram: I AM thy shield, and thy exceeding great reward* (Gn 15:1).

All the promises of God are immutable in the eternal Son, *For all the promises of God IN HIM are yea, and IN HIM Amen, unto the glory of God by us* (2 Cor 1:20). Good works, bad works, or no works, does nothing to accomplish the sinner's justification before God. *No man is justified by the law in the sight of God, it is evident* (Gal 3:11). We are *justified freely by his grace through the redemption that is IN CHRIST JESUS* (Rom 3:24).

God-given faith is not in faith, justification, righteousness, or the law. The evidence of justification is made sure to us by the substance of faith, *the substance of things hoped for, the evidence of things not seen* (Heb 11:1). True faith is in Christ alone, *whom God hath set forth to be a propitiation through faith in his blood, to declare his righteousness for the remission of sins that are past, through the forbearance of God; To declare, I say, at this time his righteousness: that he might be just, and the justifier of him which believeth in Jesus* (Rom 3:25).

.

DELIVERED AND RAISED

Who was delivered for our offences, and was raised again for our justification.
Romans 4:25

The accomplishment of Jesus Christ in his body of flesh while upon this earth left not one requirement of divine justice unfulfilled. For all whom he loved and represented, the triune God is infinitely and sublimely satisfied in his only begotten Son. The very essence of SATISFACTION is satisfied! The perfection of his work is the glorious excellence of his person. Only with eyes of faith can we look upon the illustrious one *who was delivered for our offences, and was raised again for our justification.*

There is nothing left to time and chance, or to the will and work of man. He was DELIVERED FOR MY OFFENCES—Therefore I am delivered! He was RAISED FOR MY JUSTIFICATION—Therefore, I am justified! Please don't confuse me with worldly wisdom and weary me with many words of wit and carnal reasoning. Tell me of my Redeemer who loved me and gave himself for me! His justifying work is saturated with infinite love which will not be denied. Grace and mercy eternally flow from his high and glorious throne unto those whom he bids to drink.

The very heart of the one who lived, suffered, and died for my sin, now throbs in loving anticipation of my presence with Him, and not for me only, but for all those whom he justified. The love of God the Father manifested in God the Son in all his wondrous work guarantees safe passage for his elect through this mortal life and into his presence forevermore. *As for me, I will behold thy face in righteousness: I shall be satisfied, when I awake, with thy likeness* (Ps 17:15).

PEACE ESTABLISHED – PEACE ENJOYED

Therefore being justified by faith, we have peace with God through our Lord Jesus Christ.
Romans 5:1

All that God has purposed for his elect children shall be enjoyed by them. All blessings received by his people comes through and by the justifying peace made by the blood of our Lord. *We have peace with God through our Lord Jesus Christ* is an old truth, as ancient as God himself, *the Lamb slain from the foundation of the world* (Rv 13:8). At God's appointed time, God's anointed Lamb came to the appointed hour and place to willingly pour out his vicarious blood; thereby, finishing the work of reconciliation, justification, atonement, redemption, sanctification, glorification—i.e., salvation for his sheep. God demanded; Christ satisfied; peace was made. We had nothing to do with it. JEHOVAH-JIREH DID IT ALL!

God the Father was pleased to deliver him up. God the Son was pleased to be delivered. God Almighty in the Trinity of his sacred person is, and always has been, satisfied with the eternal work of the eternal Son executed in time. God was never our enemy. We were HIS enemy. Christ in his efficacious work made us friends with God. You see, *when we were enemies, we were reconciled to God by the death of his Son, much more, being reconciled, we shall be saved by his life* (Rom 5:10). Now there is peace.

However, being dead in sin by nature, we knew nothing of this great and wonderful peace in Christ. Again, in his time, yea, in our time, God sent his Word, his Spirit, revealing Christ and giving life. *And because ye are sons, God hath sent forth the Spirit of his Son into your hearts, crying, Abba, Father* (Gal 4:6). Now, By faith in Christ, we can with understanding say, *we have peace with God through our Lord Jesus Christ, by whom also we have access by faith into this grace wherein we stand, and rejoice in hope of the glory of God* (Rom 5:2).

PEACEFUL TRIBULATIONS

We glory in (find peace in) *tribulations also.*
Romans 5:3

It is only by the grace of God wherein we stand with faith in Christ that we have a good measure of peace in the tribulations of life afforded to us by his good providence. *These things I have spoken unto you, that in me ye might have peace. In the world ye shall have tribulation: but be of good cheer; I have overcome the world* (Jn 16:33). No matter what the believer's situation in life, we can always be confident knowing *tribulation worketh patience; And patience, experience; and experience, hope: And hope maketh not ashamed; because the love of God is shed abroad in our hearts by the Holy Ghost which is given unto us.*

Our Lord overcame the world of adversity for his sheep so that we may have peace and consolation within our hearts through the experience of his omnipotent care for us. There is no difference in his permissive will and his perfect will. What he permits he has perfectly purposed; therefore, magnifying and vindicating his purposeful promise. *All things work together for good to them that love God, to them who are the called according to his purpose* (Rom 8:28).

What shall we say then of our trials, troubles, tribulations, adversities, distresses, our own sin, faults, and failures, as we acknowledge our own wretchedness? May we have peace as well as remorse! *What shall we then say to these things? If God be for us, who can be against us?* (Rom 8:31). Tribulations are of great benefit to those whom the *love of God is shed abroad in their*

211

hearts by the Holy Ghost because we know that *when we were yet without strength, in due time Christ died for the ungodly*. The greater our tribulations the more we experience *the peace of God, which passeth all understanding,* (which) *shall keep your* (our) *hearts and minds through Christ Jesus* (Phil 4:7).

We charge ourselves with sin and worthy of tribulations. We find him guilty in overcoming our sin with the peace he made for us to experience, BY THE BLOOD OF HIS CROSS! Not that we CONTINUE IN SIN, *that grace may abound. God forbid* (Rom 6:1).

FOR WHOM DID CHRIST DIE?

For when we were yet without strength, in due time Christ died for the ungodly.
Romans 5:6

The sufficient and efficient cause and accomplishment of the salvation of God's elect (from election to glorification) is the person and work of the incarnate Son of God, Jesus Christ our Lord. His life, death and resurrection accomplished and secured their salvation to infinite perfection. Those for whom Christ died are identified in this world by virtue of their fallen human nature as spiritually dead, unrighteous, ungodly sinners, without strength, and enemies of God. Christ did not die for PRETTY GOOD FOLKS, GOOD CHRISTIANS, or even RIGHTEOUS PEOPLE—HE DIED FOR SINNERS! *When Jesus heard it, he saith unto them, They that are whole,* think they are good, *have no need of the Physician, but they that are sick* (awakened to their helpless estate): *I came not to call the righteous (*self-righteous)*, but sinners to repentance* (Mk 2:17).

Upon regeneration, those for whom Christ died will always have the same estimation of themselves in light of their carnal nature revealed unto them by the Holy Ghost. *This is a faithful saying, and worthy of all acceptation, that Christ Jesus came into the world to save sinners; of whom I AM CHIEF* (1 Tm 1:15). *When Simon Peter saw it, he fell down at Jesus' knees, saying, Depart from me; for I AM A SINFUL MAN, O Lord* (Lk 5:8). *And the publican, standing afar off, would not lift up so much as his eyes unto heaven, but smote upon his breast, saying, God be merciful to ME A SINNER* (Lk 18:13).

All are sinners before God. But not all know it and confess it. All to whom God in efficacious grace reveals their sinnerhood, he will graciously and efficaciously reveal Christ as their salvation.

"He is all my righteousness,
I stand in him complete
and worship HIM."

THE GIFT BY GRACE

But not as the offence, so also is the free gift. For if through the offence of one many be dead, much more the grace of God, and the gift by grace, which is by one man, Jesus Christ, hath abounded unto many.
Romans 5:15

In preaching the Gospel we often use the term "free grace." One reason for this is to distinguish the difference between God's grace and how WORKS-RELIGION ignorantly defines grace. The difference is simple, GRACE and WORKS. It is by our self-righteous works we are condemned. It is by his free grace we are *justified freely by his grace through the redemption that is in Christ Jesus* (Rom 3:24). The free gift of grace is Jesus Christ and all we have in Him. The offence of disobedience by one man, Adam, brought the sentence of death upon all men.

The obedience of one man—Jesus Christ—in life and death, yields life for the dead. The Lord Jesus Christ and all the spiritual blessings his people have and enjoy in him are absolutely FREE! This *one man, Jesus Christ* lovingly, freely, efficaciously, graciously, perfectly, and eternally, gave himself in all respects and demands required by divine justice to God's satisfaction, securing the salvation of his people without their aid or assistance. The *offence* has it's work—DEATH! The *free gift* has his work—LIFE!

THE MILITANT CONQUEST OF GRACE

That as sin hath reigned unto death, even so might grace reign through righteousness unto eternal life by Jesus Christ our Lord.
Romans 5:21

The power of sin and deception is incomprehensible. The heart of man by virtue of his fallen nature is deceitful and desperately wicked beyond human understanding. God alone knows the depth and darkness of the abyss into which the soul of man plummeted when he sinned against the holiness and justice of God and in which he remains until this day and shall forever remain.

"Dark the stain that soiled man's nature,
long the distance that he fell."

The end of sin is death. It is not annihilation, but rather perpetual death and eternal separation from God. Left untouched by omnipotent grace there is no hope of recovery whatsoever. However, thanks be unto God, there is one (only one) Hope for the hopeless! One cure! One remedy! There is one person and one work that sin is powerless against—The sovereign grace of God in Christ Jesus our Lord. *Where sin abounded, grace did much more abound* (Rom 5:20). The Lord Jesus Christ conquered death by his death for all of his covenant loved ones.

The grace of God like a mighty army conquered every enemy and foe. Every sin and transgression of those he loves was destroyed with precise accuracy and irresistible force. The death of Christ appears to be weakness to some, but the redeemed of the Lord, by faith, views his vicarious death as it really is—the victorious conquest of our Redeemer over sin and death for us. What he did is timeless.

The effect of his death is and shall be a wonder and admired in him and his elect throughout time and eternity. The Lord Jesus Christ is our Mighty Saviour—*Who is This that cometh from Edom, with dyed garments from Bozrah? This that is glorious in his apparel, traveling in the greatness of his strength? I that speak in righteousness, mighty to save* (Is 63:1).

THE LIVING DEAD

*That as sin hath reigned unto death, even so might grace reign
through righteousness unto eternal life by Jesus Christ our Lord.
What shall we say then? Shall we continue in sin, that grace may
abound? God forbid. How shall we, that are dead to sin, live any
longer therein?*

Romans 5:21, 6:2

As sin and death reigns in the unregenerate, grace reigns in
those who live in Christ. Not to minimize the importance of
the believer's conversation in this world which honors Christ and
his Gospel, the text and context of the verses before us speak of
the effectual work of God the Spirit in his persevering, preserving
presence in his people. We do not reign over our sin, it is the
grace of God by the righteousness of Christ in us that reigns over
sin. Although we are very much aware of our sin, we are dead to
sin because we are alive in Christ.

We do not live in sin, we live in Christ—*For ye are dead,
and your life is hid with Christ in God* (Col 3:3). The Holy Spirit
is confirming to us the impossibility of living in Christ and living
in sin at the same time—*How shall we, that are dead to sin, live
any longer therein*? Paul is also answering the sarcastic argument
many make against the grace of God—Shall we sin more that the
grace of God will abound more? He says, *God forbid*! The life of
a child of God is a mystery to the world, and somewhat a mystery
to ourselves, because we still live in this body of death.

The difference is, we simply believe what God says and
we *reckon ourselves to be dead indeed unto sin, but alive unto*

God through Jesus Christ our Lord (Rom 6:11). We reckon that's the way it is because that's the way God says it is. The child of God is alive and dead at the same time. Some day soon we shall lose the dead and there will only remain the life, that eternal life which is in Christ Jesus our Lord. I speak to the dead because it is only the dead that can hear. *Verily, verily, I say unto you, The hour is coming, and now is, when the dead shall hear the voice of the Son of God: and they that hear shall live* (Jn 5:25).

FORGIVENESS OF SIN

Romans 6:10

Forgiveness of sin is not God merely looking the other way and saying, "I understand, you cannot help what you are and what you do, so I will not hold it against you." Sin is an offense against the holy and just God and MUST BE PUNISHED! For sin to be forgiven there must be a sacrifice— a sinless sacrifice. The forgiveness of sin is by a bloody sacrifice. Our sins were not forgiven by the perfect life of Christ, but by the atoning death of God's Lamb. For God to forgive our sin, divine justice must be satisfied. That is what our Lord did for us. *For in that he died, he died unto sin once* (Rom 6: 10).

"I RECKON"

*Likewise reckon ye also yourselves to be dead indeed unto sin,
but alive unto God through Jesus Christ our Lord.*
Romans 6:11

The child of faith has the unnatural privilege and ability to embrace divine truth even when diametrically opposed to human reasoning. The believer in Christ serves up his carnal mind as enmity and in opposition to God. The imparted divine nature is in agreement with God against the old nature. Everything in my being tells me that I am nothing but sin, and sin is all I can do. The Word of God tells me this. My experiences in life tell me this. *For I know that in me (that is, in my flesh,) dwelleth no good thing: for to will is present with me; but [how] to perform that which is good I find not. I find then a law, that, when I would do good, evil is present with me* (Rom 7:18).

However, not voiding the truth of who and what I am in this flesh, I RECKON myself to be dead indeed unto sin and alive unto God through Jesus Christ my Lord! The child of God is dead on two counts. He is dead to the law because *by him all that believe are justified from all things, from which ye could not be justified by the law of Moses* (Acts 13:39), and dead to sin because *once in the end of the world hath he appeared to put away sin by the sacrifice of himself* (Heb 9:26). When I look at myself, even in light of the Scriptures, I would most despair in unbelief. However, as he gives grace to look to Christ, I can reckon myself dead to sin and alive unto God in Christ Jesus my Lord.

218

"Free from the law, O happy condition,
Jesus has bled and there is remission,
Cursed by the law and bruised by the fall,
Christ hath redeemed us once for all."

"ALIVE UNTO GOD"

Likewise reckon ye also yourselves to be dead indeed unto sin,
but alive unto God through Jesus Christ our Lord.
Romans 6:11

True faith ultimately receives the Word of God without question. The faith that God's Spirit gives in regeneration believes the unbelievable and comprehends the incomprehensible. How can we who are so sinful and dead unto God be dead unto sin and alive unto God? By grace through faith we reckon (know) it to be so, because God made it so through Jesus Christ our Lord. The sanctifying work of God the Spirit in regeneration receives the love of the truth, embracing the Son of the living God in all his glorious work.

The spiritual birth of the child of God renders death to the old man of sin daily. That which God freely gives by grace is the spring and substance of life. The one who is alive unto God through Jesus Christ our Lord, has a new heart that throbs with desire and love for Christ, his Gospel, his work, his church, and the growth of his kingdom on this earth.

SHALL WE SIN?

What then? shall we sin, because we are not under the law, but under grace? God forbid.

Romans 6:15

The result of the accomplished work of God the Spirit in the regeneration of a sinner is the impartation of new life, spiritual life, the Spirit of Christ. *But ye are not in the flesh, but in the Spirit, if so be that the Spirit of God dwell in you. Now if any man have not the Spirit of Christ, he is none of his* (Rom 8:9). This new life is a dramatic change from the old man, which remains very much alive and well. The new man lives by new desires, and new motives. Believers may do many of the same things that are within themselves GOOD THINGS. He may even refrain from doing BAD THINGS. But now they come with new motives and new desires springing from a new heart. On the other hand, because we are now under grace, the true child of grace does not conclude that he has the freedom to live after the flesh. He does not have the attitude that SINCE SALVATION is by the sovereign grace of God, "it is of no consequence what I do or don't do, whether I am committed and faithful or not."

This attitude reveals faith in a doctrine rather than a desire and love for Christ. The child of grace desires to live his life before God and man in a way that honors and magnifies the glory of his God, because he loves Him. *For this is the love of God, that we keep his commandments: and his commandments are not grievous* (1 Jn 5:3). We do not excuse ourselves from being committed to Christ, his Gospel and his church because we are under grace. Neither do we commit ourselves to be faithful to justify ourselves before God because we are under the law. Living by grace is simply living out our life in this world believing on Christ, looking to Christ, loving Christ, desiring to be faithful and committed to him for his great name's sake. Without this God-given desire, all is a sham and will be revealed for what it is in our daily life, and in eternal condemnation.

There is therefore now no condemnation to them which are in Christ Jesus, WHO WALK NOT AFTER THE FLESH, BUT AFTER THE SPIRIT (Rom 8:1).

THE GIFT OF GOD

For the wages of sin is death; but the gift of God is eternal life through Jesus Christ our Lord.
Romans 6:23

B lessed contrast! All that God's children receive is from him, and in every respect a gift. All that we receive comes to us through and by the Lord Jesus Christ, and him alone. God has given unto us eternal life and this life is in his Son. He has blessed us with all spiritual blessings in Christ Jesus our Lord. All the works of man are vain and their reward is death. No matter how sincere, no matter now noble, no matter how much praised by others, there will be no work accepted by God, other than that which is perfect in every respect. There will be no flesh glory in his presence. All the GOOD WORKS of man are self-righteous in nature and an abomination to God, if not preformed by faith in Christ and for the glory of God. This is impossible for the creature to do apart from Christ working in us both to will and to do his good pleasure.

The Gift of God to the sinner is Christ! Without him there can only be condemnation and death. *Many will say to me in that day, Lord, Lord, have we not prophesied in thy name? and in thy name have cast out devils? and in thy name done many wonderful works? And then will I profess unto them, I never knew you: depart from me, ye that work iniquity* (Mt 7:22-23). All that we need, all that we have, all that we desire for time and eternity, we have been given in Christ. *Not by works of righteousness which we have done, but according to his mercy he has saved us.* The Lord Jesus Christ is ours, and all that he is and has is ours by virtue of his electing love and sovereign grace.

All else is sin and worthy of death by virtue of man's fallen, self-righteous nature. This is simple and easy to understand, yet cannot be believed and embraced apart from a work of almighty grace in the heart of the sinful creature. The believer rejoices that *of him are we in Christ Jesus, who of God is made unto us wisdom, and righteousness, and sanctification, and redemption* (1 Cor 1:30).

CHRIST DID

For what the law could not do, in that it was weak through the flesh, God sending his own Son in the likeness of sinful flesh, and for sin, condemned sin in the flesh.
Romans 8:3

The law in this context is essentially the perfections and demands of divine justice requiring nothing less than exact conformity and obedience to the demands of it by all sinful men. The law of God could not make that which is less than perfect, perfect. The law could never make that which is unrighteous,

righteous. The law could never make that which is unholy, holy. The law could never make that which is unjust, just. The weakness of the law to do so is not found in the law, but in sinful man.

The law can only condemn and punish sin. Sinful flesh can never render anything more than what it is—sin. Neither can the law make a clean thing out of an unclean thing. Therefore, we must conclude the law is helpless to put away sin and justify the ungodly, and so man is helpless to fulfill and satisfy the law, because he is SIN-FULL. BUT CHRIST DID! Our blessed Redeemer condemned his loved ones' sin to death by his perfect obedience, and justified the ungodly by his vicarious death. Thank God for substitution! Here we see the impossible brought to pass—*The things which are impossible with men are possible with God* (Lk 18:27).

Our Lord Jesus Christ did what neither the law nor man could do. GOD SENDING HIS OWN SON IN THE LIKENESS OF SINFUL FLESH was the ONLY answer to the unanswerable question—*how should man be just with God?* (Jb 9:2). When someone asks me, "Who saved you?"— I can now truthfully say, "Christ did!" When someone asks, "Who obeyed the law of God to infinite satisfaction?"— I can truthfully say, "Only one Man did, Christ!" The Lord Jesus Christ condemned my sin in his flesh by his perfect obedience and bloody death, and I am thereby justified before the law of God. Is this not THE BEST of news for a helpless sinner?

EXAMINE YOURSELVES

But ye are not in the flesh, but in the Spirit, if so be that the Spirit of God dwell in you. Now if any man have not the Spirit of Christ, he is none of His.

Romans 8:9

Those to whom God has revealed his blessed Son have been made keenly aware of their sinful nature. Our sinful nature is exposed by his sinless nature. Our sinful nature is confirmed by the Word of God, and by the indwelling Spirit of God. To deny this is insanity. However, those to whom God by regeneration has imparted the Spirit of Christ has a new nature. It is new as opposed to the old man, or the sinful nature. Christ dwells in them, effecting life where there was none before.

The believer lives with this new life every day in the experience of grace and in the experience of life. In the text and context of the above verse there are two distinct persons. One does not have the Spirit of Christ dwelling in him; the other does. These two men are still men but vastly different. The impartation of spiritual life is our salvation because *if any man have not the Spirit of Christ, he is none of His.* The impartation of spiritual life is *Christ in you, the hope of glory* (Col 1:27). *Christ in you* separates the living from the dead. God imputes the righteousness of Christ to our account, establishing our righteousness, thereby justifying the believer. He imparts the righteous Christ to us and thereby gives life to those whom he justified. We cannot have the one without the other. Those sinful creatures who have the Spirit of Christ gladly confess both their sin and *The Lord our Righteousness.*

Examine yourselves, whether ye be in the faith; prove your own selves. Know ye not your own selves, how that Jesus Christ is in you, except ye be reprobates? (2 Cor 13:5).

REGENERATION AND KNOWLEDGE

But ye are not in the flesh, but in the Spirit, if so be that the Spirit of God dwell in you. Now if any man have not the Spirit of Christ, he is none of his

Romans 8:9

This is a plain and simple declaration of God. Those who have God given faith in Christ for all their salvation, have the Spirit of Christ dwelling in them. Although men may have learned some truth intellectually, it is not possible to have spiritual life, or love and embrace the truth of God, apart from the regenerating work of God the Spirit indwelling the believer upon conversion. This miraculous work of omnipotence is the effectual impartation of the life (Spirit) of Christ to dead sinners, which is—*Christ in you, the hope of glory* (Col 1:27).

Not taking away from the importance, yea, the necessity of sound doctrine, I believe there is far too much emphasis placed and pressed upon poor sinners as to WHAT we know, rather than WHO we know. It is not WHAT we know that is of life giving efficacy, it is vital union with the Son of God, who is our life—*I in them, and thou in me, that they may be made perfect in one; and that the world may know that thou hast sent me, and hast loved them, as thou hast loved me* (Jn 17:23). By God's grace, I am determined to press upon men to come to Christ, to look to him in whom all truth is revealed, received, and embraced by the power of his blessed Spirit. There seems to be great satisfaction by many when men give mental accent to doctrinal truth. However, in the Scriptures and in the experience of grace, there is life, hope, joy, peace, and rest only in knowing Christ by his blessed Holy Spirit, which he has given us.

What I am saying is this: If the Lord Jesus Christ dwells in me by his Spirit, I have eternal life, which is his life. If Christ does not live in me by his Spirit, I am still DEAD in trespasses and sin, and do not know Him, no matter HOW MUCH I know. The most evident effect of *Christ in you* is LOVE! Love for Christ, love for his Gospel, and love for the brethren. *Beloved, let us love one another: for love is of God; and every one that loveth is born of God, and knoweth God. He that loveth not knoweth not God; for God is love* (1 Jn 4:7—8).

PRAYER

We know not what we should pray for as we ought.
Romans 8:26

Prayer is for ourselves, not for God. It is we that need to commune with Him; he needs not us. God only receives that which he gives. These things we must know to understand the need, use and privilege of prayer—*Likewise the Spirit also helpeth our infirmities: for we know not what we should pray for as we ought: but the Spirit itself maketh intercession for us with groanings which cannot be uttered. And he that searcheth the hearts knoweth what is the mind of the Spirit, because he maketh intercession for the saints according to the will of God* (Rom 8:26).

God makes us to feel our need for him, and to cry out to him in thanksgiving for grace, mercy, and help in our time of need. Prayer does not CHANGE THINGS—It is God, who never changes, that changes things according to his will for the good of his people and for his glory. We ask because he says *ASK!* We receive because he is gracious to give. Prayer is the blessed privilege whereby his people come boldly to his throne and asking with confidence that he will do what is best, according to his wisdom, justice, and holiness.

The blessing of prayer is accessible only by the Lord Jesus Christ. Christ is our intercessor. We come to God by Him. Not just any one can come to God in any way. We pray to God by faith in Christ—*seeing he ever liveth to make intercession for us.* The heart of true prayer is thy *will be done!*

GOD'S PROVIDENCE

And we know that all things work together for good to them that love God, to them who are the called according to his purpose.
Romans 8:28

All of the suffering and misery in the world is a result of sin. There is no one immune to sin and its consequences, and its effect upon this flesh. However, the child of God is immune to its eternal consequences, which is condemnation before God. The Lord Jesus Christ was made sin for us and satisfied God the Father in making full payment for our sin and transgression, in his vicarious death upon the cross of Calvary.

God, in his wisdom and love, turns the sin and suffering, troubles and trials, pain and grief that Christians experience in this world for our good. So, all the BAD things are really GOOD things for the believer, from the hand of omnipotent grace and mercy. *And we know that all things work together for good to them that love God, to them who are the called according to his purpose* (Rom 8:28).

May God help us to remember we are but pilgrims and strangers here, and all things in God's providence are for our good. He will be glorified in his people, as we live by faith in him who loves us and gave himself for us. There is a great measure of peace, even in adversity, in submission to him who does all things well.

But as for you, ye thought evil against me; but God meant it unto good, to bring to pass, as it is this day, to save much people alive. (Gn 50:20).

THE LAW OF LOVE

He that spared not his own Son, but delivered him up for us all, how shall he not with him also freely give us all things?
Romans 8:32

Essentially, law is that which governs one's actions whether it be inward or outward. The best illustration of this is the moving cause of the incarnation of the Lord Jesus Christ—*Herein is love, not that we loved God, but that he loved us, and sent his Son the Propitiation for our sins* (1 Jn 4:10). The love of God in Christ our Redeemer is the moving cause of the elect's salvation. The law that sent Christ into the world to save sinners is the law of love.

Likewise, the believer's love for Christ is the motivation of his work of faith and labor of love. All else done in the name of Christ in religion is nothing more than a servile law with hope of reward or fear of punishment. Whatever we do, if love for Christ is not the moving cause, it is done in self-righteousness and for vain glory. Many, I fear, do what they do, whether little or much, because they feel that it is a duty, or out of necessity, or so they can feel good about themselves. These usually put limits and restraints upon themselves, fearing they might short themselves in some way. Where there is no love for Christ, the pleasures, comforts and security of the flesh, will have preeminence. This is true in every area of one's life, whether it is the study of God's Word, attending the worship services, giving, bearing others burdens, and in every area of commitment.

When God saves sinners, he gives them a heart like his heart, a heart of love. The children of God have been regenerated by his Spirit. They have a desire and a love for Christ, his Gospel, their brothers and sisters, that moves them in kindness, tenderness, and generosity, without regard for reward or fear of loss. This is a spiritual matter, a matter of the heart that God alone can govern. And govern he does by his sovereign, eternal love. *The love of God is shed abroad in our hearts by the Holy Ghost which is given unto us* (Rom 5:5).

THE STUMBLING STONE

As it is written, Behold, I lay in Sion a Stumblingstone and Rock
of offence: and whosoever believeth on him shall not be ashamed.
Romans 9:33

I n this verse, *Sion* is the church of the Lord Jesus Christ, while
the *Stumblingstone and Rock* is Christ himself. Those who
seek to be justified by their own works are those that stumble and
fall, because they BELIEVE NOT on Christ for all their
righteousness. Those who believe on him shall not be ashamed,
confounded, or fall.

The Lord Jesus Christ is our righteousness—period! If he
is not, we have none—period! Self-righteousness is the offending
characteristic of our depraved human nature before God. The
imputed and imparted righteousness of Christ is the hope and
salvation of God's elect.

Self-righteousness embodies unbelief, doubt, rebellion,
and hatred for God and his Christ. Self-righteousness is an
abomination to God, because it exalts the creature above the
Creator. The unbeliever is offended and stumbles upon Christ and
his righteousness.

The righteousness of Christ humbles the child of God and
exalts the Lord Jesus Christ. Those who have submitted
themselves to the righteousness of Christ, willingly and gladly
renounce their own righteousness, which is of the law, and
embrace Christ and his righteousness.

Christ is the Stone and Rock of our salvation. *God forbid*
that I should glory, save in the cross of our Lord Jesus Christ, by

whom the world is crucified unto me, and I unto the world (Gal 6:14).

A BELIEVING HEART

For with the heart man believeth unto righteousness; and with the mouth confession is made unto salvation.
Romans 10:10

If we have a believing heart it is a precious gift from God. I fear that many believe the Gospel of the Lord Jesus Christ only with the mind, much as we believe anything that we consider to be true. It is only by the impartation of spiritual life that we can believe on the Lord Jesus Christ to the saving of the soul. *A new heart also will I give you, and a new Spirit will I put within you: and I will take away the stony heart out of your flesh, and I will give you an heart of flesh* (Ez 36:26). The new heart that God gives, not only believes with understanding and acceptance, it embraces the Lord Jesus Christ in love, adoration, praise and worship. Therefore, as his love for and commitment to us is manifest, so will our love and commitment to him be manifest— *with the mouth confession is made unto salvation.*

This confession of the child of God is not only the words that we say, it is the life that we live. *I am crucified with Christ: nevertheless I live; yet not I, but Christ liveth in me: and the life which I now live in the flesh I live by the faith of the Son of God, who loved me, and gave himself for me* (Gal 2:20). Although imperfect by virtue of our sinful nature, the believer in this world has a God-given love for Christ and his Gospel, which are inseparable—that is; Christ, the Gospel, and the believer are inseparable—Read Ephesians 3:14-21. Where there is no heart-love for Christ there will be no heart-commitment, and for the most part very little outward commitment.

However, it is equally as true that outward commitment without inward love is nothing but a straw house built upon self-righteousness, and will fall in God's appointed time. We would be wise to ask ourselves this question: "Does my professed love for Christ constrain me to be committed and faithful to Him, his Gospel, and his church?" By God's grace, we must look to him and his Word for the answer. I pray that he will make known unto us his glorious person, and in knowing him we will be able to say in our hearts, *I have esteemed the words of his mouth more than my necessary food.* And as Peter, *Lord, thou knowest all things; thou knowest that I love thee.*

A BELIEVING HEART

For with the heart man believeth unto righteousness; and with the mouth confession is made unto salvation.
Romans 10:10

Consequential to his fallen nature, the heart of man does not, cannot, and will not believe God. In man there is no natural faith in Christ. Man's heart is deceitful and desperately wicked. Man is self-centered, self-righteous and self-glorifying. If we do believe the Word of God, if we do have faith in Christ, it is because God in sovereign grace and mercy has given us a new heart. Believing with the heart is much more than a mere verbal agreement and mental accent to Biblical facts, as propagated by false preachers and teachers pressing upon men to accept Jesus as their personal saviour.

A BELIEVING HEART IS ONE THAT lives unto God, embracing, loving, seeking, rejoicing in the precious Redeemer of their souls, the Lord Jesus Christ.

A BELIEVING HEART IS ONE THAT hungers and thirsts after the righteousness of Christ, and has a God-given abhorrence of sin and self.

A BELIEVING HEART IS ONE THAT daily takes up his cross, denying his own righteousness, repenting of his sin and unbelief and follows Christ by faith.

Those whom God has given life and faith in Christ love the Gospel. Not just any so-called Gospel. They love the truth as revealed in the Lord Jesus Christ. It is utter nonsense to imagine that a sinner to whom Christ has been revealed in the preaching of the Gospel does not love to hear Christ preached, and has no desire to be committed to the Gospel. To profess to be saved and yet have no desire or use for the Gospel is a contradiction.

The natural man is persistent in his pursuance of the things that satisfies his carnal cravings, even to the extreme. Likewise, the believing heart will not be denied of that one thing which satisfies the longing of his soul; the Object of his faith; the Lord Jesus Christ. *One thing have I desired of the LORD, that will I seek after; that I may dwell in the house of the LORD all the days of my life, to behold the beauty of the LORD, and to enquire in his temple* (Ps 27:4).

WITH THE HEART

With the heart man believeth unto righteousness; and with the mouth confession is made unto salvation.

Romans 10:10

Considering previous verses to the above text, we understand this verse is concerned with the Lord Jesus Christ being his people's righteousness and all their salvation. As it is possible to believe anything as fact in the mind, the inspired Word of God makes a distinction of the difference in natural mental accent to this precious truth and the faith that God gives his people in regeneration.

Believing on the Lord Jesus Christ with the heart is impossible for man apart from the gift of faith. Believing with the heart is the efficacious work of God the Spirit in the giving of spiritual life. Without exception, every child of God that has been given faith in Christ, confesses gladly and thankfully before the world, *The LORD hath brought forth our righteousness: come, and let us declare in Zion the work of the LORD our God* (Jer 51:10). Our confessing Christ does not make us righteous. Neither does it seal or secure our salvation. The believer's confession of Christ is a voluntary, natural act of the indwelling Spirit of grace. The believer expresses outwardly that which he loves and that which gives all glory and honour to Christ. Anyone can confess anything with the mouth. Only those who know Christ in a vital union can confess him with the heart, in the context of our verse.

This mouth confession is a heart confession. It is with the *NEW HEART* we live unto God, worshipping Him, loving Him, trusting Him, looking unto Christ as the Author and Finisher of our faith. The affections of the believer's heart is *set on things above, not on things on the earth. For ye are dead, and your life is hid with Christ in God. When Christ, who is our life, shall appear, then shall ye also appear with him in glory* (Col 3:2-4).

"EVEN SO THEN AT THIS PRESENT TIME"

Even so then at this present time also there is a remnant according to the election of grace.
Romans 11:5

Elijah, upon observing the supposed ruin of Israel and slaughter of God's people and the worship of false gods, was convinced he was the only prophet of God left, and they would soon kill him. His great concern was not for his life but the Gospel. When he took his complaint to God he found the encouragement that he needed. God said, *I have reserved to myself seven thousand men, who have not bowed the knee to the image of Baal.*

We are much like Elijah in this respect. The children of God often become discouraged and fearful as we look around and inside ourselves. The adversary is real and the flesh is weak. There is no doubt the enemy far out-numbers us. Our adversary is at liberty (as much as God will allow him) to use whatever means he can devise to further his cause against Christ and his kingdom. The believer has only one defense—GOD! *Unto thee, O my strength, will I sing: for God is my defense, and the God of my mercy* (Ps 59:17). Elijah's God is the God we worship, and we are not alone *even at this present time.* Elijah's encouragement was not that seven thousand had not bowed to Baal, but that God answered, *I HAVE. Even so at this present time,* Christ is on the throne ruling and reigning for his people, and they will not bow to any other god. This is *according to the election of grace.*

What shall we then say to these things? If God be for us, who can be against us? (Rom 8:31).

IMMEASURABLE RICHES

O the depth of the riches both of the wisdom and knowledge of God! how unsearchable are his judgments, and his ways past finding out!

Romans 11:33

The wisdom, knowledge, judgments, and ways of God our Saviour are infinitely rich in glory and grace, in the accomplished redemption of fallen sinners. His ways are so unfathomably deep, those who experience his grace will spend the rest of their days, here and in eternity, searching and finding it out! The wisdom and ways of the incarnate God can only be known by divine revelation and the power of God in regeneration. Even then, the entirety of his love, mercy, and grace is incomprehensible, because of the weakness of our sinful intellect.

By God's amazing grace he gives faith, which believes and receives his Word without question. By faith we understand that we are of him, *in Christ Jesus, who of God is made unto us wisdom, and righteousness, and sanctification, and redemption* (1 Cor 1:30). *The riches of his grace in his kindness toward us through Christ Jesus* (Eph 2:7), originates in *the depth of the riches both of the wisdom and knowledge of God* and are according to his unsearchable judgments and ways manifest in Jehovah our Saviour. These blessings of the wisdom and knowledge of God reside in our Redeemer, the Lord Jesus Christ. They are bequeathed to his people freely and eternally. *Blessed be the God and Father of our Lord Jesus Christ, who hath blessed us with all spiritual blessings in heavenly places in Christ* (Eph 1:3). The rich blessings of the child of God consist not of earthly possessions, but rather in the Lord Jesus Christ himself.

Therefore let no man glory in men. For all things are yours (1 Cor 3:21).

ABOVE REPROACH

For even Christ pleased not himself; but, as it is written, The reproaches of them that reproached thee fell on me.
Romans 15:3

To set the record straight, I am not above the reproach of others. I wish I were. I have failed, and do fail, in just about every way imaginable. If I have not laid my hand to do it, or withheld my hand from doing it, I have considered it. I plead guilty to all charges. There is no way to justify or excuse our sin. Therefore we must conclude, as does the Word of God, *In this flesh dwelleth no good thing.* Repentance before the throne of grace is no alternative for the believer, it is his daily portion. Our Lord has promised: *If we confess our sins, he is faithful and just to forgive us our sins, and to cleanse us from all unrighteousness* (1 Jn 1:9).

There is only one that is above reproach. He is our substitute, the Lord Jesus Christ, who was made a reproach (sin) for us. *For even Christ pleased not himself; but, as it is written, The reproaches of them that reproached thee fell on me* (Rom 15:3). He had no sin of his own, but made our sin his sin, so much so that justice declared he *hath made him to be sin.* In Christ, the child of God is above reproach; *who shall lay any thing to the charge of God's elect? It is God that justifieth. Who is he that condemneth? It is Christ that died, yea rather, that is risen again, who is even at the right hand of God, who also maketh intercession for us* (Rom 8:33-34). However, in this flesh, in this world, as mortal, decaying human beings, we are faulty and corrupt, prone to sin and disgrace.

Sometimes one worm imagines himself better than another worm, because he has not fallen into the same quagmire as his brother. This is only the sin of self-righteousness! Oh, to be free from this flesh! Some day we will. *So when this corruptible shall have put on incorruption, and this mortal shall have put on immortality, then shall be brought to pass the saying that is written, Death is swallowed up in victory* (1 Cor 15:54).

THE BLESSING OF CHRIST

And I am sure that, when I come unto you, I shall come in the
fulness of the blessing of the gospel of Christ.
Romans 15:29

W hen I come to preach the Gospel of Christ to you, I come
not in my own name, but in the name of him whose name
is above every name, declaring his merit, and beauty, his
righteousness, and his glory. When we come to hear the Gospel
of Christ preached, we come not in our own name, but in his
name. May God help us to worship in the fulness of the blessing
of the Gospel of Christ.

THE GOSPEL – THE POWER OF GOD

For the preaching of the cross is to them that perish foolishness;
but unto us which are saved it is the power of God.
1 Corinthians 1:18

T he preaching of the cross encompasses the declaration of the
whole of the person and work of our Redeemer. Therefore,
the center, sum, and substance of the Gospel message is the Lord
Jesus Christ. There can be no credibility given to any message
that has any thing or person, other than Christ, as its center as a

Gospel message. Likewise, neither can those who preach any other message than *Jesus Christ, and him crucified* (1 Cor 2:2) be correctly identified as Gospel preachers. *But though we, or an angel from heaven, preach any other gospel unto you than that which we have preached unto you, let him be accursed* (Gal 1:8).

The power of God is manifested by his Spirit to his people by a two-fold means in their salvation.

THE WORD OF GOD—*For our gospel came not unto you in word only, but also in power, and in the Holy Ghost, and in much assurance* (1 Thes 1:5).

THE PREACHING OF IT—*For after that in the wisdom of God the world by wisdom knew not God, it pleased God by the foolishness of preaching to save them that believe* (1 Cor 1:21).

There can be (and is) an abundance of GOOD THINGS being said, and a lot of WORTHY CAUSES being promoted in the world of Christendom. Nevertheless, it is only the message of *Jesus Christ and him Crucified* that God uses to reveal his glory and power in the salvation of poor sinners. To THEM, this singular message preached in simplicity is utter foolishness. *BUT UNTO US WHICH ARE SAVED it is the power of God*!

FREE GRACE

*Now we have received, not the spirit of the world, but the spirit
which is of God; that we might know the things that are freely
given to us of God.*

1 Corinthians 2:12

W E often use the term "free grace" but I wonder how many
understand its true meaning by experience. To really
appreciate something, of necessity we must experience it. To give
an example; with all our being, we may believe there is warmth
by the fireside, yet if we remain bound outside in the cold, we
will never experience and appreciate the warmth of the fire.

So it is with the grace of God. Only those who have been
brought by God's omnipotent, sovereign, irresistible grace to
Christ, that bask in the enjoyment, comfort, and reality of its
freeness. There is nothing we can do to merit or earn God's
wondrous favor of grace. Salvation is solely owning to the
pleasure and purpose of God. God, constrained only by his
everlasting love for his children, freely sent his blessed Son into
the world. The Lord Jesus Christ, God's dear Son, freely, gladly,
joyfully, and without reservation suffered and gave his life a
ransom for us. We had absolutely nothing to do with the great
work of redemption.

What God did in Christ for his people, he did freely.
Then, thanks be unto God, in his time he sent his Word by the
power of his Holy Spirit and brought us to Christ. This he did
freely, giving us life, revealing himself to us in the experience of

grace. Now, having experienced the grace of God in Christ Jesus our Lord, the believer's life is an experience of free grace.

Some may conclude that I place too much emphasis upon experience. Judge my words however you must. I agree it is truth that we are not saved by experience. However, it is equally true that where there is no experience there is no life. There is a vast difference between head knowledge and believing with our heart.

CHRIST OUR PASSOVER

Christ our Passover is sacrificed for us.
1 Corinthians 5:7

The word *Passover* first appears in the Scriptures in Exodus 12:11. *And thus shall ye eat it; with your loins girded, your shoes on your feet, and your staff in your hand; and ye shall eat it in haste: it is the LORD'S Passover.* Here in Exodus the *Passover* is identified as *the LORD'S Passover.* LORD'S is conspicuously capitalized prophetically identifying the LORD JESUS CHRIST as the sacrifice offered up to God for his loved ones in the fullness of time (Gal 4:4). This has never changed and will never change. He is THE SACRIFICE, and he is THE ONLY SACRIFICE for sin. Because of his sacrifice the wrath and judgment of God has passed over his people and death will never come near them. Here in 1 Corinthians, he is identified as *Christ OUR Passover.* Thanks be unto God, he has made him our Passover sacrifice! *Of him are ye in Christ Jesus, who of God is made unto us wisdom, and righteousness, and sanctification, and REDEMPTION* (1 Cor 1:30).

Once the Lamb was slain and the blood applied, the Israelites were to eat the sacrifice. The sacrifice was to become one with them, symbolizing faith in the substance and the accomplishment of that which was offered. Although the saints have always been one with Christ in God's eternal purpose of grace as Christ stood as *the Lamb slain from the foundation of the world* (Rv 13:8), we become one with him in regeneration as we partake of him by God given faith.

In regeneration, by faith in his blood, we can truly say *Christ our Passover is sacrificed for us.* What a wondrous confession of faith! What blessed assurance! What beautiful ground and foundation for worship! All those that know him by faith *eat it* (Christ) *in haste* (readily and thankfully). *Whoso eateth my flesh, and drinketh my blood, hath eternal life; and I will raise him up at the last day. For my flesh is meat indeed, and my blood is drink indeed. He that eateth my flesh, and drinketh my blood, dwelleth in me, and I in him* (Jn 6:54-56).

THIS IS MY BODY, WHICH IS BROKEN FOR YOU

And when he had given thanks, he brake it, and said, Take, eat: this is my body, which is broken for you: this do in remembrance of Me.

1 Corinthians 11:24

The sufferings of our Lord in his flesh are not a matter of insignificance. The pain and agony he suffered in his body stirs the compassion of all those that love Him. It would be heartless not to be touched with the feelings of his infirmities, as by them he is touched with ours. We all justly merit suffering because all we are in the flesh is sin. But not Jesus. His suffering was the reward of his people's sin, not His. Every pain inflicted upon our Redeemer was ours. He willingly made them His. Indeed there could be no efficacy in our suffering, but thanks be unto God there is in His. The inward travail of his soul for us is incomprehensible and infinitely meritorious. However, his suffering and death as a man is as vital, and inseparable in his justifying work in redemption. The full price must be paid.

The word *broken* is used to relate all of his physical sufferings, which progressively intensified and finally culminated in his vicarious death. In order for his sufferings and death to be efficacious to all his loved ones, the Bread of life must be broken. He *brake it, and said, Take, eat: this is my body, which is broken for you. He* willingly brake the bread and gave it to whom he would, symbolically showing us he was suffering for his particular people making us partakers thereof. The word *broken* also means GIVEN. *And he took bread, and gave thanks, and brake it, and gave unto them, saying, This is my body which is given for you* (Lk 22:19).

Every piercing, scourging, and anguish inflicted upon his sinless body was predestinated by Almighty God and executed in time accordingly, by the hands of you and me. As he represented us in his broken body, those that pierced him represented us as well. We might well say, "We are guilty of his death," and "He is guilty of our salvation." However, in his accomplishment, I must *declare, I say, at this time his righteousness: that he might be just, and the justifier of him which believeth in Jesus* (Rom 3:26).

WHY DID CHRIST DIE?

*For I delivered unto you first of all that which I also received,
how that Christ died for our sins according to the scriptures.*
1 Corinthians 15:3

The death of our Lord Jesus Christ was more than a judicial rendering of the demands of God's holy law for the punishment of our sins. Indeed it was that, however, the reason of our Redeemer giving his life a ransom for his sheep is equally important, and is much too often passed over in our haste to be doctrinally correct. The divine motive of this incomprehensible transaction was the everlasting love God for his children. *In this was manifested the love of God toward us, because that God sent his only begotten Son into the world, that we might live through him* (1 Jn 4:9).

Had there been no love for us there would have been no Redeemer provided. The glory of God is most perfectly and completely revealed by the Son when he gave his life for those he loved. Oh what love, wondrous love, for me was shown! When by faith we see our Saviour dying, we must not only see justice satisfied, we must see God's love fulfilled, magnified, and glorified! *Now when I passed by thee, and looked upon thee, behold, thy time was the time of love; and I spread my skirt over thee, and covered thy nakedness: yea, I sware unto thee, and entered into a covenant with thee, saith the Lord GOD, and thou becamest mine* (Ez 16:8).

God is satisfied as he rests in his love! Not only did Christ die to satisfy the justice of God legally, he died to express his love and that we might live forever with him in glory. The love of God and the death of Christ is in such harmony that justice smiles, closes the book, strikes its gavel, and declares from the courts of heaven, echoing throughout eternity, "Case closed. All charges against the accused are dismissed." Now if that is not good news for a wretch such as the likes of me, I don't know what is!

> "I'm redeemed by love divine!
> Glory, Glory, Christ is mine!"

COVENANT PROMISES

2 Corinthians 1:20

God Almighty is a covenant God. His very being, character, and attributes, makes his Word, purpose, promises, and covenant unalterable and everlasting. The Godhead, the Father, Son and Spirit, are inseparable in the scheme and execution of all things in time and eternity. The Lord Jesus Christ is that manifestation of the invisible Godhead. *In him dwelleth all the fulness of the Godhead bodily* (Col 2:9). It is in Christ our Redeemer that we see God's purpose of grace for his elect, his promise to his people, and the glory of his accomplishment. You see, there is nothing in the way of grace contrived by vain mankind. The way of salvation, and the execution of salvation of chosen sinners, is the fulfillment of the covenant of God the Father, God the Son, and God the Spirit. Who are we, that we should imagine entering into this divine wisdom and work of the Almighty?

As far as God is concerned, All the work of Christ is done—*For we which have believed do enter into rest, as he said, As I have sworn in my wrath, if they shall enter into my rest: although the works were finished from the foundation of the world* (Heb 4:3). The sum of God's covenant promises is fulfilled in Christ our Lord in one declaration; *For all the promises of God in him are yea, and in him Amen, unto the glory of God by us* (2 Cor 1:20). Dear child of God, rest assured that when Christ said, *It is finished*, IT IS FINISHED! In him is our assurance of the enjoyment of the everlasting salvation of our soul.

THE BELIEVER'S TREASURE

But we have this treasure in earthen vessels, that the excellency of the power may be of God, and not of us.
2 Corinthians 4:7

By God's grace, the child of God is different than those who do not know Christ. Every person is an earthen vessel, but the believer has a treasure, which the unbeliever does not have. This makes the difference. God has given his people this treasure he may receive the glory, and not us. This treasure is a gift of God to poor sinners who are undeserving and powerless. From this text, let us consider a threefold treasure which I believe comprises the whole of the believer's life in this world.

The first, without which there would be nothing else, is CHRIST. The Lord Jesus Christ is the greatest treasure that one could have.   Everything else is but dung compared to Him. To have Christ is to have everything. *But of him are ye in Christ Jesus, who of God is made unto us wisdom, and righteousness, and sanctification, and redemption* (1 Cor 1:30). One could have all of this worlds goods, but without Christ all would be nothing—*Christ is all, and in all* (Col 3:11).

Second, the believer's great treasure in this world is the Gospel OF THE LORD JESUS CHRIST. The Gospel is the record that God has given to his people concerning his Son and their redemption in Him. The Gospel is the revelation of Jesus Christ, the living Word of God. The child of God treasures the Gospel more than anything in the world because it speaks of him who is altogether lovely. The one who has the Gospel has the greatest of treasures and would dare to die than part with it. The desire and treasure of the believing heart is to HEAR THE GOSPEL OF CHRIST PROCLAIMED.

Third, to the believer, the preaching of the Gospel is the great joy and rejoicing of his heart. To hear the truth of our Lord Jesus Christ proclaimed is a treasure from God, without which the believing sinner cannot live. Those who can live in this world without consistently hearing the preaching of the Gospel live in this world without Christ. He *that is of God heareth God's words: ye therefore hear them not, because ye are not of God* (Jn 8:47). We have this treasure because God, in his sovereign grace, is pleased that we have it. The excellency of the power of God is Christ, and he is revealed in the preaching of the Gospel to chosen earthen vessels, which is *the power of God unto salvation to every one that believeth* (Rom 1:16).

"FOR WHICH CAUSE WE FAINT NOT"

For which cause we faint not; but though our outward man perish, yet the inward man is renewed day by day.
2 Corinthians 4:16

The child of God is not immune to the afflictions that come upon the unbeliever. Unlike the unbeliever, all that happens in a Christian's life is a trial of faith. Whether it is prosperity or poverty, health or sickness, life or death, God uses these experiences to cause us to look to him for all things, teaching us these things are temporary and soon will pass. The faith God gives us in his Son looks beyond this physical life. Faith sees the unseen and believes the unbelievable. The faith that God gives glorifies Christ in the life of the believer, as we look to him for all things both temporary and eternal. We faint not because his grace keeps looking to Christ and believing his promises to us.

LOVE'S PERSUASION

For The Love Of Christ Constraineth Us
2 Corinthians 5:14

A ll of mankind are driven by one of two undeniable inward powers or passions. We are born into this world with a love for self, a love for the things of the world, and a love for every thing that will satisfy our fleshly appetite. Those who are born from above have a love for Christ and the things which are not of this world. The child of God has both, yet the latter has preeminence and dominion, and will ultimately prevail in the course of time and events. This insatiable desire and appetite directs the path of the believer's life.

The Scriptures term this "constraining" love. This love is twofold in respect to God's love for his people. Because of his love for us, we love him with the love that he has given us. We have often heard LOVE defined as COMMITMENT, DEDICATION, DEVOTION, FAITHFULNESS, etc. However, these are not love. Rather, these are the evidences of existing love. Where these abide there is love. Where these do not exist there is no love. All men have love, but all men do not love Christ.

The object is non-existent in the hearts of those that know not Christ, and the evidence is clearly revealed. The Word of God declares that *If any man love the world, the love of the Father is not in him* (1 Jn 2:15), and that *if any man love God, the same is known of him* (1 Cor 8:3). A profession of love for Christ without commitment, devotion, dedication and faithfulness to him and his work is like a dead body with only a name tag on it's toe. The constraining love of Christ does exactly that; it constrains us. It moves, persuades, and compels us to come to Christ; to love and worship, desiring the things of God. My prayer is: *That Christ may dwell in your hearts by faith; that ye, being rooted and grounded in love, may be able to comprehend with all saints what is the breadth, and length, and depth, and height; and to know the love of Christ, which passeth knowledge, that ye might be filled with all the fulness of God* (Eph 3:17-19).

ALL THINGS ARE OF GOD

And all things are of God, who hath reconciled us to himself by Jesus Christ, and hath given to us the ministry of reconciliation.
2 Corinthians 5:18

This passage speaks primarily of the great act of reconciliation, which is the work of God in Christ alone. The phrase *all things are of God* includes all that Jehovah (the unchanging, eternal, self-existent God, the great *I am, that I am*) purposed to do. Every THING is a direct, intentional, purposeful result of the sovereign decree of Almighty God. Those who do not know God, those who do not believe the Bible, may call this view of the Almighty fatalistic or hyper-Calvinistic. Nevertheless, God is God or he is not God. No man invented this wonderful truth. It is declared throughout the Scriptures; *Declaring the end from the beginning, and from ancient times the things that are not yet done, saying, my counsel shall stand, and I will do all my pleasure* (Is 46:10).

All THINGS are of God in the old creation, and all THINGS are of God in the new as well. The great work of redemption and all that pertains is by the sovereign pleasure and good-will of

Jehovah-Jireh. *I will ransom them from the power of the grave; I will redeem them from death: O death, I will be thy plagues; O grave, I will be thy destruction: repentance shall be hid from mine eyes* (Hos 13:14). The Incarnate God came into the world he created and sustains, and by the Word of his power, to accomplish a work which he purposed from everlasting. Namely, the eternal redemption of all he was pleased to redeem—*Neither by the blood of goats and calves, but by his own blood he entered in once into the Holy Place, having obtained eternal redemption for us* (Heb 9:12).

All THINGS are of God in regeneration as well. It is he who gives life and faith in the Lord Jesus Christ. If he did not do it, it would not be done. Man will remain in death and darkness except he say, *Let there be Light*. And when he says *Let there be Light,* there WILL be Light!

SUBSTITUTION – GOD'S MYSTERY

For he hath made him to be sin for us, who knew no sin; that we might be made the righteousness of God in Him.
2 Corinthians 5:21

The incomprehensible wondrous works of the triune God in the redemption of sinners, defies all finite human logic, and frustrates the understanding of mankind. From the incarnation of the eternal Son of God to the glorification of the sanctified ones there remains a treasure of divine secrets known only unto Him. Even for his chosen people there are *unspeakable words, which it is not lawful for a man to utter*. Often we have a hankering to delve into the unrevealed mysteries of the infinite mind, and consequently gather unto ourselves confusion.

When an attempt is made to explain that which God is pleased to retain in his storehouse of wisdom, there arises a polluted fountain of intellectual poison, gendering pride, causing strife and division. God's ministers are called and sent to declare what God has revealed. When we go beyond divine revelation we are promoting self rather than the glory of God. In our text God has declared, *he hath made him to be sin for us, who knew no sin; that we might be made the righteousness of God in Him.* Any deviation from this would be heresy. This is the Word of God. Need we say more? The theme of all Scriptures is the Lord Jesus Christ, his redemptive, substitutionary work. The ultimate substance and accomplishment of that work is, *he hath made him to be sin for us, who knew no sin; that we might be made the righteousness of God in him* to the praise of his glory and grace.

This is the crystal clear revelation of God Almighty concerning his blessed Son. I cannot answer for others, but as for me, I cannot explain the triune God, the incarnation of Christ, the actual guilt of my sin being laid upon Christ, the death of one who is God in the flesh, the resurrection of the dead Lamb, the regenerating work of God the Spirit, the glorification of once dead sinners, except—DIVINE WISDOM AND OMNIPOTENCE! REVEALED TRUTH!

O the depth of the riches both of the wisdom and knowledge of God! how unsearchable his judgments, and his ways past finding out! (Rom 11:33).

A PRESENT SALVATION

Behold, NOW is the day of salvation.
2 Corinthians 6:2

Yesterday is gone. We do not have the promise of tomorrow. NOW is all we have. I know that I cannot save anyone. I know that you cannot save yourself. However, the Gospel is preached for a verdict. I pray that we would be blessed of God TODAY to see the beauty of Christ and all that is in him for sinners such as ourselves.

STRENGTH IN WEAKNESS

My grace is sufficient for thee: for my strength is made perfect in weakness. Most gladly therefore will I rather glory in my infirmities, that the power of Christ may rest upon me.
2 Corinthians 12:9

Sinful men come to Christ by the almighty power of God's irresistible grace. We come willingly and humbly because he has made us willing, by humbling our hearts to see our sin and helplessness, and his love, mercy, and grace, through the preaching of the Gospel. The same grace and faith that first brought us to Christ supports and comforts the child of God in all of life's trials. *I am crucified with Christ: nevertheless I live; yet not I, but Christ liveth in me: and the life which I now live in the flesh I live by the faith of the Son of God, who loved me, and gave himself for me.* (Gal 2:20).

Those who do not look to Christ, separating themselves from the Gospel, look within themselves and to the world for comfort and therefore often despair. This should not be surprising, because there is no real, lasting, peace and assurance anywhere but in Christ and his Gospel. Believers are not immune to trouble and trials, but they have the constant and enduring promise of God in Christ and the Gospel that his grace is sufficient, and he will NEVER leave or forsake us. Those that live outside and away from the Gospel have no promise of peace and help in life's many trials. We do not come to Christ for our troubles to end; yet those who come to him, find in him strength and faith to persevere day by day.

THREE GREAT DIFFERENCES

There be some that trouble you, and would pervert the gospel of Christ.

Galatians 1:7

The first perversion of the Word of God is recorded in Genesis 3:4. *And the serpent said unto the woman, YE SHALL NOT SURELY DIE.*

This declaration made by the serpent was a blatant lie. Since then, all false religions, false preachers and false teachers have followed suite. Although there are many perversions and differences between the true and the false, I believe they can be summed up in three.

THE BASIS OF ALL FALSE RELIGION IS THEIR GOD. The god of false religion in no way resembles the God of the Bible. The only true and living God, as revealed in the Scriptures, is HOLY, RIGHTEOUS, JUST, SOVEREIGN, IMMUTABLE, INFINITE, OMNIPOTENT, OMNISCIENT AND OMNIPRESENT. The god of false religion is limited by the creature in every capacity and therefore is no god at all.

THE PERSON AND WORK OF THE LORD JESUS CHRIST. The Lord Jesus Christ is God manifest in the flesh, and in him dwells all the fulness of the Godhead bodily. He is the infinite God and perfect humanity. In him alone there is salvation for sinful man. He alone is the sinner's substitute and sacrifice. He is our wisdom, righteous, sanctification and redemption. He alone is our Great High Priest, our advocate and intercessor. All for whom he died shall be saved with an everlasting salvation, without exception. The christ of false religion in no way resembles the Christ of the Bible. As the Christ of God is the express image of the true and living God, so does the christ of false religion bear the image of their false god—he can be no more. He is a pathetic imposter. He is a product of man's depraved imagination with no power, no ability, and not worthy of any glory, honor or praise. Therefore he is not christ at all.

THE CONDITION OR STATE OF MAN. The Scriptures declare that man is a fallen creature. We are sinful creatures within and without. The Word of God reveals that we have no desire for Christ, no ability to come to Christ, and that we are dead in trespasses and sin. In unregenerate man there is no faith or capacity to believe on Christ. Man's will is in bondage to sin and self and can never be otherwise apart from the power of God. The Scriptures declare that man has no righteousness before God and can never attain unto the righteousness that God will accept. False religion embraces the blasphemous idea that man is not so bad at all. It teaches and preaches that God places all men on a savable plane and salvation is according to his own supposed FREE WILL. False preachers declare salvation is by works rather

256

than by the grace of God. They affirm that man has the ability to let God save sinners if they so choose. They believe they can establish a righteousness that God will accept by their own good works. There is a vast difference—study the Scriptures!

"WHEN IT PLEASED GOD"

Galatians 1:15-16

It never occurred to me that God is sovereign over all things, only doing that which pleases Him, only when he is pleased to do so, until God in grace and mercy revealed his Son to me through the preaching of the Gospel. This great truth, which is revealed throughout the Scriptures, leaves man at the disposal of our infinite, omnipotent, just, and holy God. Contrary to the popular opinion of false preachers and false professors, salvation is of the Lord—from start to finish. Any message, any preacher, or any professor of Christianity that gives credit, ability, or the determining choice to man in the matter of regeneration is anti-God and anti-Christ.

Salvation is in the hand of the Saviour! Grace comes only from him who said, *I will be gracious*! Mercy is received only from him who said, *I will be merciful*.

It pleased God to choose his people before the world was made—*According as he hath chosen us in him before the foundation of the world* (Eph 1:4).

It pleased God to send his Son to be the propitiation for his people's sin—*Herein is love, not that we loved God, but that he loved us, and sent his son to be the propitiation for our sins* (1 Jn 4:10).

It pleases God, in his time, to call his elect to faith in Christ by the preaching of the glorious Gospel of his Son—*For after that in the wisdom of God the world by wisdom knew not God, IT PLEASED GOD by the foolishness of preaching to save them that believe* (1 Cor 1:21).

It pleased God to create the world and all that is therein—*Thou art worthy, O Lord, to receive glory and honour and power: for thou hast created all things, and for thy pleasure they are and were created* (Rv 4:11).

It pleases God to uphold all things by the Word of his power—*Who being the brightness of his glory, and the express image of his person, and upholding all things by the word of his power, when he had by himself purged our sins, sat down on the right hand of the Majesty on high* (Heb 1:3). And, THANK GOD!

It pleased him to make us his people! *For the LORD will not forsake his people for his great name's sake: because IT HATH PLEASED THE LORD TO MAKE YOU HIS PEOPLE* (1 Sm 12:22).

What God does not do will never be done. What God has done will never be undone, because *IT PLEASED GOD*!

IDENTIFICATION OF THE BELIEVER

The life which I now live in the flesh I live by the faith of the Son of God, who loved me, and gave himself for me.
Galatians 2:20

The mark of spiritual circumcision of the heart is faith in Christ. The believer's life in this world is governed by the new heart, which is freely given and sanctified by the Spirit of the living God to a preeminent faith in Christ. The abiding presence of *Christ in you* reveals a distinct new life in contrast to our inherent, carnal heart and nature. This is entirely a work of the omnipotent Spirit of God. The child of God is identified and known by his living relationship with Christ.

The believer is identified by a new heart, not a renovation (repair, redecoration, or remodeling) of the old. *A new heart also will I give you, and a new Spirit will I put within you* (Ez 36:26). Spiritual circumcision is only comparative to fleshly circumcision in the identification of a particular people—*He is a Jew, which is one inwardly; and circumcision is that of the heart, in the spirit, and not in the letter* (Rom 2:29). The burden of emphasis is significantly directed to the heart that recognizes *the Son of God, who loved me, and gave himself for me,* and therefore in response, loves *him who first loved us* (1 Jn 4:19). The God-given love for Christ moves the believer to worship, adoration, gratitude and commitment.

The new heart has a discernment of truth and error. The child of God knows the voice of his Shepherd and has an undeniable will to follow Him—*And when he putteth forth his own sheep, he goeth before them, and the sheep follow Him: for they know his voice. And a stranger will they not follow, but will flee from him: for they know not the voice of strangers* (Jn 10:4-5). God the Father identifies his children by giving them a heart for Christ. All else will ultimately be revealed as uncircumcision, which is unbelief and identifies those who perish.

THE FRUIT OF THE SPIRIT

The fruit of the Spirit is love . . . If we live in the Spirit, let us also walk in the Spirit.

Galatians 5:22-25

Those who belong to Christ believe his Gospel, and are committed to Christ, his Gospel, and to one another. Believing the doctrinal truths of the Gospel as fact, but not in heart and practice having and living the fruit of the Spirit, is a contradiction to the Scriptures and to our profession of faith in Christ. What I am saying is this: If we are truly Christ's, we have the fruit of the Spirit, which is love, joy, peace, longsuffering, gentleness, goodness, faith, meekness, temperance, and have crucified the flesh with the affections and lusts.

This is a work of God in the new man created in Christ Jesus. The children of God are not hasty to judge a brother and are quick to forgive, because God, for Christ's sake, has forgiven us. Love is the foundation of the believer's life of faith. We love Christ, his Gospel, and the brethren because God first loved us and sent his Son to die for us, and has given us of his Spirit. The child of God is prone to think the best instead the worst, especially when it involves a brother or sister in Christ. The Spirit of God in the heart of the child of God causes us to seek peace and pursue it. The fruit of the Spirit is to heal and mend rather than cause division and strife.

Charity (love) suffereth long, and is kind; charity envieth not; charity vaunteth not itself, is not puffed up, Doth not behave itself unseemly, seeketh not her own, is not easily provoked, thinketh no evil; Rejoiceth not in iniquity, but rejoiceth in the truth; Beareth all things, believeth all things, hopeth all things, endureth all things (1 Cor 13:4-7).

The family of God is a spiritual family begotten by God himself. They are the body of Christ of whom he is the head. Being one in him we bear the same fruit unto his glory. The people of God are the kindest, gentlest, most generous, forgiving people in the world. Therefore, *let all bitterness, and wrath, and anger, and clamour, and evil speaking, be put away from you, with all malice: And be ye kind one to another, tenderhearted, forgiving one another, even as God for Christ's sake hath forgiven you* (Eph 4:31).

INCOMPREHENSIBILITY – DEFINED

For if a man think himself to be something, when he is nothing, he deceiveth himself.

Galatians 6:3

Were God not pleased to reveal himself and his work to his people in Christ, we would comprehend nothing of spiritual nature. *Incomprehensibility* is simply the lack of ability to understand. It is only by faith (revelation by the Spirit of God) we are enabled to understand the things of God.

It is of no consequence to try to make spiritual things palatable or reasonable to the flesh of natural man by carnal reasoning. *Incomprehensibility* of the things of God is a virtue of us all, by nature.

However, to comprehend is a virtue of those to whom God has given spiritual life in Christ. Therefore, if we do know the truth as it is in Christ Jesus, we have no reason to glory in ourselves; *But he that glorieth, let him glory in the Lord* (2 Cor 10:17).

Thus, we conclude that those who promote themselves to be spiritual, intellectual giants are eaten up with *incomprehensibility*, knowing nothing at all, and don't even know it! *For if a man think himself to be something, when he is nothing, he deceiveth himself* (Gal 6:3).

ARE THERE CHRISTIANS WHO ARE NOT FAITHFUL

Paul, an apostle of Jesus Christ by the will of God, to the saints which are at Ephesus, and to the faithful in Christ Jesus:
Ephesians 1:1

There is no need to define the word *faithful* because everyone knows what it means. It appears 82 times in 78 verses of the Bible. In the 54 times it appears in the New Testament it is used in regard to Christ's faithfulness to his Father, the SHEEP, and the SHEEP's faithfulness to their Shepherd. There can be no doubt as to our Lord's faithfulness to his people. Those who belong to him experience this every day. But we have a greater proof than that of our experiences. We have his Word! He is perfectly and always faithful. He *shall not fail nor be discouraged* (Is 42:4. *Jesus Christ, who is the Faithful Witness* (Rv 1: 5).

Now, what about the other side of the coin? Are his people faithful? Are there Christians (real Christians) who are not faithful? The question is not "do they sin?" or "are they perfect in the flesh as their Lord is perfect?" Yes! His people are faithful. No! There are no Christians who are unfaithful. The true child of God's life proves it. This is not only my personal view based upon observation. This is the judgment of the holy writ. *No servant can serve two masters: for either he will hate the one, and love the other, or else he will hold to the one, and despise the other. Ye cannot serve God and mammon* (Lk 16:13).

The title of the believer renders the same truth, *The faithful in Christ Jesus* (Eph. 1:1). The foundation of this truth is based upon his faithfulness: *Being confident of this very thing, that he which hath begun a good work in you will perform it until the day of Jesus Christ* (Phil 1:6).

The Object of the believer's faith is Christ; *Looking unto Jesus the Author and Finisher of our faith. . .* (Heb. 12:2). The believer's life is a life of faith; *The just shall live by faith* (Rom. 1:17). And it is the HE who is faithful unto his Lord that receives a crown of life; *be thou faithful unto death, and I evil give thee a crown of life* (Rv. 2:10).

The idea that some of Christ's sheep live an unfaithful life is the invention of unconverted preachers to make false professors feel comfortable in their licentiousness. To insinuate God has a people he has called to faith in his Son who remain unfaithful, is to deny God's faithfulness to his people. The title CHRISTIAN identifies a faithful people.

THE BEST OF EVERYTHING

Blessed be the God and Father of our Lord Jesus Christ, who hath blessed us with all spiritual blessings in heavenly places in Christ:

Ephesians 1:3

The child of God is not forsaken in poverty and ruin. He is not left to fend for himself in the garbage and filth of the world and religion. He is not left to walk in the blindness and darkness of error. There is nothing negative or despairing about the sheep of Christ our Lord. God's children have the best of everything.

THE TRUE AND LIVING GOD IS OUR GOD AND WE ARE HIS PEOPLE—*God hath said, I will dwell in them, and walk in them; and I will be their God, and they shall be my people* (2 Cor 6:16).

GOD IS FOR HIS PEOPLE—*What shall we then say to these things? If God be for us, who can be against us?* (Rom 8:31).

GOD WORKS ALL THINGS IN PROVIDENCE FOR HIS PEOPLE'S GOOD—*And we know that all things work together for good to them that love God, to them who are the called according to [his] purpose* (Rom 8:28).

GOD HAS NOT WITHHELD ANY SPIRITUAL BLESSING FROM US—*Blessed be the God and Father of our Lord Jesus Christ, who hath blessed us with all spiritual blessings in heavenly places in Christ* (Eph 1:3).

NOT ONLY HAS HE FORGIVEN OUR SIN, HE HAS GIVEN US THE VERY RIGHTEOUSNESS OF CHRIST—*For he hath made him to be sin for us, who knew no sin; that we might be made the righteousness of God in him* (2 Cor 5:21).

THERE IS NOTHING LACKING IN THE BELIEVER'S LIFE—*And ye are complete in Him, which is the head of all principality and power* (Col 2:10).

GOD'S PEOPLE WALK IN THE LIGHT AND GLORY OF GOD BY FAITH THAT HE HAS GIVEN—*Ye are all the children of light, and the children of the day: we are not of the night, nor of darkness* (1 Thes 5:5).

It would be impossible to number and articulate all we have as God's children. But to sum it up, in Christ we have the best of everything. If Christ be ours and we be His, there is nothing more to be desired. He has freely given all that we have, because he loves us and is pleased to do so. I may not look like much or appear to have much by the world's estimation, but by God's grace, I have the best of everything.

ACCEPTED IN THE BELOVED

He hath made us accepted in the Beloved.
Ephesians 1:6

For a sinful creature such as I am to be accepted by God is one of the most amazing declarations of the Gospel of Christ. Often, to be accepted by others, we must meet and conform to certain criteria conformable to THEIR standards and rules, and justified by THEIR understanding and convictions. However, our Lord declares that sinners are accepted by him in Christ, according to the riches of his grace. Every sinner that God saves, he saves in Christ. Those saved are all partakers of his grace and one in Him. All are freely justified, forgiven, and members of his body. The *us* in the passage speaks of the ONENESS, which every believer enjoys in Christ.

We are accepted because God the Father forever loved us in Christ. We are chosen in Christ, redeemed by Christ, clothed with the righteousness of Christ, and therefore accepted in Christ. Being in agreement with God, every believer accepts one another much the same way; as accepted in the *Beloved;* Sinners forgiven, sinners justified, sinners accepting each other because of the sovereign grace of God in Christ Jesus our Lord. There is nothing that can separate us from the love of God, which is Christ Jesus, our Lord. And it is as equally true that nothing can sever the body of Christ and destroy the love we have for each other because it is born of God. It is true that while we are in this flesh we will have disagreements and misunderstandings. But these things should never cause us to separate and distance ourselves from the fellowship of other sinners whom God has accepted in Christ.

True, there can be no fellowship in the Gospel with those that do not believe and preach the true Gospel of Christ. But those who love Christ, his Gospel, and one another should seek to be ready to forgive, restore, and even give the brother the benefit of doubt. Dogmatism is a good thing, if it is not used as a weapon in the hand of pride. Compromise should be unheard of, if we are certain and understand all the facts. This I understand, all that are accepted in the Beloved are sinners saved by the grace of God. We are all just alike in the flesh—SINNERS, and we are all alike in Christ—ACCEPTED.

THE GOSPEL OF YOUR SALVATION

In whom (Christ) *ye also trusted,* AFTER *that ye heard the word of truth, the gospel of your salvation: in whom also* AFTER *that ye believed, ye were sealed with that Holy Spirit of promise*
Ephesians 1:13

The WORD OF TRUTH—THE GOSPEL, is synonymous with Christ.

What I am saying is this: Christ is the Word OF TRUTH, and without Christ there is no true Gospel. We cannot have one without the other. The Lord Jesus Christ is revealed in the Gospel, therefore, without the Gospel there is no saving knowledge of Christ. The preaching and hearing of THE GOSPEL—THE TRUTH, is vital to God calling chosen sinners to Christ by his sovereign, irresistible grace. *For after that in the wisdom of God the world by wisdom knew not God, it pleased God by the foolishness of preaching to save them that believe* (1 Cor 1:21). God's ordained way and means of saving sinners is shown to us in this; *But we are bound to give thanks alway to God for you, brethren beloved of the Lord, because God hath from the beginning chosen you to salvation* THROUGH SANCTIFICATION OF THE SPIRIT AND BELIEF OF THE TRUTH. (2 Thes 2:13).

To say that we were saved BEFORE we heard the Gospel of our salvation (which is the Word OF TRUTH), is a contradiction to the Word of God. False preachers and a false Gospel have their place in God's great scheme of things, but it is not to the salvation of men's souls. It is to the praise of the glory of God's justice and to the condemnation of those who preach it and believe it. A misrepresentation of the truth of God can only lead to a false faith in a false god, and a false hope in a false christ. Those of God's elect who were saved while in Egypt were not saved by bowing to the Egyptian gods, they were saved by his grace, when he sent his messenger to them with a word from Him.

This is God's ordained way; *So then faith cometh by hearing, and hearing by the Word of God* (Rom 10:17). The preaching of the Gospel of Christ is not just another way of preaching Christ, IT IS THE ONLY MESSAGE OF THE BIBLE, and the only way that God uses to reveal Christ savingly to his people. *For the preaching of the cross is to them that perish foolishness; but unto us which are saved it is the power of God* (1 Cor 1:18). Are we going in a different direction or have we just changed horses and continuing in the same direction? To hang on to a false profession made under a false Gospel glorifies a lie and dishonors the glorious Gospel of God's redeeming grace, which we now profess to believe.

"WHICH IS HIS BODY"

And hath put all things under his feet, and gave him to be the head over all things to the church, which is his body, the fulness of him that filleth all in all.
Ephesians 1:22-23

The church of the living God, the mystical body of Christ, is a glorious church not having any spot of sin or blemish, as a result of the propitiatory work of our Redeemer. We are one in and with Christ of whom it is written; *In him is no sin.* Living with the knowledge of our perfection in Christ in this fleshly body condemned to death because of sin, is a humbling experience of God's revealed grace. The effects of seeing our union with Christ in regeneration are abundant in blessings and benefits, which redound to his glory. We are comforted and assured in him who is sovereign over all things to our eternal good, *And hath put all things under his feet. He* who is our Wisdom is our HEAD that knows and sees all things, and therefore governs all things providentially for our good—*and gave him to be the head over all things to the church.*

Then there is the sweet fellowship we have with him together. We are united in one body, mind, and accord. Our union with Christ brings us together as one body at his feet to worship him and hear his Words, which are life unto us. Our union with him is a union begotten of love. That union abides in love for him and one another, and causes us to seek the good of our brethren, forgiving, forbearing, and patiently bearing with the faults and failures of others for Christ's sake—*And be ye kind one to another, tenderhearted, forgiving one another, even as God for Christ's sake hath forgiven you* (Eph 4:32).

It is a misnomer to bear the name of CHRISTIAN and be filled with malice, jealousy, envy, hatred and strife. If we truly know Him, we are those of whom it is written, *Now ye are the body of Christ, and members in particular* (1 Cor 12:27). We, as believers, should have one objective, one goal, one desire, *Whether therefore ye eat, or drink, or WHATSOEVER YE DO, do all to the glory of God* (1 Cor 10:31).

WHO IS SAVED?

For by grace are ye saved through faith; and that not of yourselves: it is the gift of God.
Ephesians 2:8

Saved is a term that is used rather loosely in the realm of religion. Generally, those that use this term are making reference to an experience they have had or a commitment that they have made based upon their free will in ACCEPTING JESUS AS THEIR PERSONAL SAVIOR, or their assent to certain laws or doctrines. As a result of what they DO, they say they are *saved.* This concept of being *saved* is nothing more than a legalistic, self-righteous, works religion, which glorifies man and dethrones God.

The verse and context before us reveals that sinners are saved by the grace of God—PERIOD!—*BY GRACE ARE YE SAVED.* Who is saved?—Those who are saved by the grace of God through Christ Jesus our Lord. Those who are saved are those who WERE dead in sin. God, in grace and mercy, has now sovereignly, and on purpose given them spiritual life in regeneration. Those who are saved are those to whom God has imputed Christ's righteousness, having justified them by his bloody sacrifice. Those who are saved are those to whom he has revealed himself through the preaching of THE GOSPEL, thereby giving them faith in Christ alone. Those who are saved are those who know Christ and believe on Christ for ALL their salvation.

They believe, love, and are committed to the Gospel of the Lord Jesus Christ. It is not those who possess the truth that are saved, it is those whom the truth possesses. It is not those who profess Christ that are saved, it is those whom Christ possesses that are saved. It is the result of being vitally united and one with Christ that gives us faith in, love for, and commitment to the Lord Jesus Christ and his Gospel. This is all the work of God from beginning to end.

Those who are saved are those who faithfully, consistently, hear the Gospel. They seek out every opportunity to worship God with the brethren, and to be taught of God. This is their joy and comfort. This is not a law to them; it is their desire. Men do what they want to do. Their spiritual desire overrides the desires of the flesh to be entertained and to seek the comforts and pleasures of this world. A little religion will satisfy only those who profess to be saved. Those who are saved can never get enough of Christ.

THE LOVE OF CHRIST

To know the love of Christ.
Ephesians 3:19

The love of Christ for his church passes knowledge. That is, his love is only known by experience as he reveals himself to us by his Spirit in his Word. His love for his people is incomprehensible by natural, human understanding, and can only be known by his people. Christ's love for his sheep was manifest in that he laid down his life for us. Anyone may believe that he died for sinners, but only those for whom he died really know and experience his love. The love of Christ is sovereign, free, strong, and enduring. There is no other love by which we may compare his love, not even our love for Him. His people do love

Him, but only because he first loved us. Absolutely nothing in time or eternity can diminish or separate us from his love. What comfort! What assurance! To know the love of Christ!

GOOD FRUIT

And be ye kind one to another, tenderhearted, forgiving one another, even as God for Christ's sake hath forgiven you.
Ephesians 4:32

*B*e *kindly affectioned one to another with brotherly love; in honour preferring one another* (Rom 12:10). *But as touching brotherly love ye need not that I write unto you: for ye yourselves are taught of God to love one another* (1 Thes 4:9). *Let brotherly love continue* (Heb 13:1).

Love, kindness, tenderness, forgiveness, longsuffering, and generosity are God-given virtues of his people toward each other. So much so that it is said; *We know that we have passed from death unto life, because we love the brethren. He that loveth not his brother abideth in death* (1 Jn 3:14).

God's people seek peace and are willing to sacrifice for it. The sheep of Christ are not rude and haughty, preferring themselves over others. They are humbled before God, and before each other, as Christ humbled himself and became obedient unto death for us. God works the same in each of his children, from the pastor in the pulpit to the youngest believer. This is the work of the almighty Spirit of grace.

To hold grudges, malice, and to be unkind to a brother or sister, is not the disposition of one whom Christ has forgiven and accepted in love. Being cold toward and ignoring anyone (especially a member of the body of Christ) is not a virtue of one that walks with God. Jealousy and envy cannot be named among those whom God has taught by experience that we too are full of sin and mistakes in this flesh. When these feelings arise in our hearts, we are immediately driven to our knees at the feet of him who has forgiven us, and again we must ask for forgiveness.

May God help us to begin this year with new commitment to him and to each other, as we are members one of another in the body of Christ. May we make a special effort to show forth the love of God in word and in deed to all the brethren, to the glory God.

Seeing ye have purified your souls in obeying the truth through the Spirit unto unfeigned love of the brethren, SEE THAT YE LOVE ONE ANOTHER WITH A PURE HEART FERVENTLY (1 Pt 1:22).

WALK IN LOVE

And walk in love, as Christ also hath loved us, and hath given himself for us an offering and a sacrifice to God for a sweetsmelling savour.
Ephesians 5:2

Here we see the motive for the performance of all duties and responsibilities (which are really privileges and blessings) of believers in regard to Christ and each other. The child of God needs no law or rules to direct him in his walk or govern his life. He has what he needs—Christ's love for him. With Christ and his love for us in view, how could we not love him and our brethren? The love of God shown in Christ giving himself for us *is shed abroad in our hearts by the Holy Ghost which is given unto us* (Rom 5:5). This love is manifest in our conversation, or walk, not just our lip service—*My little children, let us not love in word, neither in tongue; but in deed and in truth* (1 Jn 3:18).

Our Lord, constrained by love, lived his life for his sheep and died for his sheep. Because he loves his own, he now provides, protects, comforts, forgives, intercedes, and blesses us with all spiritual and temporal blessings. On this earth, he walked in love until his death, and now reigns in love at the right hand of the Father. It is his desire (which shall be accomplished) that all whom he loves shall be with him in Glory, eternally. Is this not the motive and attitude of those who know Him—To be like Him?

My brethren, because he walked in love for us, everything will be all right. As the body of Christ walks in love for Him, his Gospel and for one another, everything will be all right. As we are mere mortals, there will be difficulties, trials, and misunderstandings. However, as we walk in love, as Christ gave himself for us and loves us, we will have peace and seek peace. We will give comfort be comforted. We will forgive and be forgiven. *Seeing ye have purified your souls in obeying the truth through the Spirit unto unfeigned love of the brethren, SEE THAT YE LOVE ONE ANOTHER with a pure heart fervently* (1 Pt 1:22).

A GLORIOUS CHURCH

That he might present it to himself a glorious church, not having spot, or wrinkle, or any such thing; but that it should be holy and without blemish.
Ephesians 5:27

When we see ourselves in our own eyes, and if we could see ourselves through the eyes of others, *glorious* would not be one of the adjectives with which we would be described. Isaiah said, *Woe is me! for I am undone; because I am a man of unclean lips, and I dwell in the midst of a people of unclean lips.* Paul said, *Christ Jesus came into the world to save sinners; of whom I am chief.* Peter said, *Depart from me; for I am a sinful man, O Lord.* The child of God is very much aware of his sinful nature, yet he is aware, as well, of his new nature in the Lord Jesus Christ.

The Lord Jesus Christ gave himself for his people that he might present them to his Father a *glorious church, not having a spot, or wrinkle, or any such thing; but that it should be holy and without blemish.* The church of the living God is a glorious church, because they were loved and chosen of God in Christ before the foundation of the world. In time, the Lamb of God, according to God's eternal purpose of grace, actually (not symbolically or figuratively—[if it were such we would only be symbolically and figuratively saved]), wrought a perfect righteousness for them, was made sin for them and punished for it as their substitute, to the satisfaction of God's divine justice.

The church of the living God is a glorious church, because in time, God the Spirit, by the preaching of Christ, calls them to himself, imparting his divine nature and imputing the blessed perfect righteousness of Christ to their account. The elect of God, called by his grace, has the very life of Christ and is clothed with his righteousness. By faith he has given, we understand that in this flesh dwells no good thing, but in Christ we are accepted by the Father in the perfection of his glorious virtues.

The person of Christ, the work of Christ, and the sheep of his pasture are inseparable, for he says, *The glory which thou gavest me I have given them; that they may be one, even as We are one* (Jn 17:22). Thank God for that blessed, vital, union that we have in Christ! Let the intellectuals and theologians quibble over words and terms if they choose. The truth of God is that every child of God is justified and righteous in the Lord Jesus Christ, and is therefore glorious in his sight.

THIS IS A GREAT MYSTERY

We are members of his body, of his flesh, and of his bones.
Ephesians 5:30

Here the apostle speaks of the believer's relation with Christ, which he symbolically illustrates by the marriage relation of a husband and wife. Our spiritual union with Christ is a great mystery in that it has a divine substance and meaning, which is beyond human understanding. The believer's union with Christ is such a one of eternal origin.

We ARE chosen in him before the foundation of the world. We ARE in him when he lived upon this earth, having assumed sinless human flesh, as he fulfilled all righteousness. We ARE one with him when he expiated our sin in his death upon his cross. We ARE one with him in his resurrection and glorification. We ARE in him as he is now seated in heaven in his resurrection body.

His church (His bride) is one body, having many members, yet joined together with Him, he being the Head. Our union with Christ infinitely supersedes all human intellect, and can only be embraced as truth by divine assistance. This wondrous truth does not void the reality of our natural depravity and lost estate as the sons of Adam, nor our own guilt, which is lively in our nativity and continues in our fleshly body. Our depravity and eternal union with Christ required the person and work of our Redeemer, and the work of his Omnipotent Spirit in regeneration. The latter reveals and applies the former. The purpose of God never changes, yet his purpose changes many things, bringing all things into harmony with, and according to his purpose. The salvation of his elect church is according to his *eternal purpose of grace in Christ Jesus our Lord* (Rom 8:28-30). From election to glorification, divine Inspiration records all in the PAST AND PRESENT TENSE, revealing this union is accomplished in eternity, in time, and in the consummation, when Christ shall deliver up the kingdom to his Father. Again, *This is a great mystery: but I speak concerning Christ and the church* (Eph 5:32).

THIS VERY THING

Being confident of this very thing, that he which hath begun a good work in you will perform it until the day of Jesus Christ.
Philippians 1:6

*T*his *very thing* is not just an important thing. It is the very heart, soul, sum, and substance of the Gospel of God our Saviour. This one verse sums up the message of the whole Bible. Every context of the Scriptures declare the successful accomplishment of Jesus Christ in the flesh, in the eternal redemption of his elect unto their final glorification, according to the sovereign will and purpose of the triune God. *This very thing* is; the Redeemer of Israel did not, cannot, will not, in any way, shape, form, or fashion fail in the performance of the everlasting salvation of all those intended.

To make reference to Christ as Redeemer and conclude that he failed to redeem anyone that he intended to redeem, is a misnomer. It is a lie! Our text plainly and unequivocally declares that HE began it, and WILL PERFORM IT until its completion.

Although the Lord Jesus Christ accomplished our redemption by his vicarious death, the effects of his work is to effectually, finally, and eternally present all whom he redeemed *to himself a glorious church, not having spot, or wrinkle, or any such thing; but that it should be holy and without blemish* (Eph 5:27). If *this very thing* is not the center of the message that we preach and believe, we are not preaching the Gospel of Christ, and we have no reason for any confidence at all. Our text says that he will, not WE will.

All false religions and false preachers say the opposite. I say to you with confidence, If Jehovah (God our Saviour) has BEGUN a good work in you, he will COMPLETE that work! This is not just a matter of being doctrinally correct; this is a matter of life and death, truth and error, and the glory of God, or the exaltation of a maggot.

DOES YOUR CONVERSATION MATTER?

Let your conversation be as it becometh the gospel of Christ: . . . that ye stand fast in one spirit, with one mind striving together for the faith of the gospel.
Philippians 1:27

I am thankful that we have the promise of God to save his elect in spite of our weaknesses and failures. However, we as our Lord's representatives here on earth, have the awesome privilege and responsibility to conduct ourselves in a manner that becomes the Gospel of Christ. We can never alter God's purpose, yet it is our desire to encourage each other in the faith and encourage those we come in contact with who do not know Christ, to continue in the presence of the Gospel, knowing that this is the means whereby God calls sinners to faith in Christ.

There may be some that God sends to us that have never heard the Gospel, or faithfully attended a church at all. It is our hope they will continue to come and hear and believe. We should never coddle, pamper, praise, and overly lavish anyone with attention. However, we should always show everyone kindness, courtesy, show ourselves to be friendly, and never do or say anything to discourage. May we never compromise the truth or depend on the flesh, but may we never forget that God uses means. It is our desire that he would be pleased to use us for his glory, in the furtherance of his kingdom. There may be things that we must overlook and maybe even endure for the sake of the Gospel. I know that God's people have exercised great patience with me many times, even now. Should I not do the same?

I pray never again to be a stumblingblock or a discouragement to anyone by my own words, actions or attitude. If the Gospel offends, so be it. Whatever men do and why they do it, is between themselves and God. Whatever we do or say as professing believers, may we do and say it for the glory of God and the Gospel's sake, that his great name not be reproached because of us.

CIRCUMCISION OF THE HEART

For we are the circumcision, which worship God in the spirit, and rejoice in Christ Jesus, and have no confidence in the flesh.
Philippians 3:3

Circumcision was the distinguishing mark of the Jewish nation. It was a physical reminder of God's covenant with Abraham. It had a spiritual meaning as well. It signified purification of the heart, or an inward circumcision effected by the Spirit of the living God. Although Paul was a Jew, he was making reference to the latter. This inward circumcision of the heart has at least three characteristics, which distinguishes the *holy nation* of God from all others; even the earthly Jewish nation.

The first we see is that only the true, spiritual circumcision worships the true and living God. All others worship false gods. Only those whom God has given spiritual life in his Son in regeneration worship Him. And they ALL worship him in spirit and in truth.

Second, we see that spiritual Israel rejoices in Christ Jesus. The true child of God joys in Christ and salvation in Him—*Whom having not seen, ye love; in whom, though now ye see him not, yet believing, ye rejoice with joy unspeakable and full of glory* (1 Pt 1:8). Worshipping God and rejoicing in Christ Jesus is truly a heart work gendered by the Holy Spirit of God. It is not a ceremonial or physical effort.

Third, we see that those who worship God in Spirit and rejoice in Christ Jesus have no confidence in the flesh. The flesh is the natural man—OUR SELF. To have confidence in self as pertaining to salvation in any respect is to have no confidence in Christ. The true circumcision looks to Christ alone, by God given faith in regeneration. We look upon the flesh as vile, deplorable, wretched, and miserable. The flesh is not to be trusted—*The heart* (the natural man) *is deceitful above all things, and desperately wicked: who can know it?* (Jer 17:9). These three characteristics are the undeniable marks of a true child of God. We worship God in Spirit and in truth. We rejoice and have confidence in Jesus Christ alone.

DUNG FOR A DIAMOND

Yea doubtless, and I count all things but loss for the excellency of the knowledge of Christ Jesus my Lord: for whom I have suffered the loss of all things, and do count them but dung, that I may win Christ.
Philippians 3:8

The individual to whom Christ has been revealed in sovereign regeneration has been given a brand new perspective concerning the value of himself, and the necessity of prominence among the high and mighty of this world. Anything that would be a rival against the child of God's view of the Lord Jesus Christ is only esteemed as worthy of being cast out as filth. The worst of our filth is our best. Our own righteousness is our abomination.

Our goodness is a cesspool of iniquity. The believer's desire for Christ and his righteousness progressively and perpetually causes contempt for SELF. *I have heard of thee by the hearing of the ear: but now mine eye seeth thee. Wherefore I abhor (hate) myself, and repent in dust and ashes* (Jb 42:5-6). This is not progressive sanctification; this is the effect of growing in grace and knowledge of Christ. Although nothing changes as to our relationship with Christ, we increasingly have a clearer view of him and of ourselves.

By God's grace we will finally realize we have given up nothing! What is dung compared to a diamond? What is this world compared to Christ? Who am I compared to Christ? There is nothing to compare with the glory, beauty, and worth of Christ; being found in him and clothed in his righteousness.

> "He is all my righteousness!
> I stand in him complete
> and worship Him!"

We hear a lot in religious circles about self-esteem and how to be better Christians, thereby attaining more of what we desire in this world and in the end a greater reward in heaven. This does nothing more than cultivate the anti-Christ self-righteousness that dominates the proud hearts of every unbeliever. The child of God is made to give it up daily.

We are constrained to be in agreement with the inspired words of the Apostle, *For I know that in me (that is, in my flesh,) dwelleth no good thing* (Rom 7:18).

THAT I MAY KNOW HIM!

That I may know Him, and the power of his resurrection, and the fellowship of his sufferings, being made conformable unto his death.

Philippians 3:10

That I may know the Lord Jesus Christ! Not just know some THINGS about Him, but to KNOW HIM in the sweet fellowship of his Word and Spirit—to know Him, to see Him, to hear Him, and to commune with him here in faith, which he has given; soon to be in his presence forever! Do I count all else but dung that I may know Him? Does all else disappear into nothingness in the light of his glory? Does all that I am in this flesh melt into a cesspool of muck, as I look upon the Lamb of God? If not, then I fear I do not know Him. If yes, then I rejoice with unspeakable joy in the knowledge of him that is altogether lovely! *I know whom I have believed* (2 Tm 1:12).

FORGET IT!

Forgetting those things which are behind, and reaching forth unto those things which are before, I press toward the mark for the prize of the high calling of God in Christ Jesus.
Philippians 3:13

The child of God is constantly aware of the blessings of yesterday, as he remembers God's hand of mercy and grace upon him both spiritually and providentially. These things we are not to forget, but we can not rely upon and rest in those things which are behind. We are to *lay aside every weight, and the sin which doth so easily beset us* (today), *and let us run with patience the race that is set before us* (today) (Heb 12:1).

Yesterday is past and *ye know not what shall be on the morrow* (Jas 4:14).

We live by faith. *Now the just shall live by faith* (Heb 10:38).

We walk by faith. *For we walk by faith, not by sight* (2 Cor 5:7).

We stand by faith. *For by faith ye stand* (2 Cor 1:24).

Therefore we die in faith. *These all died in faith* (Heb 11:13).

Our life's work as a child of God is not done until faith is done—today's faith! The Apostle said, *I have fought a good fight, I have finished my course, I have kept the faith* (2 Tm 4:7). We are not saved by works, we are saved by grace through faith. Yet, it is equally true that *as the body without the spirit is dead, so faith without works is dead also* (Jas 2:26). DEAD FAITH is no faith at all. The believer must not look back and be at ease or presume with good intensions on tomorrow, but rather look to Christ today and press forward by faith.

It is good to remember the work that God has done in us, but we are to forget it as our necessary substance for today. Today we must *reach forth unto those things which are before, and press toward the mark for the prize of the high calling of God in Christ Jesus.* Salvation is a present work of grace in the heart carried on by faith that God gives. Faith in Christ is sufficient for today, and it will be sufficient for tomorrow as well.

ENEMIES OF CHRIST

For many walk, of whom I have told you often, and now tell you even weeping, that they are the enemies of the cross of Christ:
Philippians 3:18

Throughout eternity, the person and redemptive work of the Lord Jesus Christ will shine as the gemstone of the revealed purpose of almighty God. The incarnation of Christ, and his work of redemption in the salvation of the elect, is the heart and soul of all that God has done and is doing in the creation of all things. It is the beauty and glory of heaven. The person and work of Christ is the theme of all Scripture, and he is the Lamb in the midst of the throne in heaven. He is the light, life, and joy of the saints on earth, and the wonder of saints and angels in glory. He glorified the Father here on earth, and is now glorified with the glory that he had with the Father, *before the world was* (Jn 17:5).

All the attributes and virtues of God are wonderfully, explicitly, yet incomprehensibly, displayed in the glorious person and perfect redemption of sinful men by the Lord Jesus Christ.

To mar this glorious truth with man and his demented religion would be the work of a madman. The proponents of so-called free will and human merit are enemies of God and his Christ, and enemies of men's souls. Christ alone is worthy of praise, honor, and glory, because he alone redeemed us to God by his *own blood* (Heb 9:12). This is his people's song here on earth and in heaven; *And they sung a new song, saying, THOU ART WORTHY to take the book, and to open the seals thereof: for thou wast slain, and hast redeemed us to God by thy blood out of every kindred, and tongue, and people, and nation* (Rv 5:9).

THE ELECTION RESULTS ARE IN

Knowing, brethren beloved, your election of God.
1 Thessalonians 1:4

I never cease to be amazed (although I shouldn't be) that so many make the mere knowledge of a system of doctrine to be their anchor of hope for eternal salvation. Nothing could be more deadly than holding the truth of God in unrighteousness, *for the wrath of God is revealed from heaven against all ungodliness and unrighteousness of men, who hold the truth in unrighteousness* (Rom 1:18). As is clearly revealed in our text, those who are chosen by God the Father, redeemed by God the Son, and regenerated by God the Spirit not only believe the truth, they also have a new heart, a new Spirit, and therefore a new life.

The elect of God upon regeneration love Christ and believe all truth as is revealed in Him. The result of divine election in Christ is a new creature. They not only have a HEAD for sound doctrine, they have a *new HEART* for Christ. It is obvious when CALVINISTS, THE REFORMED, or anyone, argues, debates, and glories in points of DOCTRINE, they are preaching themselves rather than Christ Jesus the Lord. It is amazing (although it shouldn't be) how men love to amuse themselves with themselves, rather than simply and singularly preaching Christ and all truth in Him.

My question is, DO WE KNOW CHRIST IN VITAL UNION BY HIS BLESSED SPIRIT, OR HAVE WE LEARNED SOME DOCTRINE? Have we come to CHRIST by his efficacious grace, or have we come to THE DOCTRINES? Precept without the PERSON is cold, hard, legal, dead and damning. The greatest evidence of being one of God's elect is believing on Christ, falling in love with Christ, resting in Christ, joying and rejoicing in Christ, and as a result, commitment to his Gospel and his church.

Yes, I believe the five points. They are the summation of the Gospel. However, the knowledge of them is not my salvation. Again, the result of divine election is *that they might know thee the only true God, and Jesus Christ, whom thou hast sent* (Jn 17:3).

Conclusion: One may learn doctrine and yet may never know Christ. However, everyone that knows Christ believes and loves the truth.

IN EVERYTHING GIVE THANKS

In every thing give thanks: for this is the will of God in Christ Jesus concerning you.
1 Thessalonians 5:18

The child of God has every reason to be thankful. We are truly thankful to him for all things, both spiritual and providential. He has given us the knowledge that all things to us-ward who believe are for his glory and for our good—*And we know that all things work together for good to them that love God, to them who are the called according to [His] purpose* (Rom 8:28).

The Psalmist said in Psalm 116:12, *What shall I render unto the LORD [for] all his benefits toward me? He* proceeds to answer the question this way: Worship, praise, thanksgiving and obedience. As he contemplates the multitude of God's tender mercies toward him, he is overwhelmed, and so are we. This realization brings us in worship and submission to the feet of him who loved us and gave himself for us. For this we must thank him as well, for it is only by his grace that we bow to his loving Lordship.

As we have been permitted to come together with our brethren, family, and friends this past week, may we look back and TRULY THANK HIM FOR ALL THINGS.

PURPOSE AND PROVIDENCE

And the very God of peace sanctify you wholly; and I pray God your whole spirit and soul and body be preserved blameless unto the coming of our Lord Jesus Christ. Faithful is he that calleth you, who also will do it.

1 Thessalonians 5:23-24

Divine providence is the unfolding of divine purpose in time. God's eternal purpose and providence is essentially and vitally connected with the Lord Jesus Christ, his redemption of those whom he has loved with an everlasting love, and his bringing them to eternal glory. All things in time are ordained by Almighty God to this glorious two-fold end; the glory of God and the eternal good of the children of God—*And we know that all things work together for good to them that love God, to them who are the called according to his purpose* (Rom 8:28). Everything, EVERYTHING! that transpires in time, from beginning to end, is concerned with the salvation and preservation of God's elect, and his glory therein.

There is no person or no thing brought into existence that does not move according to his great design. Every atom is subject of divine omnipotence to the praise of the glory of the same. Therefore, we confidently conclude without fear or trepidation that God and his Christ is and will be glorified in all things. We, his people, are saved with an everlasting salvation.

My brethren be assured, every trial, sorrow, affliction, failure, success, joy, and happiness, is meticulously attended by divine Omniscience: Omnipresence and scrutiny, to perfection—

Faithful is he that calleth you, who also will do it. Our Lord Jesus Christ, *who being the brightness of his glory, and the express image of his person, and upholding all things by the word of his power, when he had by himself purged our sins, sat down on the right hand of the Majesty on high* (Heb 1:3). May our God give us rest in his blessed Son, knowing that present and future history is charted by unfailing love and certain success.

THANK YOU, THANK YOU, THANK YOU

We are bound to thank God always for you, brethren, as it is meet, because that your faith groweth exceedingly, and the charity of every one of you all toward each other aboundeth.
2 Thessalonians 1:3

I understand that a true child of God does not covet glory and honor for himself for the deeds that he does for others. We know we receive every thing from our Heavenly Father, and he must receive the glory. Sometimes, we even cringe when someone recognizes us or gives us a heartfelt THANK YOU.

When I say I THANK YOU, I truly THANK YOU! I appreciate you and the expression of love you have shown. There is an UNSPOKEN UNDERSTANDING among the family of God when we say THANK YOU, that without him we would have nothing and could do nothing. He alone is ultimately worthy of praise and thanksgiving. Therefore, with this understanding, it is always good to convey our gratitude to others for their kindness with a hardy THANK YOU! How rude it would be to never say THANK YOU!

Having said all of that, Robin and I THANK YOU, THANK YOU, THANK YOU. *We are bound to thank God always for you, brethren, as it is meet.*

UNBELIEVING CHRISTIANS?

But we are bound to give thanks alway to God for you, brethren beloved of the Lord, because God hath from the beginning chosen you to salvation through sanctification of the Spirit and belief of the truth.

2 Thessalonians 2:13

There is no such animal as a Bible believing Christian that doesn't know and believe the Gospel of God's redeeming grace in the Lord Jesus Christ. However, there are those who perpetually promote themselves by trying to bridge the gulf between free will, Armenian, works religion, and the Gospel of the free grace of God. There is absolutely no agreement between the two.

Gospel preachers and Christians don't have a need to return to the Gospel. By the grace of God, they have ALREADY come to Christ, and they DO believe and preach the Gospel. Those who don't believe it and preach it have not yet been regenerated and called. Regeneration by God the Spirit, and belief of the Gospel is the distinguishing difference.

The preaching of the Gospel is the means whereby God, in sovereign grace and mercy, calls his elect to faith in Christ Jesus. *For after that in the wisdom of God the world by wisdom knew not God, it pleased God by the foolishness of preaching to save them that believe* (1 Cor 1:21). There is not one whom God has called by his Spirit, and revealed the Lord Jesus Christ to, that continues to follow false preachers and a false Gospel. *When he putteth forth his own sheep, he goeth before them, and the sheep follow Him: for they know his voice. And a stranger will they not follow, but will flee from him: for they know not the voice of strangers* (Jn 10:4-5).

The revelation of Christ to a dead sinner is salvation and the revelation of the truth. *In whom ye also trusted, after that ye heard the word of truth, the gospel of your salvation: in whom also after that ye believed, ye were sealed with that Holy Spirit of promise* (Eph 1:13).

Are there those who are saved (Christians) who do not believe and love the Gospel? Emphatically NO! *But ye believe not, because ye are not of my sheep, as I said unto you* (Jn 10:26).

ETERNAL REDEMPTION

In whom we have redemption through his blood, even the forgiveness of sins.
Colossians 1:14

The exact and effectual redemption of God Almighty's elect church is an eternal redemption secured by one man, the Lord Jesus Christ, God's sacrificial Lamb. The redemption accomplished in time by our surety did not originate in time; neither will it cease in time. Christ is the *Lamb slain from the foundation of the world* (Rv 13:8). He was the Lamb on the cross (1 Pt 1:18-20), and he is now the Lamb in the midst of the throne (Rv 7:17). Time makes no impression on the purpose of God. The purpose of God dictates all past, present, and future history in time. Therefore, we have redemption in Christ through his blood, even the forgiveness of sins, without beginning and without end, according to God's eternal purpose of grace.

Christ died for us in time, and we are given faith and regenerated in time, as a result of God's everlasting love for us manifested in the vicarious blood-shedding of the Christ of God. *We have redemption* can only be said of and by those who have Christ—*But of him are ye in Christ Jesus, who of God is made unto us wisdom, and righteousness, and sanctification, and redemption* (1 Cor 1:30). This will never change! Heaven and earth shall pass away, but the redeemed have never been and will never be unredeemed! *For thou wast slain, and hast redeemed us to God by thy blood out of every kindred, and tongue, and people, and nation* (Rv 5:9).

Christ has obtained that which the triune God purposed. His people have obtained it as well, because he obtained it for us. *Neither by the blood of goats and calves, but by his own blood he entered in once into the holy place, having obtained eternal redemption for us* (Heb 9:12). Away with universal redemption and the free will of man! Thank God for his free will in the eternal redemption of once dead, chosen sinners—Even the forgiveness of sins!

THE FORGIVENESS OF SINS

In whom we have redemption through his blood, even the forgiveness of sins.
Colossians 1:14

All sin originates in the heart, and is against God. All mankind are sinners by virtue of our fallen nature. We do what we do because we are what we are. We sin because we are sinners. The forgiveness that counts must come from the one who is sinned against—God!

With him THERE IS FORGIVENESS. *If thou, LORD, shouldest mark iniquities, O Lord, who shall stand? But there is forgiveness with thee, that thou mayest be feared* (Ps 130:3-4).

Forgiveness of sin with the Lord is much more than just words. Sin must be actually and completely put away forever—*I will forgive their iniquity, and I will remember their sin no more* (Jer 31:34). The motive for forgiveness of sin is the eternal love of God. The work of forgiveness is the substitutionary work of the Lord Jesus Christ. Because God DID love his people, and has ALWAYS loved his people, he sent his Son to put away their sin by the sacrifice of himself. *Herein is love, not that we loved God, but that he loved us, and sent his Son to be the propitiation for our sins* (1 Jn 4:10).

The forgiveness of our sin originated in the heart, mind, and purpose of God, and was accomplished in time in the person and work of Christ, *In whom* (Christ) *we have redemption through his blood, even the forgiveness of sins* (Col 1:14). Not only are our sins forgiven in Christ, WE are forgiven!

The proof, or evidence, of our being forgiven is God given faith in Christ. This faith of God's elect reveals to us our acceptance before God in Christ. He *hath made us accepted in the Beloved. In whom we have redemption through his blood, the forgiveness of sins, according to the riches of his grace* (Eph 1:6-7). Faith reveals to us that we are not under the condemnation of the law of God, because we are forgiven in Christ. *There is therefore now no condemnation to them which are in Christ Jesus* (Rom 8:1).

Therefore, it is by the grace of God alone that we are forgiven. There is no way that man can atone for sin, or make himself acceptable before God, by some outward reformation. Forgiving is what God does, without our help. If we seek forgiveness, it is because we ARE forgiven, and by his grace we will know that we are.

Be it known unto you therefore, men and brethren, that through THIS MAN is preached unto you the forgiveness of sins: And BY HIM all that believe are justified from all things, from which ye could not be justified by the law of Moses (Acts 13:38-39).

NEW PRINCIPLES OR NEW LIFE?

To whom God would make known what is the riches of the glory of this mystery among the Gentiles; which is Christ in you, the hope of glory

Colossians 1:27

A PRINCIPLE is an underlying law or assumption required in a system of thought. New or different principles may be acquired by serious and deliberate determination of the mind and ability of the intellect. The result is a change in the manner of our thinking, and consequently is manifest in our behavior and actions. This is possible and attainable by the natural man if he so desires.

This is not necessarily new life. It is rearranging the old. Therefore it is conceivable that one may convert to Calvinism (the doctrines) by mere exercise of the intellect, and yet remain spiritually dead. New life, spiritual life, is obtained ONLY by the regenerating work of the omnipotent God imparting the righteous Lord Jesus Christ to the once dead sinner. The believer now lives by Christ IN him, not new principles. I know this is a great mystery and inconceivable to the natural man, but it is so; *To whom God would make known what is the riches of the glory of this mystery among the Gentiles; which is Christ in you, the hope of glory* (Col 1:27).

Knowledge of the truth of things is not life. Christ is life—*When Christ, who is* (notice w*ho is* is supplied) *our life, shall appear, then shall ye also appear with him in glory* (Col 3:4). With life in Christ, there is indeed new principles. However, these new principles are the operation of the new heart, which is governed by desire and love for Christ, and the knowledge of Him. In truth then, *Christ liveth in me: and the life which I now live in the flesh I live by the faith of the Son of God, who loved me, and gave himself for me* Gal 2:20).

Having a new nature, the believer is now in constant warfare with the old man; *For I know that in me (that is, in my flesh,) dwelleth no good thing* (Rom 7:18). NOW HE CANNOT EVEN TRUST HIS KNOWLEDGE, he must look to Christ alone for assurance. This is the operation of the grace of God in the new heart.

May God help us to examine ourselves, *whether ye be in the faith; prove your own selves. Know ye not your own selves, how that Jesus Christ is in you, except ye be reprobates?* (2 Cor 13:5).

COMPLETE

And ye are complete in Him, which is the head of all principality and power.

Colossians 2:10

COMPLETENESS in the positive spiritual sense has been a stranger to mankind since the fall of Adam. Man is complete only in the sense that he is completely sinful, and completely spiritually dead, which is negative as to his relationship with God. Proverbs 27:20 says that *the eyes of man are never satisfied.* COMPLETE suggests being whole, fulfilled, satisfied, nothing lacking. In man there is a void, an emptiness, which he continually attempts to fill with all that he knows to utilize, which is all that is in the world—the lust of the flesh, the lust of the eye, and the pride of life.

So man spends his life trying to fill an abyss with things that are perpetually changing and dying. Any happiness, contentment, satisfaction, or gratification is temporary and short lived that is derived from the things of the world. Only those who have the Lord Jesus Christ as the Object or their faith and Anchor of their soul are complete. This completeness, where it really matters, is the believer's relationship with God and his satisfaction. All the elect are complete in Christ and therefore accepted by God in Him. By revelation in regeneration, the child of God, by faith, is enabled to see and enjoy this relationship, and therefore looks to Christ. He finds peace, satisfaction, contentment and fulfillment, which is not of this world, and which is eternal, everlasting, and therefore complete.

Those that continually seek out the things of the world to find happiness and contentment are in a sad state, because their world and dreams are vanishing, and will soon disappear before their eyes. Those that are complete in Christ and look to him for all things are in a happy state, and will soon leave this world where every thing is temporary. We will be no more complete then, than now. However, we will be able to enjoy Christ without the cares and temptations of this fleshly tabernacle in which we live in this world. Where, and to whom, do we find ourselves looking to find consolation and happiness; to ourselves and the things of the world, or to Christ?

The child of God is *Looking unto Jesus the Author and Finisher of our faith; who for the joy that was set before him endured the cross, despising the shame, and is set down at the right hand of the throne of God* (Heb 12:2).

"CHRIST, WHO IS OUR LIFE"

When Christ, who is our life, shall appear, then shall ye also appear with him in glory.
Colossians 3:4

Our life consists of that which captivates our affections. Those things that we love, cherish, and hold dear to our heart are the center of our life. Our thoughts, time, and attention are drawn toward, and gravitate around, that which excites our senses and brings us pleasure. The Lord Jesus Christ and the things of God is the center, sum, and substance of the believer's life. The apostle Paul said it this way; *For to me to live is Christ* (Phil 1:21).

If Christ is not our life here, then when he shall appear, we will not be with him in glory. The believer does the things that he must do, to the end he can do that which he desires to do—that is to be taken up with the things of God. God has taught us, and is teaching us, that *life is more than meat, and the body is more than raiment* (Lk 12:23). He does this by revealing the beauty of the person of the Lord Jesus Christ to our hearts, and keeping him ever before us. The child of God is not consumed with the things of the world. We are in the world but not of the world. *Love not the world, neither the things that are in the world. If any man love the world, the love of the Father is not in him* (1 Jn 2:15).

The people of God are committed to Christ and his church. Not just outwardly, but inwardly as well. To the believer duty becomes a privilege, and faithfulness a way of life. Christ, who is our life, is the strength by which we perform, and the zeal by which we accomplish, that which he works in us for his glory and our good. To those that know him, The Lord Jesus Christ is not just someone to save them from hell and take them to heaven; not just someone to heal them when they are sick; not just someone to rescue them from their troubles. He is their life!

He that hath the Son hath life; and he that hath not the Son of God hath not life (1 Jn 5:12).

THE BELIEVER'S DISPOSITION

Put on therefore, as the elect of God, holy and beloved, bowels of
mercies, kindness, humbleness of mind, meekness, longsuffering.
Colossians 3:12

This verse, as well as the preceding and following verses,
reveals how our deportment and disposition should be, as
becomes a child of God. Our attitude toward others, especially
those who profess to know Christ and believe his Gospel, is one
of love and tenderness. They may not always fit our mold as to
how we think they should be and do, yet we must be kind and
patient, and always try to give them the benefit of the doubt,
knowing that our judgments are imperfect as well. It is never
becoming to our profession to be rude, withdrawn, and callous
toward others. It is love and kindness that heals and helps, rather
than indifference and coldness.

I am not saying that we should agree with everyone and
everything, compromising what we know to be the truth. I am
saying that as much as God will give us grace in our hearts, we
are to be approachable and friendly. *A man that hath friends must*
shew himself friendly: and there is a friend that sticketh closer
than a brother (Prv 18:24). Speak kindly and be hospitable to all
men, especially those who profess to know Christ, even when
maybe sometimes others are not so with us.

Often we tend to show our feelings of disagreement with
others by intentionally ignoring them and distancing ourselves.
Many times these issues have nothing to do with the Gospel
directly, and our fellowship and friendship can be maintained, if

we would but be consistent in our attitude of love toward the brethren. I may disagree with you, but may God help me to be kind and approachable, as one that cares.

IS THERE HOPE?

Paul, an apostle of Jesus Christ by the commandment of God our Saviour, and Lord Jesus Christ, our hope.
1 Timothy 1:1

Almost everyone has a *hope*. Some hope there is no God. Some hope physical death is the end. Some hope in Buda. Some hope in Mohammad. Some hope in the pope. A vast multitude of folks among Calvinists, Arminians, Baptists, Methodists, Presbyterians, and Pentecostals, etc., hope in themselves. Their hope is their works and intellect. However, those who hope in any one or any thing, other than the Lord Jesus Christ and his righteousness, really have no hope. The hope of the child of God is more than an anticipation of heaven and the avoidance of hell. Our hope is a person, the Lord Jesus Christ— *Looking for* THAT BLESSED HOPE, *and the glorious appearing of* THE GREAT GOD AND OUR SAVIOUR JESUS CHRIST (Ti 2:13).

The hope of the believer is a present hope. That is to say, not just wishing that something might transpire in the future— WHICH HOPE WE HAVE *as an anchor of the soul, both sure and steadfast, and which entereth into that within the veil* (Heb 6:19). The hope of the child of God is a living hope, not just a documented creed or contract, but a hope that *ever lives* within the veil *to make intercession for us.* If we were drowning, it would be better to be in the arms of a lifeguard than just

KNOWING there was a wooden throne on the beach with a sign that says LIFEGUARD.

Where THIS HOPE is, there is no danger or despair—*who shall separate us from the love of Christ? [shall] tribulation, or distress, or persecution, or famine, or nakedness, or peril, or sword? As it is written, For thy sake we are killed all the day long; we are accounted as sheep for the slaughter. Nay, in all these things we are more than conquerors through him that loved us. For I am persuaded, that neither death, nor life, nor angels, nor principalities, nor powers, nor things present, nor things to come, Nor height, nor depth, nor any other creature, shall be able to separate us from the love of God, which is in Christ Jesus our Lord* (Rom 8:35-39).

SAVED, SAVED & SAVED!

Who hath saved us, and called us with an holy calling, not according to our works, but according to his own purpose and grace, which was given us in Christ Jesus before the world began.

2 Timothy 1:9

Paul, an apostle of the Lord Jesus Christ, writes to the young evangelist Timothy (and to all believers) by the inspiration of God, denouncing salvation by our works, and insisting the salvation of his elect is by his own purpose and grace, and is an eternal salvation. The phrase *who hath saved us* reveals three vital Gospel truths which are stated in this verse's context.

1. We learn our being *saved* was something that was a DONE DEAL from all eternity—*before the world began.*

2. We learn the elect's salvation was necessarily wrought by the person and redemptive work of Christ our Lord in the wondrous display of his grace, as our substitute and sacrifice. The execution of our ordained salvation was completely accomplished by our Redeemer when he said, *It is finished, and bowed his head and gave up the Ghost.*

3. Only those to whom Christ has revealed himself can truthfully say, "I am SAVED," and that because he *hath called us with a holy calling,* and made us *partakers of the divine nature.* Upon regeneration we can truthfully say, he *hath saved us* in eternity by purpose, decree, predestination and covenant—all in Christ. Beloved, now we can say, *we are the sons of God* (1 Jn 3:2).

Our salvation has always been secure in our surety, but we didn't know it in time until we heard the Gospel of our salvation and believed—*In whom ye also trusted, after that ye heard the word of truth, the gospel of your salvation: in whom also after that ye believed, ye were sealed with that holy Spirit of promise,* (Eph 1:13), and were given life by his omnipotent Spirit—*according to his mercy he SAVED US, by the washing of regeneration, and renewing of the Holy Ghost* (Ti 3:5).

We were *saved* before the world began. We were *saved* when Christ died for us. We were *saved* when he quickened us who were dead in trespasses and sin. We are *saved* eternally.

THE GLORIOUS GOSPEL

According to the glorious gospel of the blessed God, which was committed to my trust.

1 Timothy 1:11

There are very few things GLORIOUS in this world. GLORIOUS essentially means, HAVING OR RADIATING THE PERFECTIONS OF THE DIVINE. Certainly, nothing connected with fallen man could truthfully be termed as "glorious." This adjective can only describe things that are not of this world; things far superior to that of corruptible flesh.

IN and OF have two very different meanings. Our Lord makes the distinction clear—*And now I am no more IN the world, but these are IN the world, . . .They are not OF the world, even as I am not OF the world* (Jn 17:11, 16).

All glorious things in this world are connected with the *GLORIOUS GOSPEL OF OUR BLESSED GOD!* Paul wrote, *According to the glorious gospel of the blessed God, which was committed to my trust* (1 Tm 1:11). The Gospel is glorious because it is of God. The Gospel is in the world, but not of the world. The Word of God is not the word of man, but the WORD OF GOD! We are assured that, *For ever, 0 LORD, thy word is settled in heaven* (Ps 119: 89).

The saints are IN the world, but they are not OF this world. They are not born of this world—*Being born again, not of corruptible seed, but of incorruptible, by the Word of God, which liveth and abideth for ever* (1 Pt 1:23). Neither are they citizens of this world. The children of God are, *no more strangers and foreigners, but fellowcitizens with the saints, and of the household of God* (Eph 2:19).

The children of God IN the world, but who are not OF the world, *are a chosen generation, a royal priesthood, an holy nation, a peculiar people; that ye should show forth the praises (glory) of him who hath called you out of darkness into his marvellous light. Which in time past were not a people, but are now the people of God: which had not obtained mercy, but now have obtained mercy.* The Gospel of God is glorious, and all that it begets is glorious. All that is not connected with the Gospel will perish. All that is connected with the Gospel, in which the glory of God is revealed in the Face of Jesus Christ, will radiate God's glory here in this world, and the world to come. *For all flesh is as grass, and all the glory of man as the flower of grass. The grass withereth, and the flower thereof falleth away: But the word of the Lord endureth for ever. And this is the word which by the gospel is preached unto you* (1 Pt 1: 24-25).

THE GLORIOUS GOSPEL

The glorious gospel of the blessed God.
1 Timothy 1:11

Glorious means WONDERFUL, MAGNIFICENT, SPLENDID. To me, these adjectives seem much too weak to describe the Gospel of God's free and sovereign grace in Christ. To the sinful soul (namely mine), who has been brought to the Lamb of God, forgiven all sin, clothed with the righteousness of Christ, and accepted by God the Father into his everlasting Kingdom, there is no mind to comprehend, or tongue to tell, of the glory and preciousness of the *gospel of the blessed God!*

The *glorious gospel* reveals four great truths from which all truth springs, and are vital in the begetting of spiritual life in the hearts of chosen sinners:

1. WHO GOD IS. God the Father, in the Trinity of his sacred persons, is God Almighty in his glorious attributes and infinite being. He is the one God of heaven, earth and all places, unto whom all men, angels, powers, and principalities are subject. He is omniscient, omnipotent and omnipresent!

2. WHO JESUS CHRIST THE LORD IS. HE is God Incarnate. He is the God-man in whom all the fulness of the Godhead dwells bodily. He is he who was made flesh and dwelt among us; full of grace and truth; full of truth to reveal God; full of grace to redeem his people; separate from sinners; in whom is no sin; he who is now seated in the throne of God; ruling and reigning for his church, as their Great High Priest and intercessor.

3. THE SINFULNESS AND DEPRAVITY OF THE HUMAN HEART. All men are spiritually dead by nature. Man by his first birth is a God hater and a rebel. There is not one spark of spiritual life inside or outside mankind. Man has no ability to do anything to commend himself to God; neither does he have the desire to do so. His mind, heart and ways are against God. Man is a sinner against God Almighty.

4. SALVATION IS BY THE PURPOSE, GRACE AND POWER OF GOD; manifested and wrought in the person and work of God's Son, the Lord Jesus Christ, and revealed to his people by the preaching of the Gospel. Christ's sheep are totally, fully, completely, and finally saved by the grace of God apart from any works of man—*by grace are you saved* (Eph 2:8).

I believe this is *the glorious gospel of the blessed God.* It is more wonderful than words can describe, to those who know Him.

THE OLD, OLD STORY!

This is a faithful saying, and worthy of all acceptation, that CHRIST JESUS CAME INTO THE WORLD TO SAVE SINNERS; *of whom I am chief.*

1 Timothy 1:15

When I was a little boy, my Uncle Boss would tell me stories of things which happened to him when he was young. I loved to hear them over and over again. It seemed as if I was present in his experience. There was one or two favorites that I would always ask him to tell. Those stories, although old, never grew old to me. They were always new and exciting.

This is the way it is when a child of God hears the Gospel of our Lord Jesus Christ. It is the same, yet never grows old or boring. It is new and exciting every time we hear of our Redeemer and his great love for us. This is our favorite story, so much so that we desire no other. Only those, and all those, whom he lovingly relates it to, are mesmerized by the substance of it and the sweet tones by which it falls upon the ear of the heart and soul. Late in the evening, after Uncle Boss's work was finished, I would anticipate sitting by him on the front porch and listening to him repeat those stories! The child of God looks forward with great anticipation to meeting with other believers and hearing God's preacher tell them, one more time, of him who loved them and gave his life for them—*I was glad when they said unto me, Let us go into the house of the* LORD (Ps 122:1). This faithful saying, and the ONE that is worthy of all acceptation, is worth repeating over and over and over again—*Christ Jesus came into the world to save sinners!*

This story, though as old as God himself, is always timely, soothing, and refreshing to the quivering, thirsty heart that hungers and thirsts after the Water of life. *As the hart panteth after the water brooks, so panteth my soul after thee, O God* (Ps 42:1). No one made me cross the road to hear Boss's stories. Often I was there before he was, waiting for him! I would drop what ever I was doing and high-tail it over there! It was where I wanted to be.

Who loves the Gospel and who doesn't, is evident. You will find those who love it on the FRONT PORCH waiting, because they have a need for, and only find satisfaction and comfort in, Christ in the Gospel, and the Gospel in Christ. Those who do not love the Gospel, will probably be found looking over some land they bought, or proving an ox, or bonding with their spouse (Lk 14:18-20), or anything else that comes up that is satisfying and gratifying to the fleshly appetite.

THE HEART OF THE GOSPEL

This is a faithful saying, and worthy of all acceptation, that Christ Jesus came into the world to save sinners.
1 Timothy 1:15

There is no debate. Tthere is no other message declared in the Bible, other than Christ Jesus the Lord. In his name, person, and work is all the revealed will of God concerning himself, and the redemption of his people. SALVATION IS BY HIM ALONE, IN HIM ALONE, AND FOR HIS GLORY ALONE—This is the Gospel (Good News!). Some would attempt to bring man into the

308

picture, and give the creature credibility and glory in the matter of salvation, perverting the Gospel of God, but they have already failed in their self-righteous pursuits. Christ has already accomplished the work predestinated by God from all eternity. What hope! What peace! What comfort for poor, wretched sinners, who other-wise could have no hope! To God be the glory; Great things he has done! A so-called Gospel that cunningly inserts man's will, man's works, man's intellect, or man's anything as a share-holder of Christ's glory and work is no Gospel at all. Rather, it is the thesis of a blundering fool who knows neither God or his Son.

The HEART of the Gospel is just that—The HEART of Christ! All true doctrine is manifest in the person and work of CHRIST. Religion is knowing ABOUT Christ. Salvation is KNOWING CHRIST! Religion is knowing DOCTRINE. Salvation is KNOWING THE CHRIST of the doctrine!

Now as always, there are those who would rather argue and debate, and make issues of things that neither they or their hearers can comprehend, than plainly and singularly declare the glory of God in Christ to undeserving sinners such as ourselves.

Not to minimize the importance and necessity of doctrinal truth, but rather point men to where it is found, where it is preached, and where salvation is promised. *I determined not to know any thing among you, save Jesus Christ, and him crucified* (1 Cor 2:2).

What I am saying is this: If we dot all the I's, cross all the T's, and cover all the points, not knowing and preaching Christ with a believing and knowing heart, the heart of the Gospel is not there. Just as well, it is impossible to preach Christ and not set forth true and sound doctrine.

CONTENTMENT – GREAT GAIN

But godliness with contentment is great gain.
1 Timothy 6:6

Men of corrupt minds, and destitute of the truth, suppose that gain is godliness, and seek contentment in materialism, using religion as a means of advancement. This is the commentary of all false professors and religions from the pew to the pulpit. This is nothing more or less than a system of works clothed with self-righteousness.

Godliness is being in agreement with God, and being content with all that he does. Godliness and contentment has more to do with the inward man than the outward man, although what we are inwardly is manifested in who we are and what we do outwardly. Such were Simon Magus and his followers (Acts 8:9-13). The unbeliever can only be satisfied when he has what he desires materially, physically, and emotionally. But when this is achieved, it is short-lived, because *the eyes of man are never satisfied* (Prv 27:20).

The believer seeks and finds happiness, pleasure, and contentment in the God of providence and the providence of God. Any other way is not gain, but rather a snare. The heart of the unsaved religionist will choose that which satisfies his fleshly desires, and makes his place in this world feel more secure, over the things of God every time. Most of the time his choice is seen outwardly. *Be content with such things as ye have: for he hath said, I will never leave thee, nor forsake thee* (Heb 13:5), is not just a rule to follow for the believer, it is a way of life. Those whom God is teaching to be content in this world are not of this world. They have the fruit of the Spirit which is *love, joy, peace, longsuffering, gentleness, goodness, faith, meekness, temperance: against such there is no law. And they that are Christ's have crucified the flesh with the affections and lusts* (Gal 5:22-24).

DOUBT AND UNBELIEF

For the which cause I also suffer these things: nevertheless I am not ashamed: for I know whom I have believed, and am persuaded that he is able to keep that which I have committed unto him against that day.
2 Timothy 1:12

Every child of God struggles with doubt, at times. We question our relationship with Christ. Am I His? Do I really know Him? Am I only going through the form and ceremony of religion? Have I just come into agreement with a doctrine? We say that we do not doubt Him, but that we doubt ourselves—we question our own experience. Although some will not admit it, we all sometime have these thoughts and uneasy feelings. The truth is, we are not doubting ourselves, we are really doubting Him. Doubtful feelings do not come from the faith which he has given. These feeling and thoughts are dishonoring to him who is *able to save them to the uttermost that come unto God by Him, seeing he ever liveth to make intercession for them* (Heb 7:25).

The Apostle, giving glory to Christ said *I know whom I have believed, and am persuaded that he is able to keep that which I have committed unto him against that day* (2 Tm 1:12). It is when we are looking to ourselves for merit and acceptance before God, rather than Christ, that doubts and unbelief arise in our hearts. It is true, we are admonished to examine ourselves, and to never presume upon the grace of God, yet be assured that nothing can separate us from the love of God which is in Christ Jesus our Lord (Rom 8:38-39). The great sins of doubt and unbelief are to be repented of, as well as all sins of the flesh (1 Jn 1:9).

THE EXPERIENCE OF LIFE

I know whom I have believed, and am persuaded that he is able to keep that which I have committed unto him against that day.
2 Timothy 1:12

To have something and have no experience of, or experience with, that which we have, would be comparable to being alive, but in a comatose state. It would be like marriage to the love of our life, yet never seeing or being with, or having met the one whom we love. Would this not be a miserable (or maybe an impossible) existence? Is this the portion for God's children while we are here in this world? Is this what God has ordained for his people? Are we to have only the mere knowledge of him and not have the presence of his life, love, mercy and grace, and be partakers of his divine nature (2 Pt 1:4)? What about the faith in Christ that gives peace, joy and rest in our hearts, and enables us to worship him in Spirit, *For the kingdom of God is not meat and drink; but righteousness, and peace, and joy in the Holy Ghost* (Rom 14:17).

What about the blessed fellowship we have with the Father and with the Son? *Truly our fellowship is with the Father, and with his Son Jesus Christ* (1 Jn 1:3). I am convinced (by the Word and Spirit of God) that being ONE WITH CHRIST is more than a HEAD-WORK. It is a HEART-WORK. It is the work of almighty grace that imparts spiritual life to dead, ungodly sinners, or there is no life (Eph 2:1 & Ez 37:14). In the giving of that life, Christ, by his Spirit, begins his eternal abode in them—*I in them, and thou in me, that they may be made perfect in one; and that the world may know that thou hast sent me, and hast loved them, as thou hast loved me* (Jn 17:23). This is the mystery revealed concerning Christ and his church (Eph 5:30-32). True, salvation is not in a feeling or an experience, but it is equally true, there is no life where there is no feeling and experience,.

There seems to be some tormenting fear of the truth of the nearness, realness, and presence of the living Lord in some who present themselves as theologians and intellectual giants. Nowhere in the Bible is it even suggested that salvation is KNOWING FACTS or having NEW PRINCIPLES. SALVATION IS KNOWING CHRIST IN LIVING, VITAL, UNION! *And this is life eternal, that they might know thee the only true God, and Jesus Christ, whom thou hast sent* (Jn 17:3). And again, *I will dwell in them, and walk in them; and I will be their God, and they shall be my people* (2 Cor 6:16).

Now, to get the horse in front of the cart—Those that are in Christ believe the truth, and do have new principles. *A new heart also will I give you, and a new spirit will I put within you: and I will take away the stony heart out of your flesh, and I will give you an heart of flesh* (Ez 36:26). The sinful creature remains dead until Christ comes and gives life, and when he does give life, the unworthy, ungodly, dead, corrupt creature lives, and knows it by experience and the revealed Word of God.

COMMON FAITH

To Timothy, mine own son after the COMMON FAITH: *grace, mercy, and peace, from God the Father and the Lord Jesus Christ our Saviour.*
Titus 1:4

The *common faith* of which Paul speaks, does not mean that it is ordinary or plain, or that every one possesses this faith. The faith spoken of is peculiar only to those to whom God has given it (Eph. 2:8-9). It is called *like precious faith* (2 Pt 1:1). It is the SAME FAITH that all who know Christ have. This precious faith has one precious object—CHRIST! *Unto you therefore which believe he is precious* (1 Pt 2:7). This *common faith* looks only to Him—*Looking unto Jesus the author and finisher of our faith* (Heb 12:2).

WITHOUT EXCEPTION, ALL those who have this faith know Him, love Him, believe his Gospel, follow Him, and are committed to Him. Faith in Christ is the brand or mark which identifies and distinguishes his people from the world. This *common faith* is the bond that unites and makes his church to be one in Him.

This *common faith* makes reference to the Gospel, as well. Those who have this faith AGREE WHOLE-HEARTEDLY upon the person and work of Christ, and salvation in him alone. ALL to whom he has given faith, believe and rejoice in God's sovereign grace and glory, revealed in the face of Jesus Christ. Those who have this faith have renounced all righteousness, even their own, and submit themselves to the righteousness of God. This *common faith*, this *precious faith*, is the life of the child of God—*I am crucified with Christ: nevertheless I live; yet not I, but Christ liveth in me: and the life which I now live in the flesh I live by the faith of the Son of God, who loved me, and gave himself for me* (Gal 2:20). *For therein is the righteousness of God revealed from faith to faith: as it is written, The just shall LIVE BY FAITH* (Rom 1:17).

Without this faith it is impossible to know God, worship God, or please him in any way. Faith never exalts itself, but rather exalts it's object, which is The Lord Jesus Christ.

" THINGS THAT ACCOMPANY SALVATION"

But, beloved, we are persuaded better things of you, and things that accompany salvation, though we thus speak.
Hebrews 6:9

As election, predestination, justification, calling, adoption, sanctification, and glorification are connected in the salvation of sinners, so is faith, repentance, brotherly love, joy, peace, longsuffering, gentleness, goodness, faith, meekness, temperance, commitment, and perseverance. The latter is the result of the former and is the fruit of the Spirit. Where the latter is not manifest there can be no scriptural claim of the former. Good intentions never realized are not virtues of the Spirit of God. The grace of God in salvation lays claim not only on the heart and soul, but on the life of it's object as well.

What we are inwardly by God's grace, will govern who we are outwardly, as we live by faith in Christ in this world. The child of God earnestly desires, seeks, and longs to be found faithful to him that loved us and gave himself for us. We have a life of faith to live, a race of faith to run with patience, and a war of faith to fight to the finish. As God provides every thing for his people in bringing us to Christ and giving us life in Him, he does the same for us in our lives in this world—*Being confident of this very thing, that he which hath begun a good work in you **will** perform it until the day of Jesus Christ* (Phil 1:6). A profession of salvation without the *things that accompany salvation* is as a body without life.

"WHICH HOPE WE HAVE"

Which hope we have as an anchor of the soul, both sure and stedfast, and which entereth into that within the veil.
Hebrews 6:19

The believer's hope lies in the immutability of God, and in the promises he made to us in Christ Jesus our Lord. In him we have a *strong consolation*, which is the Anchor of our soul. The child of God doesn't just fancy or have a hopeful attitude that things will work out as God has promised, he has a good hope through grace in the omnipotent Lord of Glory which is sure and steadfast, which comes with God-given faith in Him. The hope of the child of God is secure in Christ. Without him there is no hope. He is our hope in this world, no matter what the circumstances. He is our hope of heaven when this life is over, no matter when this life is over—*To whom God would make known what is the riches of the glory of this mystery among the Gentiles; which is Christ in you, the hope of glory* (Col 1:27).

Our spiritual life begins with hope in Him, we persevere in this hope and we die with hope in Him—the same as faith. In this life we experience, feel and live with this hope in our Redeemer. Having believed and believing in him we are sustained, comforted, assured, encouraged, and supported by the faith and hope that he has given us in himself by the Gospel. The believer's hope is not in this world or the things of this world. The believer's hope is not in his works or performance of duty. The child of God has no hope in any thing or person other than the Lord Jesus Christ and his faithfulness. The hope, which we have, gives rest to the soul, peace to the heart and confidence in God's Word.

"My hope is built on nothing less
than Jesus' blood and righteousness.
I dare not trust the sweetest frame,
but wholly lean on Jesus name"

ENDLESS MERCY

I will be merciful to their unrighteousness, and their sins and their iniquities will I remember no more.
Hebrews 8:12

The just and irreversible punishment for sin by God Almighty is eternal death. Sin punished and sinners forgiven? How can it be? Without the possibility of the unchangeable God being coerced or influenced, he makes covenant promise to himself in loving consideration of his chosen ones. *I will be merciful to their unrighteousness, and their sins and their iniquities will I remember no more.* The execution and fulfillment of this promise is in no way contingent upon them as they are the *unrighteous* by virtue of their sins and iniquities. The certainty of this impossibility being accomplished lies in the excellent person and PROPITIATORY work of our *Great High Priest, who is set on the right hand of the throne of the Majesty in the heavens.*

Although incomprehensible to human thought, reason, and logic by virtue of our natural spiritual ignorance and insanity, God in infinite wisdom and omnipotent grace provided himself a sacrifice and substitute in whom their sin was imputed and punished. Righteousness was provided, imputed, and imparted. This Fountain of mercy flows endlessly to his chosen vessels, which he ordained for his glory before the foundation of the world, and is realized and enjoyed by them in regeneration in the experience of grace. His *mercy endureth for ever* is recorded no less than forty one times in the Bible, and in every case it is in regard to his people. The saints here on earth may confidently join David in proclaiming; *Surely, goodness and mercy shall follow me all the days of my life.*

"Come, thou Fount of every blessing,
Tune my heart to sing thy grace;
Streams of mercy, never ceasing,
Call for songs of loudest praise."

BY HIS OWN BLOOD

By his own blood he entered in once into the holy place, having obtained eternal redemption for us.
Hebrews 9:12

The ceremonial law was merely a shadow or representation of better and good things to come to the people of God. All of these spiritual blessings— redemption, adoption, acceptance, forgiveness, inheritance and much more— were to come to us through the accomplished work of our true representative and substitute, the Lord Jesus Christ. Having appeared, being sent of God, he put away his people's sin by the sacrifice of himself. Therefore, by his own blood he obtained eternal redemption for us. This he accomplished by himself. This work was his own. All those that are redeemed by his blood ARE REDEEMED—*He shall not fail nor be discouraged* (Is 42:4). All for whom Christ died shall be saved. Any other message is false and blasphemous, and robs Christ of his glory.

THE APPEARING OF CHRIST

For Christ is not entered into the holy places made with hands, which are the figures of the true; but into heaven itself, now to appear in the presence of God for us.

Hebrews 9:24

The eternal Son of God entered into the world to fulfill the demands of God's holy law for all his elect. In the accomplishment of that singular work there was a twofold work perfected—1. He wrought a perfect righteousness for his people. 2. He paid the penalty for their sin to the perfect satisfaction of divine justice.

When he was identified by his Father, God said, *Thou art my Beloved Son in whom I am well pleased.* This is what happened. This is what God purposed to do and this is what The Lord Jesus Christ did. This is the record of all holy writ. This work was not, is not, nor shall ever be, in any way, shape, form or fashion, the work of any one other than the Lord of Glory—the Lamb of God—our substitute! This is what he did THEN. Therefore, having glorified his Father in having obtained eternal redemption for us, he NOW, appears in the presence of God in Heaven—*For the Lamb which is in the midst of the throne shall feed them, and shall lead them unto living fountains of waters: and God shall wipe away all tears from their eyes* (Rv 7:17).

This is where and how we see him NOW. Not in a manger, not on a cross. We see him on the throne of his glory being our Redeemer, our Great High Priest, and our ever-living intercessor. This is how he reveals himself to his people. When we look to him by faith, which he has given, we see him as the Author and Finisher of our salvation. We do not see him as one that is a beggar, as one that is attempting to save us, as one that made salvation possible, anticipating the cooperation of man's supposed free will. We see the ONE that is mighty to save. We see one that did not fail, neither was he discouraged. This is how all Christians see Him. If you do not see him as he now appears in the presence of God, you have yet to see him as he is, and therefore do not know him as your Lord and Saviour. *THIS is life eternal, that they might know thee the only true God, and Jesus Christ, whom thou hast sent* (Jn 17:3).

WHY ATTEND THE GOSPEL?

Let us consider one another to provoke unto love and to good works: Not forsaking the assembling of ourselves together, as the manner of some is; but exhorting one another: and so much the more, as ye see the day approaching.
Hebrews 10:24-25

The church of God operates according to the law of love (with the motive of love). Although the benefits and blessings rendered to us by our loving heavenly Father is incomprehensible, we do not assemble together in his blessed name to get something from Him. We come together with the motive to render worship unto him who loved us and gave himself for us. *The hour cometh, and now is, when the true worshippers shall worship the Father in spirit and in truth: for the Father seeketh such to worship him* (Jn 4:23).

We see the glorified church in heaven doing the same. *The four and twenty elders* (representing the complete church) *fall down before him that sat on the throne, and worship him that liveth for ever and ever, and cast their crowns before the throne* (Rv 4:10). If indeed Christ is preached, there is no scriptural motive for believers to absent themselves from the worship of Christ with other believers, *For where two or three are gathered together in my name, there am I in the midst of them* (Mt 18:20). Love for Christ and the worship of Christ being the chief motive, there are many good things that flow from this.

It is an encouragement to other believers as we *consider one another to provoke unto love and to good works.* Our love for the brethren as we are one in Christ brings us together in exhortation *(exhorting one another)* to faithful worship, being of one mind, one accord, and one Spirit. Our faithful (or unfaithful) attendance of the Gospel of Christ speaks volumes to those who are without Christ. Our love (or lack thereof) for Christ, his Gospel and for each other is a witness and testimony to our lost family, friends and neighbors. God may use this means (love and faithfulness) to bring them under the Gospel and reveal Christ to them as well. However, if he doesn't, what a blessing and privilege it is to meet with those whom we love in Christ and worship him in the preaching and hearing of the Gospel!

ALL WHO BELIEVE ARE SAVED

We are not of them who draw back unto perdition; but of them that believe to the saving of the soul.
Hebrews 10:39

All those that believe on the Lord Jesus Christ are saved. They have everlasting life and this life is in God's Son (1 Jn 5:11). Not one of them shall perish (Jn 10:28). Their perseverance unto eternal glory is certain because their salvation is a work of God in Christ and it is not a work of man (Rom 8:28-30). Christ lived and died for all those whom God chose in electing love. They shall be called by his grace, quickened by his Spirit, and given faith in Christ and Christ alone. All sin being forgiven, they shall be clothed with his righteousness and presented blameless before the throne of his infinite glory (Eph 5:27). We could no more draw back than we could save ourselves. The same God that gave us spiritual life, keeps us (1 Pt 1:5). He that begun the work of salvation in us will continue to perform that work (Phil 1:6). Any doctrine that asserts otherwise is not the doctrine of God, but is false and damning (Gal 1:8).

Those that believe to the saving of the soul, grow in grace and knowledge of him as well (2 Pt 3:18). Nowhere in the Scriptures are we taught that those who know him grow out of his grace and become more ignorant of the truth. Those who profess to believe, eventually losing interest, and finally leaving the Gospel altogether are of those that draw back unto perdition (2 Thes 2:10-12).

THE EVIDENCE

Now faith is the substance of things hoped for, the evidence of things not seen.
Hebrews 11:1

It is always true that those who do not believe on Christ as he is revealed in the Scriptures look to themselves as the cause of salvation, seeking justification, righteousness, hope, and assurance in their so-called good works. To them, what they do and don't do is evidence and proof of being saved. It may be just believing there is a God, or going to church occasionally, or being baptized, or being an honest, moral person. There are even those that trust in their being in agreement with a certain doctrine as evidence of being a child of God. Can this be true? It is rather the contrary.

FAITH IN ANY THING OR ANY OTHER PERSON THAN THE LORD JESUS CHRIST HIMSELF IS FALSE FAITH, AND IS EVIDENCE THAT ONE IS YET IN DARKNESS AND UNBELIEF. The faith that God gives has one Object—Christ Jesus The Lord. Only those that have this faith have the evidence and substance of eternal life, which is Christ. We are not saved by FAITH; we are saved by CHRIST (Ti 3:5; 2 Tm 1:9). Faith reveals Christ to us. Our faith is not in our faith; it is in Christ. We look unto Jesus the Author and Finisher of our faith (Heb 12:2). The evidence is in; *Christ is all* to the true child of God (Col 3:11).

"On Christ the Solid Rock I stand,
all other ground is sinking sand."

IS IT NECESSARY?

But without faith it is impossible to please Him: for HE THAT COMETH TO GOD MUST BELIEVE THAT HE IS, *and that he is a rewarder of them that diligently seek Him.*
Hebrews 11:6

There is absolutely no coming to God apart from Christ and faith in Him. As a matter of truth, coming to Christ and faith in him is synonymous. Therefore we must conclude that there is no salvation for sinners without God given faith in the Lord Jesus Christ, who is none other than God manifested in the flesh. The

God-man is now seated on the throne of glory being his people's representative, ruling with all power and authority.

God requires faith in Christ of all his elect, and faith he gives. It is a must. Not just faith that he exists, but faith that he occupies and rules in all his offices as Prophet, Priest and King, and in his people's hearts.

Who the Lord Jesus Christ is, gives credibility and virtue to all that he has done and is doing as our representative and surety. Simply put—all that come to God must and do continually believe that he is all their salvation, plus nothing and minus nothing.

In this the believer is diligent to look to Christ alone for all things, and gladly renounces all others, most importantly self and all supposed righteousness which is of the flesh, and is nothing more than self-righteousness.

God is not pleased with anyone or anything that is done without faith in Christ, because *without faith it is impossible to please Him.*

THE NECESSITY OF FAITH

Without faith it is impossible to please Him: for he that cometh to God must believe that he is, and that he is a rewarder of them that diligently seek Him.
Hebrews 11:6

It is not a natural attribute of man to believe God's Word. It is impossible for man to believe in and trust God's blessed Son whom he has never seen and does not know. It is natural and only possible for man to trust himself, which is not faith, and leaves man with a false hope that will necessarily fail, and in the end be his destruction. God Almighty is not pleased with those that look to themselves and ignore Christ. If we ever come to God, we must come with faith in Christ alone, leaving all hope and trust in ourselves behind. Although this is impossible with man, it is possible with God. Thank God, he provides that which he requires.

Salvation is of the Lord! Faith is a gift of God—*For by grace are ye saved through faith; and that not of yourselves: it is the gift of God* (Eph 2:8). Faith in Christ Jesus comes with spiritual life in the regenerating work of the Holy Spirit. This God-given faith is not merely a mental agreement with historical facts. True faith in Christ is a living faith with heart and soul; *whom having not seen* (Jesus Christ), *ye love; in whom, though now ye see him not, yet believing, ye rejoice with joy unspeakable and full of glory. Receiving the end of your faith, even the salvation of your souls* (1 Pt 1:8-9). The means whereby God gives faith is by his Word—*So then faith cometh by hearing, and hearing by the word of God* (Rom 10:17). The Word of God is the revelation of Christ in his redemptive work.

Only by his omnipotent Spirit is his Word made effectual. There is no pleasing God apart from faith in his Beloved Son. There is no coming to Christ without faith in Him, which is not a work of the flesh. It is rather a supernatural work of God's free, irresistible, sovereign, loving grace shown toward otherwise helpless, hopeless, impotent, chosen sinners.

Did I say CHOSEN? Yes, I purposely did! (Eph 1:4; 2 Thes 2:13; 1 Pt 2:9; Rv 17:14).

HOLY DETERMINATION

Looking unto Jesus the author and finisher of our faith; who for the joy that was set before him endured the cross, despising the shame, and is set down at the right hand of the throne of God.
Hebrews 12:2

Jesus Christ is God incarnate and therefore cannot sin. Yet He, in his flesh, was afflicted and affected by sin. He endured his cross of suffering through trials, testings, temptations, sorrows, and death. He despised the shame of sin, yet he endured the consequences of it. He was tempted in every way and did not sin, yet he suffered for it. He never sinned in any way, yet he died for it—HE ENDURED IT. He underwent the penalty for it. He willingly and effectually claimed it for his own. It is not AS IF he was *made sin—He hath made him sin for us* (2 Cor 5:21). The life and death of our Redeemer was one of uninterrupted labor, toil, blood, sweat, and tears. His whole life was one of sacrifice—*He is despised and rejected of men; a man of sorrows, and acquainted with grief—Surely he hath borne our griefs, and carried our sorrows: yet we did esteem him stricken, smitten of God, and afflicted* (Is 53:3-4).

In all his life he had a holy determination that would not be denied. Whatever the price, whatever the cost, he must accomplish his covenant purpose made with his Father from everlasting. He would not be denied the glory and joy of that accomplishment! That joy set before him was to glorify God in finishing to perfection the great work of the redemption of those whom they loved. The proof of both is that he *is set down at the right hand of the throne of God. He* is no less determined that all for whom he endured the cross, despising the shame, shall endure to the same end and be with him to forever share in that joy—*if I go and prepare a place for you, I will come again, and receive you unto Myself; that where I am, there ye may be also* (Jn 14:3). Let us not be weary and faint as we consider him who endured such contradiction of sin for us. Rather, may we be determined to patiently endure all things for his glory.

CONSIDER HIM

*Wherefore we receiving a kingdom which cannot be moved, let us have grace, whereby we may serve (*worship*) God acceptably with reverence and godly fear.*
Hebrews 12:28

There is one characteristic (among many) of a people who profess to know Christ with their mouth, but whose heart is far from Him, that excels all others. That is the absence of REVERENCE for Him—*There is no fear (reverence) of God before their eyes* (Rom 3:18). This irreverence of God manifests itself in many ways. However, the absence of a desire to worship God in the Gospel of Christ stands head and shoulders above the rest. Those people whose heart is far from him treat the things of God with a casual, indifferent attitude.

The preaching, the hearing, and the consistent attendance, having a desire for heart worship in the Gospel with the people of God, does not register on their scale of priorities. Instead of trying to arrange their lives and schedules in a way as to not interfere with *the assembling of ourselves together, as the manner of some is; but exhorting one another: and so much the more, as ye see the day approaching,* they try to fit the public worship of God where there is a space in their schedule, when it is convenient for them, and they have nothing better to do. I know by experience this irreverent attitude is not a labor or a difficult exertion of the flesh. It is a willing, premeditated determination of the careless heart that comes as natural as breathing. Even when in attendance, they are separated to themselves in heart and thought.

The child of grace has a God-given desire to worship him with reverence as often as he can, and weeps in his heart when providentially he cannot. Even then he feels he comes far short. He prays for the gift of grace in his heart that will effectually deny the flesh, and to be enabled to consider *Him, who loved us and washed us from our sins in his own blood,* with reverence and heart worship.

THE BELIEVER'S ALTAR

We have an altar, whereof they have no right to eat which serve the tabernacle.

Hebrews 13:10

*A*ltar comes from the Hebrew word MIZBE'AH, meaning TO SLAY. Under the Mosaic economy there were many material altars erected for the purpose of offering up offerings and blood sacrifices. The outstanding altar that we read of was the one on the Day of Atonement (Lv 16:30 & Lv 23:27). Upon this altar the sacrifice was slain and atonement was made for sin (Not actually, but symbolically). This was done once every year. Neither the altar nor the sacrifice could put away sin for two reasons—the altar was man-made and the animal was only a beast. Never were they meant to put away sin. They were only figurative of the true sacrifice who was to come—*The Lamb of God.*

Sinful man must have both an altar and a sacrifice, which God will accept. In the Old Testament the altar and the sacrifice were viewed separately. In the New Testament, Christ is both. He is the Altar to which we come, and he is The Offering which was sacrificed for us. Coming to a bench at the front of a church building, and offering our works to God for reconciliation and ACCEPTING JESUS is the height of idolatry. Satisfaction and reconciliation was made for his people only by the sacrifice of Christ.

"By Faith"

James 2:18-26

The faith of God's elect is a gift of God, not of works (Eph 2:8). Faith in Christ is not an attribute of man. We are not born with faith, nor can we acquire faith by religious works. If we have it, God must give it. Faith has only one object—JESUS CHRIST. The Object of our faith is the Author and Finisher of it (Heb 12:2). Faith is the result of spiritual life, not the cause. Good works, which God has ordained his people unto (Eph 2:10), and performs in them (Phil 1:6), is the fruit of the Spirit carried on by the Spirit of God (Eph 5:9; Gal 5:22).

That which is not of faith is sin (or of the flesh) and unrighteous (Rom 14:23, 1 Jn 5:17). Without faith it is impossible to please God (Heb 11:6). Faith is always active in producing good works; works which honor and glorify God. Where there is no works there is no faith, and where there is no faith, all of man's works are self-righteous works. So, it is by *faith* that God has given, that we live before Him.

CONDEMNED BELIEVERS

Thou believest that there is one God; thou doest well: the devils also believe, and tremble.

James 2:19

To believe there is a God, even there is ONE God, is a mere exercise of the intellect. I am convinced that even the self-proclaimed atheist, if he were not such a liar, and would speak honestly, would render the same conclusion. The light of creation, the existence of all things, reveals God's handiwork. *The heavens declare the glory of God; and the firmament sheweth his handiwork* (Ps 19:1). His signature is clearly visible in all and to all. *The invisible things of him from the creation of the world are clearly seen, being understood by the things that are made, even his eternal power and Godhead; so that they are without excuse* (Rom 1:20). However, a mere belief in the existence of God is not saving faith.

The Object of SAVING faith is Jesus Christ in whom alone is salvation. The effect of spiritual life is God-given faith which results in embracing, loving, and worshipping Him. The result of a mere intellectual belief in the existence of God is self-righteousness based upon that belief which is nothing more that faith in SELF. It is not those who believe there is a God that have everlasting life and shall not come into condemnation. It is those chosen sinners that are in Christ (live by faith in Christ) that shall never perish. *There is therefore now no condemnation to them which are in Christ Jesus, who walk not after the flesh, but after the Spirit* (Rom 8:1). Men *do well* to believe there is one God. That is true and should be believed. However, this is nothing more than the devils do. They *also believe and tremble.*

This brings us to one conclusion: Apart from faith in Christ there is only condemnation. We cannot bypass Christ and his redemptive work and have favor with God. It is the sovereign Spirit of the living God that quickens dead sinners and reveals Christ to them. There is a difference in believing and BELIEVING!

IN BONDAGE TO SELF-WILL

James 4:17

The need to gratify the desires of the flesh and mind, willingly carrying out those desires in the face of revealed admonitions and rebukes from God, without remorse and repentance, is an evidence of slavery to sin, rebellion against God, and the absence of spiritual life. Self-justification and lame excuses attended with prideful continuance in love for self and the world reveals a Godless self-centered life, in bondage to self. *Therefore to him that knoweth to do good, and doeth it not, to him it is sin* (Jas 4:17).

THE VALUE OF CHRIST'S BLOOD

Forasmuch as ye know that ye were not redeemed with corruptible things, as silver and gold, from your vain conversation received by tradition from your fathers; But with the precious blood of Christ, as of a lamb without blemish and without spot: Who verily was foreordained before the foundation of the world, but was manifest in these last times for you
1 Peter 1:18-20.

The Lord Jesus Christ and his redemptive work is invaluable to the worthless sinner. The preciousness of Christ and his blood does not suggest or reveal the worth of a soul, but the contrary. The redemptive work of Christ reveals the worth and preciousness of Christ to the worthless redeemed sinner. The value or worth of a soul is only of worth or value having the imparted life of Christ and the imputed righteousness of Christ. Apart from union with Christ the soul of man is repugnant to all that is holy and good. The elect of God is glorious only because we are chosen in him and glorified in Him.

All that God has done and is doing in Christ for the sinner reflects his glory and virtue, not the sinners'. The sinner has none of his own. Christ did not die for sinners because they were worth saving. All men are alike by nature. The myriads of lost souls in hell are a testimony to their worthlessness. The multitude of the redeemed ones in glory is a testimony to the worth of Christ, and the preciousness of his blood. Any other view would suggest some quality or virtue in the sinner that moved God to choose him, Christ to die for him, and thus redeem him.

Nothing could be farther from the truth. This is the epitome of Armenian, free will doctrine, the heart and soul of self-righteousness. The redeemed of the Lord are of great worth only because of our relationship and union with Christ alone—nothing else. This is the case anywhere and everywhere in the Scriptures. Every time God says any thing good about any man it is always in respect to his being in Christ. May we never forget the words *IN CHRIST*.

THE MESSAGE

Ye were not redeemed with corruptible things, . . .but with the precious blood of Christ.
1 Peter 1:18-19

The redemptive work of the Lord Jesus Christ is the heart and soul of the Gospel. If this be not the message, then we have no Gospel. Who he is and what he has done and is doing is the ONLY good news for poor sinners. There are many things that need to be said and many things must be dealt with at the proper place and time, but the preaching of the Gospel is exclusively centered upon ONE person, and that is the Lord Jesus Christ. *For I determined not to know any thing among you, save Jesus Christ, and him crucified* (1 Cor 2:2).

What I am saying is this: no matter where we take our text, no matter what we title our message, the context, the heart, the theme, must be concerning Christ and his redemptive work, or we are not preaching the Gospel, and we have not heard the Gospel. Preachers can beat people over the head all they want for what they do or don't do, but nothing will change a heart except the preaching of the glorious Gospel of God's redeeming grace in Christ Jesus our Lord. *For after that in the wisdom of God the world by wisdom knew not God, it pleased God by the foolishness of preaching to save them that believe* (1 Cor 1:21). The saved one will get the DOS and DON'TS straightened out in God's time. Those who have been redeemed by the blood of Christ, and have been brought to faith in Christ, desire to please him and will grow in grace and knowledge of Him.

A Gospel message is a Gospel message only when Christ is set forth in his fulness, and the flesh is abased. Nothing will cause one to hate sin and love righteousness more than God revealing the blood-shedding of the Lamb for his sin. The MESSAGE of the Gospel is concerning a person and what that person did for sinful man—*When the fulness of the time was come, God sent forth his Son, made of a woman, made under the law, To redeem them that were under the law, that we might receive the adoption of sons. And because ye are sons, God hath sent forth the Spirit of his Son into your hearts, crying, Abba, Father. Wherefore thou art no more a servant, but a son; and if a son, then an heir of God through Christ.*

The message of God to sinners is not about corruptible things—It is the message of the blood of Christ, which *taketh away the sin of the world.*

THE BLOOD OF CHRIST

But with the precious blood of Christ, as of a lamb without blemish and without spot:
1 Peter 1:19

The blood of the Son of God is precious to the sons of God. In context *precious* simply means that the children of the living God love the blood of Christ, depend upon the blood of Christ, and esteem the blood of Christ above all things. Therefore we do not seek to remove the blood from our view, but rather seek to see the application of the blood to everything. The true believer will not tolerate a bloodless religion. Were it not for the blood of the Lamb of God there would be no redemption, atonement, reconciliation, justification, sanctification, or forgiveness of sin, and therefore no acceptance for us with God. Were it not for the sacrificial blood of Christ as our substitute, God could not be just in putting away our sin, AND WOULD NOT PUT AWAY OUR SIN! Were it not for the blood there could be no peace with God or peace in our hearts. Were it not for the blood there would be no Gospel (Good News) for sinners. Apart from the blood of Christ, all God has for the sinner is wrath and condemnation. It is only when God sees the *blood* that he will pass over those to whom the blood has been applied.

HE CARETH FOR YOU

Casting all your care upon Him; for he careth for you.
1 Peter 5:7

CARE has several meanings, two of which we see here in this verse. The first one reflects the believer's trials, afflictions, and adversities in and of the flesh. The second one, he *careth for you,* the promise of his lovingkindness and providential hand in supplying our needs. No matter how deep our sorrow, no matter how severe our pain, no matter how shaken we are by our fears, he is always with us and cares for his loved ones.

He sends those things in love that we may experience his mercy and grace in our life. He *careth for you* is more that an emotion. It is the hand of God moving in our life every day for our good and his glory. It is not everyone that receives the gracious invitation *Cast all your care upon Me.* It is not everyone to whom he says he *careth for you.*

If you do not know Him, you have nowhere to cast your care. In your care and trouble there is silence from the throne of God. However, the child of God may *come boldly unto the throne of grace, that we may obtain mercy, and find grace to help in time of need* (Heb 4:16).

TIME WILL TELL

2 Peter 1:10.

Time is really a hard thing to define. I suppose the simplest way, for me at least, is this—it is the beginning of all things and the end of all things. This I do know—God created it and someday there will be time no longer (Rv 10:5-6). In the Bible *time* is mentioned in 563 Scriptures, and in every one we see that God is in control of each event in *time*. In God's workings in providence, he uses time to reveal many things. There have been many who professed to believe on Christ, love the Gospel, and were seemingly committed to him and his work. But in time their profession proved to be a charade.

On the other hand there have been those who persevered in faith unto eternal glory, such as Paul—*I have fought a good fight, I have finished [my] course, I have kept the faith* (2 Tm 4:7). I wonder what time will reveal concerning us? *Wherefore the rather, brethren, give diligence to make your calling and election sure: for if ye do these things, ye shall never fall* (2 Pt 1:10).

TIME WILL TELL!

WALKING IN THE LIGHT

But if we walk in the light, as he is in the light, we have fellowship one with another, and the blood of Jesus Christ his Son cleanseth us from all sin.

1 John 1:7

The children of God have an unearthly bond, a spiritual union stronger than earthly ties and affections, and that union is in the Lord Jesus Christ. The blessing of that fellowship here on this earth is that common faith in him we have together, as we walk in his Gospel. Walking in the Light is walking in the Gospel, the revealed person and work of our Redeemer. As his sheep we have all things of God in common. It is impossible for the Lord's sheep to have a good, solid, lasting, loving, communicative relationship, and fellowship with someone who abhors their God, and disagrees with the truths they esteem to be of infinite worth. *Can two walk together, except they be agreed?* (Am 3:3). *Be ye not unequally yoked together with unbelievers: for what fellowship hath righteousness with unrighteousness? and what communion hath Light with darkness? And what concord hath Christ with Belial? or what part hath he that believeth with an infidel?* (2 Cor 6:14-15).

If both parties are wishy-washy and compromising, both have concluded their relationship is of more value than Christ, and there can be communication and peace. This relationship reveals that neither esteems what they claim to believe to be of vital importance. I have heard the comment, "The Gospel (or religion) should not be an issue." Christ and his Gospel (the truth) is always an issue to those that love Him. The Israel of God and Egyptian idolaters can never enjoy the sweet union and fellowship of Christ. The truth and a lie, light and darkness, love and hate, humility and pride, one or the other, govern every individual and are opposites. They can never co-exist in harmony, contentment and peace.

That which we have seen and heard declare we unto you, that ye also may have fellowship with us: and truly our fellowship is with the Father, and with his Son Jesus Christ 1 John 1:3.

IF ANY MAN LOVE THE WORLD

1 John 2:15

Why is it that some who claim to be Christians and believe the Gospel are faithful and ambitious in every aspect of their life except the Gospel and the things of God? They are faithful to their family and their job. They make sure that they have all the provisions necessary to a comfortable and pleasurable existence in this world, as much as they can. Yet, when it comes to the things of God, there is very little time, resources, or interest left. There is nothing wrong with having these things and doing these things, but should it be at the expense of the most important, most wonderful and glorious thing in a believer's life?

When I observe the tendency of this attitude in my life, and in others, I am reminded of these Scriptures: *In this was manifested the love of God TOWARD US, because that God sent his only begotten Son into the world, THAT WE MIGHT LIVE through him* (1 Jn 4:9); *Lay not up for yourselves treasures upon earth, where moth and rust doth corrupt, and where thieves break through and steal: But lay up for yourselves treasures in heaven, where neither moth nor rust doth corrupt, and where thieves do not break through nor steal: For* WHERE YOUR TREASURE IS, THERE WILL YOUR HEART BE ALSO (Mt 6:19-21); *For what shall it profit a man, if he shall gain the whole world, and lose his own soul?* (Mk 8:36); *Love not the world, neither the things that are in the world.* IF ANY MAN LOVE THE WORLD, THE LOVE OF THE FATHER IS NOT IN HIM (1 Jn 2:15).

Can it be that one who truly loves Christ, his Gospel, and his people, continually and boldly with a self-justifying attitude, live to themselves, and put the things of God somewhere in a convenience file? The most important things in our heart will be the most important things in our life. May God give us grace and boldness enough to examine ourselves in the light of his Word to truthfully answer this all important, vital, Gospel question—"Do I love Christ?"

So when they had dined, Jesus saith to Simon Peter, Simon, son of Jonas, LOVEST THOU ME MORE THAN THESE? *HE saith unto Him, Yea, Lord; thou knowest that I love thee* (Jn 21:15).

GOD'S LOVE PERCEIVED

Hereby perceive we the love of God, because he laid down his life for us: and we ought to lay down our lives for the brethren.
1 John 3:16

Out of necessity on our behalf; out of love on his behalf, Christ died for his sheep. God needs nothing—we need everything. The need of sinners and the love of God is culminated in the person and work of JEHOVAH-JIREH (The Lord will see—The Lord will provide—The Lord will be seen—in that order). The apex of God's INFINITE (not measurable: without any finite or measurable limits), unchangeable, sovereign love is perceived ONLY in God's Lamb willingly sacrificed. The love of God for sinners is ONLY perceived by those chosen sinners for whom Christ laid down his life—*HEREBY PERCEIVE WE THE LOVE OF GOD.*

It is ONLY in the VICARIOUS (done or endured by someone as a substitute for someone else) death of Christ that his sheep perceive their incomprehensible need of Him. It was only when the dying thief, with God-given eyes of faith, saw the dying Lamb of God, and in his death saw both God's love for him and his need for Christ, that he cried out for mercy, *LORD, REMEMBER ME when thou comest into thy kingdom* (Lk 23:42).

It is evident that those who embrace a universal love of God and a universal redemption do not perceive the love of God. Universalism annihilates the love of God and deifies the sinner. The holy perception of both the love of God and our great need for Christ constrains or moves the child of God to love for him and the brethren, even to the sacrificing of ourselves to him and them. *If any man come to me, and hate not his father, and mother, and wife, and children, and brethren, and sisters, yea, and his own life also, he cannot be my disciple* (Lk 14:26), *because he laid down his life for us we ought to lay down our lives for the brethren.*

LOVE FOR CHRIST

We love Him, because he first loved us.
1 John 4:19

Love for the Lord Jesus Christ never has and never will be begotten from the heart of sinful mankind. Love for Christ is a gift of God originating from his love for us. Our love for him begins when he effectually reveals his love for us in regeneration in his glorious person and redemptive work as our substitute by the preaching of the Gospel—*We love Him,* BECAUSE *he first loved us.* Christ's love for his elect never originated. His love for his people is eternal (no beginning and no end). His love for us was, and is MANIFESTED (revealed)—*In this was* MANIFESTED *the love of God toward us, because that God sent his only begotten Son into the world, that we might live through him* (1 Jn 4:9).

Our love for Christ is MANIFESTED as well—*Whosoever believeth that Jesus is the Christ is born of God: and every one that loveth him that begat loveth him also that is begotten of Him. By this we know that we love the children of God, when we love God, and keep his commandments. For this is the love of God, that we keep his commandments: and his commandments are not grievous* (1 Jn 5:1-3).

The commandment (declaration) that we have from him is that all those whom he loves, and to whom he has revealed himself, WILL LOVE HIM AND LOVE EACH OTHER—*And this commandment have we from Him, That he who loveth God love his brother also* (1 Jn 4:21).

Unregenerate man does not love God nor does he love God's people—not with the special, spiritual love that God gives. Man loves the thoughts of the benefits that Christ promises to his people, but not Christ himself. Christ's sheep's love for him is manifested in their love for and commitment to Christ, his Gospel, and his church. It is not fear of punishment or hope of reward that fuels the fire in the hearts of God's chosen to live for Him. It is love for Christ. It is not necessarily those who profess to know him and love Him, and his doctrine, that actually love Him. It is those who ACTUALLY KNOW him and necessarily manifest that LOVE, which he has given them.

He saith unto him the third time, Simon, son of Jonas, lovest thou Me? Peter was grieved because he said unto him the third time, Lovest thou Me? And he said unto Him, Lord, thou knowest all things; thou knowest that I love thee. Jesus saith unto him, Feed my sheep (Jn 21:17).

LOVE FOR CHRIST

We love Him, because he first loved us.
1 John 4:19

Many make an outward show of love for Christ who do not love him. However, some who profess to know Christ and love him make it very plain that they do not. The Word of God reveals that more do not love him than do. Many profess to know and love him who consistently reveal their lack of love for Him, his Gospel, and his church, by their careless, inconsistent behavior, and attitude toward the things of God. The former can be counterfeited, but the latter cannot.

What I am saying is this: an unbelieving church member can have all the outward evidences of being a lover of Christ, or he (or she) may not. But a true lover of Christ will manifest the evidence outwardly which comes from a heart of faith and love. Eventually, in God's time, both will be revealed.

THOSE THAT LOVE CHRIST LOVE HIS WORD. God's Word is their Food from heaven. His Word reveals Christ, being all their hope and salvation. Job said, *I have esteemed the words of his mouth more than my necessary food.* The Word of God is precious to those that love Christ. His Word is their Light, their Lamp, their comfort, and their daily Manna from God.

THOSE THAT LOVE CHRIST LOVE THE PREACHING OF THE GOSPEL. Meeting together with others that love him to hear of their Redeemer is not something they do when there is nothing else to do, or when it does not infringe upon what is pleasing to the flesh. Lack of love for Christ, his Gospel and his church is one of the first signs of apostasy. Those that love Christ desire to be faithful and committed to his Gospel and his work in whatever way they can that will honor and glorify Him. This is their life.

THOSE THAT LOVE CHRIST LOVE HIS CHURCH. They love other believers. They have a desire for the good of the body. The brotherhood of the children of God is closer than earthly family ties—*If any man come to me, and hate not his father, and mother, and wife, and children, and brethren, and sisters, yea, and his own life also, he cannot be my disciple* (Lk 14:26).

Those that love Christ desire to be in the company and fellowship of other believers and communicate with them, sharing, comforting, encouraging, edifying, and rejoicing with them in the things of God, and bearing each others burdens in times of trials and suffering. Our Lord asked Peter, *Do you love Me?* It would a good thing to ask our self this same question. Like Peter, all those who know him love Him.

DO WE LOVE CHRIST?

We love Him, because he first loved us.
1 John 4:19

When we love someone, we feel that our life would not be complete without them. We find our thoughts upon them often, and cherish the time we are permitted to be together. Without effort—that is by desire and with joy—we are committed to those we love, and are proud to be identified with them in time of persecution or peace. We are quick to defend those we love when they are attacked by the enemy. It gives us great joy and humbleness of heart to know that we have the God-given blessing to love them, and to be loved by them. DO WE LOVE CHRIST?

We love him, because he first loved us (1 Jn 4:19).

THE LAW OF LOVE

We love Him, because he first loved us.
1 John 4:19

The word LAW has many implications and applications. The one which is best suited for our subject is—A GOD GIVEN LOVE FOR CHRIST, AND DESIRE WITHIN, WHICH MOTIVATES, GOVERNS, OR REGULATES OUR LIFE AS A CHILD OF GOD. This is the determining difference between a person that knows Christ and one that just professes to be a believer. Either you got it, or you ain't. It makes no difference if folks are Calvinists, Armenians, Atheists, or any thing else. If there is no love for and commitment to Christ, his Gospel and his church, there is no life. There is overwhelming evidence that another LAW has dominion over them. It is the *Law of Sin and Death.* We could call this LAW the LAW OF LOVE OF SELF.

The child of God is governed by God's love. It begins and operates like this—*WE LOVE HIM, because he first loved us* (1 Jn 4:19). This is not an option. This is a truth. This is a law! This is love he has given us, and this love rules the believer's life. Not only do we love him who first loved us, we love all that is connected to Him. We love his Word and The Gospel. *Therefore I love thy commandments above gold; yea, above fine gold* (Ps 119:127). The believer cannot help but love the Gospel that speaks of their blessed Redeemer, he who was wounded for their transgressions and bore their grief.

The love of Christ constrains us, persuades us to love him and his Word! This is not an option. This is a truth. This is a law! Those that love the Gospel will avail every opportunity to hear of Christ when at all possible. Not only does the law of love insist that we love him and his Word—WE LOVE THE BRETHREN. *If a man say, I love God, and hateth his brother, he is a liar: for he that loveth not his brother whom he hath seen, how can he love God whom he hath not seen?* (1 Jn 4:20).

Every believer loves every other believer! We don't endure one another or put up with one another. Believers love each other, forgive each other, help each other, pray for each other, and if need be, are willing to suffer for each other for Christ's sake.

Now there are many who say they love Christ but don't. *Behold, I will make them of the synagogue of Satan, which say they are Jews (believers), and are not, but do lie; behold, I will make them to come and worship before thy feet, and to know that I have loved thee* (Rv 3:9). These are eventually manifest in that they have no love for Christ, his Gospel, or his people *because they received not the love of the truth, that they might be saved* (2 Thes 2:7-12).

COMMITMENT

For whatsoever is born of God overcometh the world: and this is the victory that overcometh the world, [even] our faith.
1 John 5:4

The Lord Jesus Christ is the believer's rule of life. In this flesh we will never be as he is in perfection, yet it is our desire. We look to Him, follow Him, and desire to be as he is in this world, *For whatsoever is born of God overcometh the world: and this is the victory that overcometh the world, [even] our faith* (1 Jn 5:4). The great work of God the Spirit in the child of God is conforming us to the image of Christ—*For whom he did foreknow, he also did predestinate to be conformed to the image of his Son, that he might be the firstborn among many brethren* (Rom 8:29).

This work will one day be complete for *we know that, when he shall appear, we shall be like Him; for we shall see him as he is* (1 Jn 3:2). In this world, in a body of flesh, the Son of Man was committed to his Father. His life as a man was a life of willing obedience—*And he that sent me is with Me: the Father hath not left me alone; for I do always those things that please him* (Jn 8:29). *Jesus saith unto them, my meat is to do the will of him that sent me, and to finish his work* (Jn 4:34). *And being found in fashion as a man, he humbled himself, and became obedient unto death, even the death of the cross* (Phil 2:8).

This is the believer's desire as well. Commitment to Christ, his Gospel, and his church is his people's way of life. The end result of this life as a child of God, honors and glorifies God the Father and God the Son—*For ye are bought with a price: therefore glorify God in your body, and in your spirit, which are God's* (1 Cor 6:20). *Let your light so shine before men, that they may see your good works, and glorify your Father which is in heaven* (Mt 5:16). There is nothing more honoring to God than being faithful to our profession of faith in Christ, neither is there anything more dishonoring to God than for one who professes to know him to be careless and negligent in the blessed privileges that he has given his people to enjoy, and that which gives him glory. May God give us grace to deny ourselves, take up our cross and follow Him.

HEALTHY, WEALTHY & WISE

He that hath the Son hath life; and he that hath not the Son of God hath not life.

1 John 5:12

To excel in health, wealth, and wisdom is to be successful in this world, according to the measure of men. Men measure men by what they possess, by their physical condition, and how smart they are. This is what men seek after; The lust of the flesh, the lust of the eye, and the pride of life. This humanistic philosophy is very deceptive. This is not the essence of life. I admit it would be great to be in perfect health, to have no want for any thing material, and to excel in intelligence. But this is not where life resides. The essence, heart and soul of real, true, life, in this world, and in all others, physical and spiritual, is in Christ Jesus our Lord—In knowing Him, being in Him, him being in us. He *that hath the Son hath life; and he that hath not the Son of God hath not life* (1 Jn 5:12). The healthiest, wealthiest, most intelligent person that ever lived is dead, bankrupt, and totally insane if Christ be not his all. The world seeks after the world. The living seek after Christ, who is their life. Are we healthy, wealthy, and wise? If we have Christ, we are!!!

But of him are ye in Christ Jesus, who of God is made unto us wisdom, and righteousness, and sanctification, and redemption: That, according as it is written, he that glorieth, let him glory in the Lord I Cor. 1: 30-31.

WEEP NOT, THE LION HAS PREVAILED

Behold, the Lion of the tribe of Judah, the Root of David, hath prevailed to open the book, and to loose the seven seals thereof.
Revelation 5:5

The scene before us is not a future heavenly ceremony to reveal someone or something which had not transpired as yet, and which was before unknown. This is the revelation of the successful work of Jesus Christ (*the Lamb slain from the foundation of the world*) in the particular, effectual and eternal redemption of his elect church. This is the revelation of the triune God's eternal covenant of grace, and the Lord Jesus Christ—the surety of that covenant, and the blessings of that covenant freely bestowed upon those whose names are eternally written in the Lamb's book of life. This is the scene from before the foundation of the world, in his incarnation, at the cross, in his resurrection, his ascension, and in his eternal glory.

This is the Gospel message, *behold, the Lion of the tribe of Judah, the Root of David, hath prevailed.* WEEP NOT! O, child of God, we must weep over our sin. We weep over our lost family members and our friends, but *weep not,* yea, rather rejoice that indeed the ransom has been paid. Our Lord has prevailed over every enemy and foe, even over sin and death, and has opened the book and declared it even so! *I am he that liveth, and was dead; and, behold, I am alive for evermore, Amen; and have the keys of hell and of death* (Rv 1:18).

There would be reason to weep if we must prevail or if he had failed to prevail, as the Arminians would have it. Indeed, there will be weeping in hell by those who trampled underfoot the redeeming blood of Christ, and perverted and abused the only means of God's grace—the Gospel of particular and effectual redemption by Jesus Christ, the Son of the living God. But for the child of God, he will say; thy *words were found, and I did eat them; and thy word was unto me the joy and rejoicing of mine heart: for I am called by thy name, O* LORD *God of hosts* (Jer 15:16).

THE GREAT WORK OF REDEMPTION

And they sung a new song, saying, THOU ART WORTHY to take the book, and to open the seals thereof: for THOU WAST SLAIN, and THOU HAST REDEEMED US TO GOD BY THY BLOOD out of every kindred, and tongue, and people, and nation.
Revelation 5:9

THE WORK OF REDEMPTION IS A GREAT WORK because of who planned and purposed it. The Lord God determined to redeem a people for himself before the world began.

THE WORK OF REDEMPTION IS A GREAT WORK because it was The Lord Jesus Christ that paid the price.

THE WORK OF REDEMPTION IS GREAT because of the price that was paid—The Lord Jesus Christ died and shed his blood for his sheep.

THE WORK OF REDEMPTION IS A GREAT WORK because it is sinners who are redeemed.

THE WORK OF REDEMPTION IS A GREAT WORK because of who it was that did not plan, purpose and pay the price—SINFUL MAN!

WHO IS WORTHY?

Worthy is the Lamb that was slain to receive power, and riches, and wisdom, and strength, and honour, and glory, and blessing.
Revelation 5:12

John saw the Lord Jesus Christ as the Lamb slain; as the Lamb in the midst of the throne; as the Lion prevailing; as the Root of David; as the exalted sovereign of all; and everlasting. What John saw concerning him is far beyond our full comprehension, yet there is one thing that our Lord God has made a living reality and embraceable to the believing heart—*worthy is the lamb!* John said in another place, he *that cometh after me is mightier than I, whose shoes I am not worthy to bear.* The worthiness of the Lord Jesus Christ renders our best as the epitome of unworthiness. The twenty-four elders fell down and worshipped Him, and in essence, said, "We are not worthy, you alone are worthy of all honour and praise and glory." Every believing heart echoes this song of the glorified church; WORTHY IS THE LAMB!

The Lord Jesus Christ is worthy because of who he is— HE IS THE ALMIGHTY! HE IS THE ANCIENT OF DAYS! HE IS THE THRICE HOLY GOD! God's holy character and all his glorious attributes are embodied in Christ's infinite being. The pen of the acclaimed scribe cannot even begin to describe his majesty and greatness. The tongue of the greatest orator must stand speechless when called upon to tell out all his worth.

He is worthy because he is the God-man! He is sinless perfection in the flesh! He is righteous! He is holy! He is undefiled! He is separate from sinners! He ALONE, the Son of

God, the Son of man, is worthy of worship. He was made sin and put away sin without sinning! Read (Phil 2:7-11).

Therefore, he is worthy because of what he accomplished. Only he could obtain eternal redemption for the elect of God. Perfect God—Perfect man—Perfect salvation for unworthy sinners! The child of God esteems him worthy because he *loved us, and washed us from our sins in his own blood, And hath made us kings and priests unto God and his Father; to him be glory and dominion for ever and ever. Amen* (Rv 1:5-6). May we never forget WHO he is. If we remember who he is we will never forget who we are. In the incandescent light of these two infinite realities we will cry from our hearts, *WORTHY IS THE LAMB!*

BORED, DISSATISFIED, AND OFFENDED

Often when men become bored, dissatisfied, and offended with the simplicity and singularity of the message of Christ and him crucified, and don't receive the attention they feel they deserve, they begin to find fault with every thing and every one else, not willing to admit what their problem really is. It would make them look bad. Eventually they will manufacture a vehicle big enough on which to ride out of town. Most often they will relocate where their flesh can be fed and nourished, no matter what is preached. As for the child of God, if Christ is preached, he is happy just to be there and worship with sinners, just like himself.

REGENERATION

O nly those who *LIVE* in Christ are able to know, see, and understand that salvation is entirely in him alone. This blessing that believers enjoy is enjoyed only because they have *EXPERIENCED* the wondrous miracle of God's saving grace in regeneration.

THERE'S A DIFFERENCE

P reachers today are licensed and ordained by the church; men of old were ordained and sent by God. Preachers today go forth armed with degrees and credentials; men of old went forth anointed by the Holy Spirit. Preachers are questioned by committees and hired to preach what the church believes; men of old came preaching "Thus saith the Lord." Preachers today give themselves to programs, visitation, and church business; men of old gave themselves to prayer and the ministry of the Word.

Preachers of today preach and men are persuaded to move their membership; men of old preached and, *they were pricked in their hearts and cried, Men and brethren, what shall we do?* Preachers today pray while the organ plays softly; Elijah prayed and the fire of God fell. Preachers today are afraid that they will offend someone; Paul was afraid that he wouldn't. If there is no offence, the cross has not been preached.

THREE SCRIPTURAL DOGMATISMS

There are three fundamental, irrefutable, absolute truths (not to the exclusion of any truth) plainly and boldly revealed in the Word of God that are essential to the honour and glory of God in the preaching of the Gospel and the salvation of the elect. Upon these truths all else stands. Without them all falls. These are so plain and simple that even I can understand them. May God help me to believe and embrace them!

The first is this—GOD IS GOD! HE is God alone. There is none other. Almighty God in the Trinity of his sacred person is holy, infinite, just, omnipotent, omniscient, omnipresent, all wise and sovereign. *Know therefore this day, and consider it in thine heart, that the LORD he is God in heaven above, and upon the earth beneath: there is none else* (Dt 4:39). He does as he pleases without any cause outside himself, and what he does is in absolute harmony with his virtues and character. And by the way, there is nothing done that he does not do! *All the inhabitants of the earth are reputed as nothing: and he doeth according to his will in the army of heaven, and among the inhabitants of the earth: and none can stay his hand, or say unto Him, What doest thou?* (Dn 4:35).

The second is this—MAN, ALL MANKIND, EVERY MAN THAT IS A DESCENDANT OF ADAM, IS A DEAD, VILE, WRETCHED, FILTHY, DEPRAVED SINNER, WITHIN AND WITHOUT, BEFORE GOD. Man is helpless and hopeless within himself. Man at his best is but a maggot in his own worth. THE STIRRING UP OF MAN'S

GOODNESS IS BUT A STINK IN THE NOSTRILS OF GOD. *We are all as an unclean thing, and all our righteousnesses are as filthy rags; and we all do fade as a leaf; and our iniquities, like the wind, have taken us away* (Is 64:6). There is not one man righteous, not one good, all are guilty of sinning against God. And not only that, there is nothing we can do about it! Only God can do something about it!

The third is this—SALVATION FOR CHOSEN SINNERS IS IN AND BY THE LORD JESUS CHRIST ALONE! The salvation of God's elect is certain. There is only one Saviour of sinners. *Neither is there salvation in any other: for there is none other name under heaven given among men, whereby we must be saved* (Acts 4:12), and he absolutely, completely, eternally accomplished salvation for those whom he loved.

Our Lord did not live his life in the flesh and die his death so sinners would have an option to choose to make him Lord of their life if they wanted to. He, without assistance, *obtained eternal redemption for us* (Heb 9:12). And all those whom he redeemed will be brought to faith in him by the irresistible, sovereign grace of God in Christ, through the preaching of the Gospel—*For after that in the wisdom of God the world by wisdom knew not God, it pleased God by the foolishness of preaching to save them that believe* (1 Cor 1:21).

A GOOD HOPE

It is only when our Lord in grace and mercy takes away our imaginary strength that we truly look to him and trust Him. This we do not learn in creeds and confessions of faith. This we are taught by him in personal relationship in the experience of grace. I only find hope in him when there is no hope anywhere else. It is easy to learn correct doctrine, but faith, hope, comfort, and rest in Christ is a living experience. Justification, redemption, atonement, sanctification and glorification are not only doctrinal truths believed in the heart, they are truths experienced in the heart in regeneration. Our Lord is our life, and all that is in him is ours. There is no hope in what I know; my only hope is in him and what he has done. May God in mercy shut us up to Christ alone!

Is God Working?

Often there is little or no visible success of the ministry of the Gospel to the world. And we who are believers sometimes find it difficult to comprehend that God is doing a work in us, among us and for us. The truth that we must not forget is that God works according to his eternal purpose. God makes all things work, and what he makes work, works all the time. Too, we must not forget that he is not through yet. We have not arrived yet and cannot see things as we will see them.

When all things are accomplished that God has purposed to do, Christ will deliver up the Kingdom to the Father. Then we will see face to face. We will see all things clearly. Also, we must remember that what the child of God sees, he sees by faith, not by sight. What we see with the natural eye is temporal; what we see by faith is eternal. Another thing we must understand is that ALL THINGS both visible and invisible, natural and spiritual, God is working toward the same end: OUR GOOD and his GLORY. Is God working in this world? Is his Gospel accomplishing anything? Are we, his children, being used of Him? I RECKON SO!! I believe God! Don't you.

THE SAINTS HARDEST STRUGGLE

The child of God must face all the afflictions that is common to the whole human race. We are not immune to family, health, financial and social problems. We all have been and will again be confronted with many hard and difficult situations. When God saves us we do not move on to EASY STREET. We then begin to fight the hardest battle that will ever be waged by anyone other than the Lord himself. This battle is with self, unbelief, doubt, hardness of heart, insincerity; things that war against the soul. The believer is the only one who knows anything about struggling with the flesh, dying daily, crucifying the flesh, self-denial, and giving SELF to the glory of God.

THE BIRTH OF THE LORD JESUS CHRIST

The birth of the Lord Jesus Christ is concerning the incarnation of God. It is concerning the ANCIENT OF DAYS becoming flesh. It is not concerning a sweet little baby Jesus rag doll lying in a manger. The incarnation of Christ is God the Father sending his Son, made of a woman, made under the law, to redeem his elect. The coming of our Lord and Redeemer into this world is about God being made flesh and subjecting himself to the scornful and ill treatment of fallen humanity, upholding and fulfilling the law of God in true righteousness and holiness, and finally being made sin and undergoing the wrath of God as his people's substitute. Christ being born into this world is concerning the manifestation of the glory of God. This man come into the world to do the will of the Father, and that he did, in every aspect. He successfully and perfectly accomplished all that God sent him to do.

The way that religion pictures the Lord Jesus Christ at Christmas time is nothing short of paganism. Of this we should not be surprised, because this is the little jesus that most folks worship 365 days a year.

The child of God worships the Incarnate Christ in Spirit and in truth, all the time. He is not a baby in a manger, hidden away in a closet somewhere all year long, and then dragged out and made a spectacle of one day a year. He is clothed in Royal apparel, seated in regal majesty and great glory at the Right Hand of God, in power and great glory.

WILLFUL IGNORANCE

Contrary to popular opinion, I believe that man's ignorance of truth is a willing Ignorance. The Scriptures declare that men love darkness rather than light and enjoy the pleasures of sin. This is evident when men hear the truth and hate it. Only a work of almighty grace in the heart will cause one to believe, bow to, and love the Gospel. The good news of the Gospel, that Christ Jesus came into the world to save sinners, will only be good news to the heart of a sinner when God awakens him to the glories of Christ and the sinfulness of his sin. Otherwise, he will remain in darkness and ignorance because he loves it there.

KNOWN OF CHRIST

There are those who know about Christ. There are those who speak of Christ. There are those who believe the doctrine of Christ. There are those who confess Christ.

Then, there are those whom Christ knows and who know Him. They believe Him. They speak of Him. They confess Him. They love Him. They are possessed with him and his Gospel.

A BUCKET WITH A HOLE IN IT

A religious person who does not know Christ may hear Christ preached and have some measure of joy in what he hears. He may have some measure of interest in what the Bible has to say. He may find some assurance and hope in what he knows, but eventually he will be empty because, like a bucket with a hole in it, religion and the flesh is full of holes, and all that is in it will run out.

BLESSED ASSURANCE

We, too often I fear, find ourselves looking inward or to THINGS for assurance. We are never encouraged by our Lord to do so. Christ said, *Look unto me*. To look anywhere else other than to Christ is folly and sin. Of that we are assured by the Word of God, which testifies of Christ and salvation in Him.

A "FREELANCE CHRISTIAN"

There are those who claim to be followers of Christ and yet will not identify themselves with him in believer's baptism, and will not commit themselves to the Gospel with a local body of believers. Therefore they feel that they are under no obligation to be faithful to attend the worship service, nor do they feel any responsibility to consistently support the Gospel monetarily or in any other way. This is the same attitude as those who argue that it is not necessary to go to church to be a Christian.

This attitude is not consistent with a heart that loves Christ, his Gospel, and his church, and longs to obey his Word. The heart of the child of God operates by love, not responsibility and obligation. These poor souls are a god unto themselves. They totally miss the joy and privilege of being free to worship the true and living God in Spirit and in truth.

A good analogy of this is a man living with a woman who will not commit himself to her in marriage. He would lose the freedom to do as he pleases, even to change partners for advantage and gratification of the flesh. There are even those who have made outward commitment and yet have no constraining love for Christ and his church. These poor deceived souls have no desire to learn of Christ nor do they find any real comfort and joy in the Gospel when they hear it proclaimed. It goes in one ear and out the other, never finding a place in the heart.

What a blessing and joy it is to the pastor and other believers in the assembly to observe those who count it a joy to be faithful and committed to Christ and his Gospel, and to one another in whatever way they can. On the other hand, it brings sadness and concern to those that love them to see those that are so casual and unconcerned about the things of God. The Scriptures repeatedly affirm that *where your treasure is, there will your heart be also* (Lk 12:34).

This is not a judgment call from this pastor; this is a crystal clear declaration from God Almighty. The only ones they are deceiving are themselves. Those that live so are tottering upon the brink of destruction—*they received not the love of the truth, that they might be saved. And for this cause God shall send them strong delusion, that they should believe a lie: That they all might be damned who believed not the truth* (2 Thes 2:10-12). Those that love the truth have a desire to be committed to it—PERIOD!

DO WE REALLY LOVE THEM?

I know that nothing we can do or say will alter the purpose of God. Those whom he has chosen in his blessed Son will be saved with an everlasting salvation. God the Father purposed it. God the Son purchased it. God the Spirit executes it. This gives us great comfort and assurance.

However, he has given his people a desire, motivated by love, to be instrumentally used of God, in the furtherance of the Gospel, which is the means whereby he calls his chosen to faith and life in Christ. And that he does. Therefore, as followers of our Lord, we are examples to all men of the grace of God whereby we have *turned to God from idols to serve the living and true God*. This is a glorious, yet serious and sobering truth.

Those who really have this desire do not have the attitude that WHAT EVER WILL BE, WILL BE, or SINCE IT IS ALL OF GRACE AND GOD WILL SAVE HIS PEOPLE ANYWAY, IT MAKES NO DIFFERENCE WHAT I DO. There are those that profess to believe the Gospel and say they desire the salvation of their children, grandchildren, family, and friends, yet by example, show that they could care less.

Their loved-ones see no real love for Christ, because they see no real commitment to the Gospel. They observe that the pleasures and comforts of this world is their priority. They see no real joy and pleasure in the things of God. They think nothing of exposing themselves and their children to a false god and a false Gospel, which is idolatry.

There are two (among many) great distinguishing characteristics of a child of God.

1. A commitment to, and a desire for the souls of men,

2. A loathing and hatred for every false way.

I would ask ourselves two vital, sobering questions, of which the answers will reveal where we really stand,

1. How important is the Gospel to me?

2. By example am I seeking the salvation or the damnation of those whom I profess to love?

My friends, the former determines the latter. May God in omnipotent grace cause us to *walk worthy of the Lord unto all pleasing, being fruitful in every good work, and increasing in the knowledge of God.*